BOOKS BY HELEN YGLESIAS:

How She Died
Family Feeling

Starting

HELEN YGLESIAS

Starting

EARLY, ANEW, OVER, AND LATE

Rawson, Wade Publishers, Inc.

NEW YORK

Grateful acknowledgment is made to the following for permission to quote lines of poetry:

Macmillan Publishing Company, Inc., for "I Shall Not Care," by Sara Teasdale, from *Collected Poems by Sara Teasdale*, copyright 1915 by Macmillan Publishing Company, Inc., copyright renewed 1943 by Mamie T. Wheless.

Random House, Inc., for lines from "Post Mortem," by Robinson Jeffers, from *Selected Poems of Robinson Jeffers*, copyright 1925, copyright renewed 1953 by Robinson Jeffers.

Norma Millay Ellis, for "What lips my lips have kissed . . ." and "My candle burns at both ends . . ." by Edna St. Vincent Millay, from *Collected Poems of Edna St. Vincent Millay*, published by Harper and Row, copyright 1922, 1923, 1950, 1951, by Edna St. Vincent Millay and Norma Millay Ellis.

Library of Congress Cataloging in Publication Data
Yglesias, Helen,
    Starting early, anew, over, and late.

    1. Self-realization—Case studies.   I. Title.
BJ1470.Y47   1978   170'.202   78-13531
ISBN 0-89256-046-0

Published simultaneously in Canada by McClelland and Stewart, Ltd.
Manufactured in the United States of America by Fairfield Graphics, Fairfield, Pennsylvania
Designed by Helen Barrow
Second Printing January 1979

For Eve Merriam

Contents

INTRODUCTION

On Starting

When I was fifty-four years of age, I quit my job, and with a sense of having taken my true life into my own hands at long last, I sat down before my typewriter to make a start on the work I had always meant to do. For me this action was so tautly filled with risk, it felt explosive. What if I failed? I had reached a sort of success: why not stay where I safely was? Twice married, once divorced, mother of three and a grandmother, very much the wife of my husband, a distinguished writer, whose person entirely filled the landscape of my emotions, I, born poor and without easy entrance into the world where I coveted a place, I had crawled in somehow, into a little corner. I was an editor on a New York-based national weekly; I was the wife of my husband, the mother of my children, the grandmother of my grandchildren, the friend of my friends. What more did I want?

I wanted to be myself, the person I had always wanted to be. I wanted to be a story-teller. And though I had wanted this before many times and made a number of earlier starts toward meeting my desire, I somehow knew that this time there would be no turning back. Seated at my typewriter, I began the work of telling a story that I had been carrying around in my head since my teens, and by keeping at the telling day after day, sheet after sheet of paper and word by word until the story was finished, I slowly became the worker I had always wanted to be—I became a story-teller, for good or bad, and in the process became, for good or bad, the person I had always secretly believed myself to be. I was born, as myself, into the real world at last.

It would seem to be late in the day to be celebrating "self-realization," as if one were discovering a new thing. If anything the celebration of the "self" has been so indulged as to have become sickening in some of its current manifestations: and it wasn't to further enhance that tradition that the idea of starting drew me as a subject. "Starting" is a loose word, applicable to almost any kind of beginning— from opening a hot-dog stand to sounding out the first notes of a symphonic composition. Both actions are starts; both may be of equal value to the starters, and indeed even to the world. But starting, in the sense in which I shall be studying it, is a process difficult to pinpoint, because the founts of starting (and the arid stretches where everything comes to a halt) are fed and starved by sources whose depths are not easily penetrated.

In this hemisphere, we have all inherited a tradition of starting in one way or another. We have all invented ourselves, just as our ancestors did—and the continent, and us, as they went along. In the process a new concept of the self came into being. We tend to think that the terrifying frontiers against which the frail self pitted itself have all been tamed, but there are new, wild spaces out there where the self still searches for its special niche. Not only is the scene wilder; the self itself appears to have become a roving beast let loose in a wilderness. Though we may be confounded as to where to go in our current explorations, surrounded as we are by quacks, gurus, and commercial faith healers, at the heart of even the silliest explorations there are real human questions clamoring for answers.

Is there any help out there? Are there any answers? How does one start to become one's self? Is it an entirely self-willed accomplishment? Is it an accomplishment at all, or simply an indulgence? Think of the opening of that hot-dog stand or the writing of the first notes of a symphony as one half of a sphere of which the self which is realized in the action constitutes the matching half. In this sense, to start is to bring the self into active existence in society. It is a commitment to trust the self in the world, and in that act of faith the individual makes a compact between the self and love, or the self and work or the self and a way of being. With great good luck, starting is a combination of the three.

But that doesn't end the questions. More crowd in. Is there "a true self"? Does it indeed exist and does its existence matter? Is there measurable damage in human and social terms when an impostor inhabits the corner of space and time reserved for a unique self—whatever that is? To do what one has always wanted to do—to be what one has always wanted to be—what does that mean?

These are some of the questions that sent me digging into the stories of the people in this book. Not all are self-willed starters. Some are unwilling victims of social catastrophes, people forced to re-create new-old selves out of the dreck dumped on them by overwhelming upheavals beyond their control. These make up the heroic stories. Others are significantly small, like my own history, which drew me to the subject in the first place. Not happiness, success, money, or fame signal that the goals of starting have been achieved, but a more intangible consummation—a declaration of unique existence, affirmed again and again in continuing action. I am here. I exist. I do what I alone can do.

It is in this tenuous sense that I hope a pattern will

emerge from these stories. If the results don't add up to a communicable process of starting useful to others, like a good recipe that may be profitably passed from hand to hand, at least a guiding thread may be discerned that can be followed, story by story, down into the fascinating labyrinth of the expressed self.

These are all true stories, though the names of the starters have been changed except where they are public persons whose stories are being retold from a particular point of view. I thank the many people who took the time to dig down into their personal histories and deepest motivations, in order to experience with me and the reader the mysterious process of starting. To name them would be to do them a disservice, but they know who they are and how deeply grateful I am for their effort and their faith. Because I strongly believe that the quick interview is often a distortion shaped entirely by the interviewee, most of the stories in this book have been amassed through long, deep probings by way of many, many hours of conversation, checked and re-checked against the facts of the person's life. In some cases, in order to round off aspects of the personality, I have gone into the stories of close family members, wives, husbands, mothers or fathers, children, companions, siblings. Because I am a woman, a Jew, a writer, and because successful men interest me, there are more stories of women, Jews, creative people, and successful men than are representative of the population. But this is not a sociological study. It is a conversation about starting, done like good gossip, by way of talk about people's lives—some discussed in depth, some in passing—but all, I hope, to the point under discussion.

My very special thanks to Eleanor Rawson, my editor and publisher, who extended the strongest support toward me and the work during a very trying period.

BOOK ONE

Autobiographical Fragment

Growing Up
IGNORANT AND EAGER

In one of my earliest memories, I see myself playing a solitary game of make-believe. (I say "game," but it seems to have been serious business with me.) I became simultaneously aware of two sounds—my own voice spilling the intimate, made-up dialogue of my private drama, and the bursting howl of grown-up laughter at my antics. I remember vividly the violent surge of shame and rage that swept over me at being discovered, and being laughed at. I must have been very young because I was not yet going to school, and I was small enough to have crept into the very center of the upside-down cave in which I had established myself as safe from eyes and ears, a protective U formed by the soft bedding of an upright folding bed, its outer walls a fortress of iron legs and springs, its warm inner padding permeated with the smell of one of my brothers who slept in it at night in the parlor.

"Parlor" has a deceptively genteel ring for the reality of what I am describing. If there were upholstered couches or chairs in the tiny room I don't remember them. There was a kerosene stove, an upright piano, a linoleum square, patterned to look like a rug, on the floor. Outside the window, the Myrtle Avenue Elevated darkened the day and made brilliant the night. The folding bed, my cave, only partly folded because it was too much trouble to remove daily its stuffing of sheets, blankets, and pillows, was therefore only partly hidden behind the half-open parlor door.

In a world made up of too little space and of many brothers and sisters, even a partly folded bed behind a partly closed door will serve as a sanctuary. The spicy, hot, competitive, male smell of the bedclothes added drama to my private place, an undertone like the thrilling piano chords and ripples which accompanied the heroines through the morbid, sexy dangers they encountered weekly at the Saturday afternoon movie house I was taken to. How exquisitely I suffered along with doll-like Lillian Gish, drifting and whirling helplessly in a black and white silence. From movie to movie, ringing changes on the same sorrows, I watched her—lovely, broken blossom, adored by a pale, pale Chink and beaten to death by a brute of a drunken father; poor orphan of the storm, banging her half-mad, delicate head against the stone wall of a prison cell. The stuff of make-believe. A serious business, nothing to laugh at. People paid good money to witness these tragedies— silvery still, imbued with a terrible, scary joy, oozing delicious sensations of pain and suffering. It was ecstacy to grieve, to cry, to wing into inexplicable elation. So why did overhearing adults laugh at me when it was exactly those same transporting sensations I was trying to get at in my make-believe play?

All the kids on the block played pretend, literally endless serial games of "You must be the father and I must be the mother. You must be the baby now and I must be the big sister. You must go to work and I must stay home to make the supper. Now the baby must get very sick and we must call the doctor. You must be the doctor . . ." But making believe with others was another game altogether. And even in those relatively tame games (where we make-believe killed off our parents and a couple of brothers and sisters), if we were surprised in our play by grown-ups, it was inevitably to the sound of laughter—coarse, guilty, grown-up laughter. To the child I was, that laughter was a killing response. It drained all natural joy from make-believe—the basis, of course, of story-telling. What had been for me an activity as easy (and private) as breathing became an unnatural "thing," wordless, shameful, shapeless, a dark secret between me and a force in life not to be acknowledged aloud but that could not be entirely suppressed either. It continued its work behind the protecting blank eyes that veil a child's real life from intruding, clumsy adults.

My parents were immigrants, a part of the great Eastern European migration of men, women, and children who fled the pogroms and persecutions of the Jews at the turn of the century. At the time I did not see them as part of a mass of human beings for whom the act of starting over—starting new, some early, some middle, and some late in life—starting again, and again, and often again—was a condition of existence and of harsh necessity of the kind that has driven other millions on similar paths in our times. I had no understanding of the social and political upheavals propelling millions of men and women into marvels of daily courageousness. Laboriously they spelled out for themselves an utterly strange way of life, disciplining their very lungs to trust the air of a total, profound, and terrifying alienness. I credited my parents with nothing but ignorance of America and turned away from them for guidance.

I sought my own way, working out my problems within the given materials—the tenements and public schools, the city parks, and the streets of the city. The special sense that middle-class doting parents convey to their most ordinary offspring—the sense of an extraordinary destiny holding its breath awaiting the arrival of their particular child—was never conveyed to me, the youngest of our large family, and I doubt that it was conveyed to any of us. We were poor. Eight people were too many for my father to provide for out of the proceeds of his tiny neighborhood grocery store. We were four sisters and two brothers (a two-year-old brother died before I was born in one of the calamitous diphtheria epidemics common before the discovery of the vaccine that wiped this illness out). We were more or less ambitious in our several ways and rather more than less at sea as to our roles and destinations.

Our parents, working hard to keep us clothed, fed, clean, and schooled, had almost no time for those intimate moments of loving parenthood that teach children the most. I saw my mother and father as two hopelessly harassed and pushed-about failures, infinitely more at sea than even I was, strangers in a place they understood less than I did. Their struggle to survive and to create a corner for us wasn't an adventure that set up any markers I was ready to use as directional signals.

Should I follow my mother into the kitchen? There she is at the round kitchen table, skillfully wielding a tapering rolling pin (brought from Europe along with her brass candlesticks and down pillows). She is transforming a large lump of dough into a fine, thin, cream-colored tablecloth. When it has been rolled so fine it seems it must inevitably tear, she lets it hang to dry, and then turns the lacey stuff into a long column, furling at the edges, and slices it into the noodles that will garnish her delicious chicken soup. I adamantly refuse such skills as my aim in life. Follow my father into his grocery store, working fourteen hours a day and barely earning enough to keep a family going? I had even less interest in that pursuit; but anyway girls didn't do such things.

What in the world *did* girls do? I had no clues as to family expectations of me—if there were any. But in the real world in which I was a child, not all girls landed in the kitchen. If they were smart they became, first, teachers and librarians, and then in descending order secretaries, bookkeepers, typists, salesgirls at the five and ten, usherettes or cashiers at the fancier movie houses, clothing models if they had the figure and the looks, looping in another direction of being smart. If they hit the bottom rung of the ladder, they fell off into prostitution; at the top, they made a good marriage. Above all I understood that a girl was expected to grow up pretty, quiet, and good, and to marry as soon as possible, getting herself off her father's back and into the care of some other man.

In the world of children's books, to which I became addicted as soon as I could read, girls became nurses, settlement house workers, governesses, music instructors and performers, and in the world of movies, where I really lived at the true hot center of my being, girls did everything. In my make-believe I assumed a new role every day, sometimes from hour to hour. I am a ballerina, a nun, an opera singer, a prostitute, a nurse, a concert pianist, an orphan, a research scientist, an actress, a governess, a bad girl, a dying tubercular, a spy, a prison inmate, a great beauty who destroys men, a pure woman who gives her life to save others in an epidemic, a drawing room sophisticate, a kindly and beautiful queen, a kept woman spending her days in idleness and vague dissatisfaction, an evangelist, a soldier masquerading in men's clothes, a pioneer, an aerial artist, a blind match girl. In my fantasies, all didn't automatically go well. Unspeakable practices were performed on my flawless body. Tragic consequences were followed by miraculous cures, renewals, and happy endings, superseded, of course, by worse events, so that the fantasies could endlessly continue, endlessly gratifying.

I was a sallow, skinny, large-eyed, big-nosed child with beautiful hair, serious and clever, no trouble to anybody but myself. With my family, I rated as a good kid, quiet and obedient. I played hooky more than I should have, but I didn't fail in school or get left back. In fact I was skipped a lot because the schools were overcrowded. I told harmless lies, and once I stole a bunch of useless stuff from the neighborhood five and ten with a group of Irish school friends who had no money to buy toys to stuff into the Christmas stockings of their younger brothers and sisters. So they claimed—though I noticed that they also swept lipsticks, rouge, stockings, change purses, and combs from the counters into the bags pinned to the insides of their coats to receive the stolen goods. I went along mostly to share in the excitement of their bold deeds. The outing was everything I had hoped for—better than a heart attack—it sent me home to mama with a sick headache. Before that, I had divvied up my collection of loot among my girlfriends when we toted up the take on a park bench. Christmas wasn't celebrated in my house; it was deplored, as the source of anti-Semitism, and like a fool I hadn't taken a thing I could use but had been drawn irresistibly to the displays of glittering tree decorations.

The following summer when I was thirteen, I went back to that five and ten to ask for a job. I was dressed in an older sister's black satin skirt and white satin blouse, my skinny legs teetering on another sister's high-heeled shoes that were too large for me. I must have been a clownish sight, my narrow anxious face garish with heavy powder, brilliant lipstick and blackest eyebrow pencil. The manager laughed at me for trying to pass myself off for fifteen, the required age to obtain working papers. He said, "Go home to your mother, will you, kid?" I was glad then that we had stolen him blind.

In all that growing-up time I had no concept of work as vocation. Work was visible, active, and coercive. Mental work was totally beyond realistic comprehension. One worked to get a salary in order to eat, pay the rent, and buy clothing in order to go to work and repeat the circle. If one was a woman one escaped this circle by marrying and entering another circle of work. Teachers and librarians were the only real live women I saw working outside of offices, stores, or kitchens.

I was prepared, in advance of meeting her, to madly love

my piano teacher (as much for herself as for her magic in transforming me into a prodigy) but she turned out to be a harsh woman who rapped my knuckles with a ruler when my hand position was insufficiently arched, and the sounds I urged upon our wheezy upright were a sobering disappointment to both of us. After a while an older sister and I went to the piano teacher's house for our lessons, because our teacher's piano was "a finer instrument."

Her apartment was suffocatingly dreary, scary, filled with dusty, hideous objects (mostly having to do with birds, embroidered, painted, stuffed, made into ceramic lamps) all suffused with a damp, stale smell. There was a daughter my age who would arrive home from Catholic school as we would be winding up our lesson—a gray-faced, mousey creature I imagined being bedded down in a closet, gathering mold. Before we would leave, she and her stern mother, with an air of bringing civilization to the natives, made a ceremony of serving us "blanc mange" which in spite of its disease ridden name was nothing but ordinary chocolate pudding made from scratch with cornstarch, whereas at home we were already serving chocolate pudding made right out of a package, a vastly superior method I was convinced. There didn't seem to be any man around. The father and husband had died or deserted them. Nothing to emulate there.

Become a school teacher? All my grade school teachers were crazy ugly old maids with rat's nest hair-dos and bad-smelling shiny black dresses that they wore day in day out without change from one end of the term to the other. The occasional teacher with a bit of plumage, and particularly the ones who were kind to me, also scared the wits out of me. One of these discovered me as a writer when I was nine or ten years old. I must have written a composition that impressed her. I have no memory of any details. Perhaps it was in my expertise at Palmer Method penmanship that she found talent. She asked me to come to school early every day for extra exercises in writing. I accepted my fate as a punishment for some mysterious wrong-doing grown-ups located in one's simplest acts, and the teacher's large, ardent, hungry blue eyes searching out my soul didn't reassure me.

I found myself so lost in this alien incident that I told nobody at home about it. My classmates were tormenting me, of course, because of the special attention I was receiving. I was ostracized and bullied, taunted as "teacher's pet," and put out of my own gang. I walked to school without companions and entered the building early, missing the talk and games that made the schoolyard before the bell rang the most exciting part of the school day. In the strange tonelessness of the empty classroom, the teacher read to me—bits from Dickens and Charles and Mary Lamb, in a voice thrilling to its own ring—and then she would assign me a subject to write about. I would oblige in my perfect penmanship, slanting the letters at the correct angle across the yellow sheets of unlined paper. Once she asked me to describe a scene of men repairing the pavement outside the schoolroom window. My composition included the phrase "the men work fastly" and when she corrected my error, she praised me, calling it an "intelligent mistake" that was "proof of my creative gift." I shrank from this talk. I thought her a nut, and when we moved from that neighborhood a few weeks later I was immensely relieved to be rid of her.

There were books at home, brought into the house by my older brothers and sisters. Most were school books, but my oldest brother had an eclectic taste for under-the-bed-clothes reading, made to order to feed the feverish imaginings of my fantasies—*Psychopathia Sexualis* was my favorite, but there was also *Sanine, The Green Hat, Journey to the End of Night, Chickie*. I had more or less vague clues as to what I was reading, but I knew that they were all forbidden and "over my head," therefore that much more delicious. Not forbidden by my parents, who didn't know enough about books to set strictures, but by my older brothers and sisters who were mainly pulling rank. If their concern for the health of my psyche had been consistent, they wouldn't have been leading me, eagerly succumbing, of course, to Saturday matinee confrontations with *The Phantom of the Opera* or *The Hunchback of Notre Dame* or the confusing biological mysteries of *The White Sister*. Where did that baby in the valise come from, was all I wanted to know. But nobody came clean.

When I was in high school, and had the facts of life and literature a bit more straightened out in my head, I entered upon a serious self-teaching project by way of a married sister's library, consisting, in its entirety, of a highly polished veneer bookcase containing fifty untouched volumes of *The Harvard Classics*—more familiarly known through its advertising as Dr. Eliot's Five-Foot Shelf. Dr. Eliot's preface bristled with missionary zeal:

> . . . a five-foot shelf would hold books enough to give in the course of years a good substitute for a liberal education in youth to anyone who would read them with devotion, even if he could spare but fifteen minutes a day for reading. . . . My purpose was to provide the literary materials from which a careful and persistent reader might gain a fair view of the progress of man observing, recording, inventing, and imagining from the earliest historical times to the close of the nineteenth century. . . . The best acquisition of a cultivated man is a liberal frame of mind or way of thinking. . . .

But my gentleman guide added a warning:

> "Although a good part of the reading provided may fairly be called interesting, there are also volumes or portions of volumes which make hard reading, even for a practiced student. . . ."

Dr. Eliot's preface was written for the 1910 edition of *The Harvard Classics*. He had by that time already retired as active president of Harvard, which he had built into the great university it is. He was in his middle or late seventies when he wrote the preface; he had come to adulthood a long time before in an era quite different from that of 1910, not to mention the 1930s, which was when I was reading him. His illusions and the maddening tone of democratic elitist condescension he displayed were widely shared attitudes of "liberal" thinkers of his time, a philosophical stance which still prevailed in the public high schools when I attended.

I entered upon my high-minded task gritting my teeth against the knowledge that to a Dr. Eliot the grubby, courageous, comic, difficult, and lively struggle of my daily existence as a member of my people, my family, and my sex, constituted a set of facts of life outside his sense of human striving. His terminology wiped me out as the person I was—and nowhere more obviously than in his exclusive use of the male gender. The reader was "he," the creative genius the reader would study was "he," and the uplift which was to result would come only to "mankind." As a Jewish girl who should be thinking about getting her skills as a typist-clerk under her belt I felt myself something of a freak injecting myself where I had little business to be. The tradition I came from strengthened this feeling. If anything, females counted for even less in the Judaic tradition than they did in Dr. Eliot's scale. Dr. Eliot, though he beckoned men to intellectual freedom *first*, didn't totally exclude women. He had himself helped to found Radcliffe as a separate and not-quite-equal women's institution.

I put irritation and resentment aside, and lured by the promise of an enlightened ladyhood I imagined as a rarefied and peaceful haven, I revved myself up to the "resolute spirit" required and applied myself. Was it inevitable that I should go straight to *The Autobiography of Benvenuto Cellini?*

What had Dr. Eliot led me to expect with his words so measured that they had stopped my flow of adrenalin before opening the book? Boredom, grinding effort, a bit of uplift, and with some luck a couple of moments of intense joy in doors opening, new sights, a flash of light. I also brought my own frozen preconceptions of Cellini—the image of an aloof, impeccable genius. The man's work was entombed in a particularly chilly hall of the Metropolitan Museum of Art, wasn't it? I was astounded. Cellini, marvelous liar and story-teller, sprang out of the sixteenth century as naturally as if he were another one of my brothers, coming straight toward me as a vivid familiar, saddled with a character even worse than mine, hustling his way in a scene as unspeakably messy as my own south Bronx, even if it *was* called the Renaissance. Could it be that the "classics" were all as wonderfully immediate as this? I never feared to pick up a classic again. That same year I read *The Golden Ass* of Lucius Apuleius with the same joyous identification. Dr. Eliot's mission had gone astray. Instead of liberal enlightenment I found conviction for a messy theory of creation and of story-telling as the art of setting down a tale with imaginative gusto, full of lies, truly told.

That summer was the last summer of my childhood. I was fifteen. I spent it in a bungalow colony in the Catskills as a kind of mother's helper for my oldest sister, the one who owned the five-foot shelf. I did the baby-sitting when my sister and her husband went out in the evening; helped make the beds and wash the dishes; took my niece and nephew on little outings to pick flowers or berries when they ripened; or led them on a walk up the hill to fetch milk from the farmhouse where the children patted the cow and the horse, and alarmed the chickens; or to bathe in a little pond in which we splashed about under a mini-waterfall of a deliciously sweet, cold brook. It was a glorious summer. There were a few other adolescents in the colony. We would go dancing at a nearby resort which let us in because we livened up the dance floor, since the guests of the place were mostly older Jewish and Russian couples who preferred folk dancing. The four young men who alternated as the three-piece band also doubled as waiters and dance partners. If we wanted the floor in good shape we had to wax it ourselves. I have never enjoyed dancing more than I did that summer.

I was in love with a boy who couldn't come to the dances.

He was dying of an illness that turned his lips a vivid purple, and when we kissed I shut my eyes before we touched, not in anticipated ecstacy as I hope he believed, but because I was afraid. For me his purple lips were the authentic color of death. Drawn and repelled. We spent hours in long stretches of kissing, left to ourselves on the screened back porch by his family. He was three or four years older than I, but his illness had so wasted his flesh and muscles that the light bones caressing me seemed those of a child. Only his lack of strength limited the extent of our dry, hot, morbid passion. He was the more attractive because of death's prior passionate claim. He wasn't sexually timid, but I knew that I could overpower him at any point, and that too was attractive, freeing me of my fears of sex with a real live male. I astonished myself by responding as if we were in one of my private fantasies. We spent hours on the back porch bewitched in exploration—"necking" and "petting" it was then called. When his family was around we talked. It seemed to me he had read everything there was to read. He quoted whole poems, not only the curriculum school-memorized verses I already knew, not only Keats's

Darkling I listen; and, for many a time
I have been half in love with easeful Death,
Called him soft names in many a mused rhyme,
To take into the air my quiet breath;
Now more than ever seems it rich to die,
To cease upon the midnight with no pain . . .

but modern, exotic poets like Robinson Jeffers.

Happy people die whole, they are all dissolved in a moment, they have
        had what they wanted,
No hard gifts; the unhappy
Linger a space, but pain is a thing that is glad to be
        forgotten . . .

He was the first person I opened up to enough to say in words, "I want to be a writer."

He had advice for me from his reading, and drew me

into literature with the passionate abandon we brought to kissing. He made me the heroine of poems—Jeffers's dancer before the temple of art, Marianne Moore's partner in developing a language even cats and dogs might understand. He urged me to live a violent, unsettled life and to take many lovers. Of course he quoted Edna St. Vincent Millay:

My candle burns at both ends,
It will not last the night,
But oh my foes and ah my friends,
It sheds a lovely light.

and every word of

What lips my lips have kissed, and where, and why,
I have forgotten, and what arms have lain
Under my head till morning . . .

but when I tentatively followed his advice and made him jealous, he tried to make me weep through Sara Teasdale:

When I am dead and over me bright April
Shakes out her rain-drenched hair,
Though you should lean above me broken-hearted,
I shall not care . . .

He became jealous when I went dancing with other boys, and he was particularly jealous of one boy who took to hanging around and following me wherever I went with the children—swimming, berry-picking—the activities too strenuous for my love. There was nothing much to recommend this new young man except his vigor, but I "necked" and "petted" with him too one night, just to try it with a strong male. The strong male was a trembling fumbler, either through fear or the discomfort of open-air lovemaking on a brilliantly cold late August night, and I worked up no feelings to compare with what I felt in the long, obsessed sessions on the back porch.

In the very last days of summer, my love's father spent a two-week vacation at the bungalow. (There was a mother

and an older sister in that bungalow too, but I have only a
vague memory of them.) The father was a dress manufac-
turer, the owner of his small business. By my standards
they were rich. They were being bled by the long illness,
obviously. Perhaps that was why they were renting in what
was a very modest bungalow colony. The father had
splurged on a splendid sports car, primarily for his son's
delight in taking long drives. The father was a slight man,
but he was able to lift his son with ease and place him in
the rumble seat where I scrambled in alongside. We spent
day after day driving through the countryside. There was a
sudden heat wave following the early cold and his father
took us driving at night as well along narrow dirt country
roads in a rushing softness of warm wind and shaken trees.
We kissed and kissed and kissed. My lips were constantly
bruised, burning with remembrance during the day and the
longing to be bruised again at night. In the middle of this
torment of bliss my sister began packing to leave. In two
days we were gone. I never saw the dying young man again.
I cannot remember his name.

Trying to Start Early
SHOT DOWN

The next year I graduated from high school and, unable to find a paying job, I set myself to writing a novel telling what it was like to be an adolescent girl in an American public high school—James Monroe High in the Bronx. I was sixteen years old. It was the time of the Great Depression, which was not then written in capital letters or understood by me to be a great social and economic disaster, but a personal time I was living through in a climate of harshness that beat my hopes to a pulp. My mother was recovering from a long illness that had drained every penny and had totally incapacitated her. My always terrifyingly strong, commanding father had been altered into a terrifyingly weak, obese, frightened invalid through the dual blows of economic collapse of his little grocery store and a massive, near-fatal heart attack. Now he lay in bed all day, plucking at the tips of his well-kept nails, crying silent tears, staring bleakly at the cracked plaster ceiling.

My father was then fifty, and my mother near sixty. The

last thing in the world they needed was another burden. What kept me sitting at the dining room table and writing a novel, living off the earnings of my brothers and sisters, was the vibrant expectation that my labors would result in a miracle. My book would be published; it would earn a lot of money; the family would be saved. Meanwhile I wasn't earning the nine, twelve, fourteen to twenty-two dollars a week (big time) that my older brothers and sisters were bringing home to help support the rest of us—my mother and father, an unemployed older brother, a part-time employed sister, and totally unemployed me. My brother, my smart brother, who was to become a real American businessman success in later years, must have sensed my fantasy view of myself as the family messiah and began to tease my by calling me "the White Hope of the Family," which didn't serve to knit up our relationship, undergoing serious unraveling under the general hardships of intense economic stress. Perhaps my brother and I would have clashed under any situation. He crowded me. He made me feel I didn't know much.

In fact I didn't know much—of life or of literature either. I went on writing, driven by the sheer, passionate need to succeed, and by a conviction that what I knew about the life I was living as an ignorant girl was real and important to communicate. My friends, my high-school gang, encouraged me. I thought them all geniuses, and they returned a like admiration. I imagined that our crowd was unique, an extraordinary group of people who luckily happened to come together in one place and all of whom were sure to make a mark in the world. Though I now know that everyone believes they ran with similar "geniuses" in high school or college, I still think I was right then. All the forces of the personality gather in adolescence, ripe to burst into glorious, naturally successive future accomplishment. It's an aberration within our society that most of this energy is squandered. There's more genius left dormant than ever comes to fruition, and most of it gets knocked off in adolescence. Adolescence is a survival trip. Many of us are sunk by the time it's over.

My family's concept of success trafficked solely in genius. Genius was the only talent that counted. What was this rare quality? Clearly, genius was not related to work. "Genius" was inexplicable—a bolt from the blue, a quick seizure culminating in a burst of achievement. A "genius," if he sat down at a desk at all (he was more likely to go walking by the sea, humming an immortal theme) sat briefly, gazed heavenward raptly, lowered his head for a second and *War and Peace* emerged, leather bound. "Genius" might also be "she"—Fanny Hurst or Edna Ferber—necessarily on a lower level, since feminine—but the same magical no-work methods applied.

Genius was flamboyant, mad, quixotic, Jewish (everybody knew that Cervantes was a Jewish genius); genius read poetry aloud, tore its hair, groaned theatrically. Genius was temperamental. I was quiet, secretive, kept my manuscript hidden under my underwear in the single drawer which was my portion of the dresser I shared with two sisters; I wrote prose, read nothing aloud. I kidded around with the rest of the family at supper and avoided fights; I joined in singing popular songs when we gathered around the piano; went along to the movies any night I was invited by a brother or sister with an extra quarter for my admission fee; and I liked to go dancing with boys to the cellar clubs that were then the gathering places of non-affluent teen-agers. I was in and out of love daily; but I kept these transports secret. Without an excess of complaining I helped my convalescent mother keep house, shop, cook, and nurse my father. I was a commonplace youngster, except for the hours I spent from nine until three every day at the dining room table filling the pages of a series of five-and-dime notebooks with my now somewhat damaged though still excellent penmanship.

Did my family take my ambitions seriously? I hardly know. Their attitudes varied. My mother accepted everything about her different children. If one of them elected to sit at the dining room table for hours at a time scribbling in a notebook, why not? It was better than loafing. Maybe some good would come of it. Look at Mischa Elman, Abraham Cahan, Paul Muni, men, true, but some women made it to the top, too—Baby Snooks and Mollie Goldberg, all poor Jews to begin with. One might as well live in hope; in crazy America anything could happen. If I wasted a few months at the dining room table, so what, I'd settle down and marry in a few years anyway.

"Marry a rich boy," was a family slogan. In our limited horizon, "rich" meant a fellow with a good steady job. My older brothers and sisters vacillated between bemused expectations and satirical cynicism (the White Hope of the Family variety). Outright resentment played its part (Why the hell doesn't she get off her ass and go out and get herself a job like everybody else?) From the last, the great gray sea of the other unemployed slaves out there saved me. There weren't any jobs. Mostly I was left alone at what was considered to be some harmless doodling, and in the course of some months I had almost finished the novel of high-school life that I was writing.

I told myself that I was writing for money, fame, and family fortune, but I was writing to validate my life—to impress myself on my times. I wanted to tell stories of New York City street kids; to describe the hot labyrinth of fantasy in which they played out their ignorance and earned their wisdom, and to report their yearnings, dramatically met, in part, within the tensions of a teeming, city high school. I knew now from my reading that all sorts of depths were dredged up by writers and deftly turned into glowing narrative. I wanted to do the same with the stuff of my existence—to make it shine with meaning for others. It was hard work. I was often deeply discouraged. I worked against a worm of conviction that I was no good and should give up, but I kept on trying, and trying harder, and then harder with the next page.

Part of the urgency of the effort was caused by the fact that I had put myself in a bad bind. If I failed in my attempt to publish a book, my only alternative was to become an office worker. I had given up any opportunity to become properly educated for a better career. In the eighth grade at grammar school I had taken a city-wide examination that won me entrance to Hunter High School—automatically followed by Hunter College, if one's grades remained satisfactory, and all of it free of charge. But at thirteen I was "boy-crazy" and the prospect of eight years in a nunnery, after as many in all girls' grade schools, was too dreary to be borne. After two days among the tight old women educators at Hunter High, still wearing velvet ribbons at their withered throats, I quit and entered the neighborhood high school—an institution with a highly disreputable academic and social standing at that time.

It was the rumor of sexual license that most attracted me. Girls were supposedly being raped in the gym fairly often. My older brother was furious that I had thrown away a good, free education and he set the punishment to fit the crime. I must enroll in the commercial course and be trained to do office work. Anything, anything, I agreed. I was bitterly sorry later, of course. I elected enough academic subjects to gain some credits toward college entrance when I graduated, but not enough for me to enter a free city college. Bennington, new then, offered a scholarship because of my excellence in English, and I could come as I was without all the proper credits, but even with a scholarship I needed a thousand dollars a year, a sum that might have been a million, it was so beyond my grasp.

It was when I was almost finished with the novel that I returned from a movie I had been taken to by a sister, to find my brother waiting up for me, my manuscript notebooks in a pile under his arm which rested upon them as if to sink them. He sent my sister off to bed, and it was a measure of the power this middle brother had achieved in our family that she, six years older than he, listened to him and left us alone—with a little nervous pat for me before she went. My brother said he wanted to talk to me about my career, and his tone dusted that word with a light coat of derision and cruel pity that turned my blood cold. For what he meant to accomplish—an all-out attack on what he considered a nonsensical delusion which was going to keep him supporting me for the rest of my destitute, bohemian, failure of a life—he had unwittingly chosen the best possible moment. Movies left me soft, bruised, vague, vulnerable. Too much chocolate candy and exaltation of the imagination, no doubt; but whatever the cause the high of the movie was inevitably followed by exhaustion, depression, and the dreary walk back to the low reality of home. In that sad shape I was in no condition to do battle for my ego, and was transfixed and defeated by the blow I saw coming at me long before it landed. Fastidious distaste was evidenced by the manner in which my brother fingered the pages of the notebooks and it altered his voice too, as if I had subjected him, by way of my manuscript, now as nauseous to me as to him, to a dirty, unhealthy, and unpleasant experience, deeply resented by him, just as he resented the unpleasant duty I had forced on him, to perform this cleansing operation for my own good.

I don't remember much of what we said to one another, or if I answered him at all. I remember the word "perverted"; "Nobody in the world is going to be interested in that perverted stuff you're writing," and of course, "genius"; "You'd have to be a genius to get away with this boring stuff, and you're no genius."

I must have been devastated, yet I fancied myself emptied of any feeling except a calm recognition of the sharpness of the reality he had shoved in my face. I went into the silent, cleaned-up kitchen. I wanted, as quickly as possible, to dispose of the physical aspects of my dirty work. I made my arrangements without switching on the kitchen light. A street lamp outside the kitchen window lit up the room sufficiently for my purpose. I ripped out handfuls of pages from the notebooks, then tore them once across and once down and stuffed them in the clean, empty garbage pail, neatly lined with newspapers. When I had filled the pail, I stopped to rest. Destruction, too, was hard work. I still had two more notebooks to go, and had to reconsider my disposal plans. A big bag would be better. I rummaged in the dark in the broom closet where paper bags were saved, and found a shopping bag large enough to hold all of the manuscript, and after destroying the last of the notebooks I transferred the other torn pages from the garbage pail to the shopping bag. I was so absorbed in my task I don't know how long my mother had been standing in the doorway watching me, before I noticed her. She startled me and I began to shake violently, as if I were being caught in the act of dismembering a corpse. My voice sounded crazy to me—perhaps because I whispered. "Get away from here, Mama. Don't watch."

My mother liked to use pet names, and she had a ridiculous one for me, Elenkoo. She called me "Elenkoo" now in a crooning, grieving reproach. "Elenkoo, Elenkoo, what are you doing to yourself? You're killing yourself. Stop killing yourself."

My mother was a naturally wise woman, and she was right; and it would take a long time before I would bring back to life the part of myself that wanted to be a storyteller.

Picking Up the Pieces
STARTING ANEW

The only possible attitude a listener can take to the story I just told, in the way that I told it, is to view my brother as the villain who squashed a young talent. I don't believe that version is the truth; though it's my truth. A particular person rejected a particular piece of writing, and the writer was too shattered to continue to write for a long time. Creativity has its mysteries, especially in the mystery of what feeds or diminishes creative power. My brother's evaluation of my talent was immensely and disproportionately important to me; he was and is a large, dominating personality and has left indelible marks on others close to him, but to dump the whole show on him would be a cop-out. Individual responsibility for the shape of one's own life is the first recognition of necessity. I believe that my real freedom began with the understanding that I was responsible for my own life.

I was a long way from that realization at the time. I went out and got myself a very bad-paying job in a printing plant, where I typed some, but mostly ran around from machine to machine carrying paper and copy and finished jobs from one skilled worker to the other. I loved the plant. It was also a relief to be rid of the dining room table and of the immense strain and pressure of facing up to a fresh blank sheet of paper, day after day. *Forget all that*, I told myself in a series of contradictory orders. *Face it, you weren't good enough. Don't think about it any more.*

Then in a surprise twist, the same brother who had so damaged me by his harsh judgment of my adolescent novel gave me one of the greatest gifts I was to receive. He paid for a trip that took me to Europe and the Mideast for many months. It was true that the trip was not planned for my benefit but as a cure for the lethargic depression that threatened to finish my father off in his fifties, and also true that my brother borrowed enough money to include my next oldest sister and myself so that my mother wouldn't worry about leaving behind her two youngest daughters, still in their teens. Nevertheless, it was a marvel—taking that trip. We sailed on an Italian boat that proceeded at the usual pace straight to Gibraltar, slowing in the Mediterranean to a leisurely tour of various ports in all the countries between us and our destination—Haifa, in what was then Palestine.

The trip took twenty-four days in all during which I was transformed from my everyday failure of a self to a fairy-tale princess, a rich American girl, in the sensationally beautiful eyes of the young Italian crew officers, for whom all American girls who sailed their steamer were necessarily rich. From not having had enough money to buy a new pair of silk hose, I was suddenly part owner with my mother and sister of a bona-fide transatlantic steamer trunk in which nested six pairs of stockings, two pairs of dancing shoes, and two Sunday night dresses, along with a dozen other costumes appropriate for travel in my new disguise. My sisters and brothers had gotten together to outfit all of us for our journey, but I had bought the Sunday night dresses myself at S. Klein on 14th Street, hunting with desperate seriousness along the racks for the exactly right ones, which as I recall now, couldn't have been more wrong for me.

My sister was a knock-out in her spiffy new outfits. The musicians of the *thé dansant* combo were already clustered around her before our ship had passed Sandy Hook. I collected some of the spin-off. By the time we reached Naples, we were being steadily courted by the pianist and the violinist. That came to some necking on deck between their work stints and a good deal of heavy sighing and sign communication to break the language barrier. They took us out to a nightclub overlooking the exquisite and smelly Bay of Naples where Vesuvius glowed and faded in the distance, a romantic cigarette in the dark, while a chorus of overweight Italian beauties on stage phonetically enunciated the American words of the by then much outdated "Yes, Sir, That's My Baby," to a blaring accompaniment from a very loud, off-key brass band. The chorus line kicked their Rubenesque legs in an operatic version of the Rockettes and waved their heavy arms listlessly, revealing a surprising amount of dark, bushy, underarm hair, and I gained some insight into my escort's fetish for kissing my shaven armpits exposed in my Sunday night dresses, a taste that had been alarmingly unaccountable to me until I saw what the native custom among beauties was.

A marvelous trip. We were abroad for about half a year. The world opened up for me in great bursts of excitement. Knowledge, which to me has always meant to taste, to feel, to see with my own eyes, rushed in on me in wave after wave of information and experience. Politics was never again to be an abstraction to me, but the actual agonies and elations of real people, vividly experienced. I had seen "politics" for myself—Italy under fascism, the poverty of the Middle East, the messy blunder that was Palestine under the Balfour Declaration—and I had become friends with some of the German refugees scrambling to get out from under Nazism and to save those they had left behind.

I had forsworn literature as a possible activity for myself, but I couldn't deny its appeal. In those days I was in love with Elinor Wylie and carried about with me wherever I went her collected poems in a faded blue binding, especially to the beach-front café in Tel Aviv where I sipped a coffee every afternoon on a terrace overlooking the sea. A young man who also frequented the same café began a conversation with me from his little table to mine one afternoon. He told me that he was an American journalist from Chicago who had settled in Palestine and was working as the Mideast correspondent for *Time*. He was a Zionist at odds with all the groups struggling with the knotty questions that bound them together and tore them apart. But we mostly talked of the book I was reading and about the book he was reading and soon he moved from his little table to mine and we were friends.

I can feel again the wonderfully dry hot air freshened by the wind from the Mediterranean, a sea colored in deep stripes that ranged from dark purple to luminescent green, and my excitement in having found a "literary" friend. *His* book was James Joyce's *Ulysses*, which he said I must read at once, and like the wind, the sea, the heat, and my excitement, I can feel Joyce's book as a texture under my fingers—the slightly rough binding and the smooth page on which a tall, sinuous S introduced "Stately, plump Buck Mulligan . . ." and led me into the heart of modern literature.

My friend worshipped at a shrine of writers new to me who was still counting Conrad as a modern writer—D. H. Lawrence, William Faulkner, Gertrude Stein, Marcel Proust. He fed them to me and I read them in a passion of communication. Why, what they were doing was what I had been aiming for in my halting ignorant blundering, but I kept that revelation to myself. My friend's real hope was to write fiction. Soon he was showing me manuscripts. Some had just been written, some had been lying around, having been rejected wherever he tried to get them published. I shocked myself with the judgment that what I had written and destroyed had been better stuff than his efforts. Should I try again? Perhaps with someone like him helping me, I could do it.

(Simone de Beauvoir tells an anecdote in *The Second Sex* that illuminates the condition I suffered from. One of her student friends trying for the baccalaureate was appalled by the enormity of the task ahead of her because, as she wailed, she had to do it "all by herself.") Grasping for help is a human reaction, but an exaggerated one in women. Females of my generation were encouraged to be helpless; they were taught to lean on others—on men, primarily—and far from that being counted a weakness in a woman, during my womanhood—the fifties—it was chalked up as psychological health. An aggressive pursuit of one's own serious work was positively frowned on by experts in the field of human relationships.

Woman's fulfillment, apart from birthing, was to come second-hand. She was allowed to be only the hulking shadow behind a brilliant man and her achieving children. The experts had her hulking because if anything went wrong with this cock-eyed picture, and it was bound to, it was her fault. If her man failed and her children committed suicide or if she went crazy, it was because she had been too aggressive, demanding, over-protective, passive, love-smothering, self-concerned, self-denying, and a dozen other conflicting evils. There was no way a woman could win her spurs in the psychological corral they herded us into, in the fifties. Some went crazy trying to bang its sides down. Some submitted and tried to make their way out deviously. Perhaps I was one of those. Perhaps I was too wounded and discouraged. I made some feeble attempts to write again, but just the sight of the blank sheet made me sick to my stomach. It seemed a tremendous fuss about nothing. What difference did it make anyway? But I hung around the edges trying to work my way in by the back door.

But when we returned from our European trip with my father cured of obesity and depression, I was still in my teens. The enchantment of my fairy-tale position had melted at the first touch of my shoes on the New York City pavement. I was right back where I had been when we left. Jobs were still scarce; I still needed to get one; and I took whatever I got. It was just before Christmas and I was hired as a temporary salesclerk in the lingerie department at Macy's. When that was over I became a temporary manuscript typist for a big printing plant. Then I was out again. I earned good money for a while as a ballroom dance instructor.

In between jobs, the New York Public Library at Forty-second Street became my university where I was majoring in the complete writings of Henry James. A young man picked me up, invited me to share his lunch at a bench in Bryant Park. He was a writer, paid by the Works Progress Administration to help compile a New York City guidebook. He was sure I could get on the project if I wanted to.

The only way into the Writer's Project of the WPA was through the relief rolls, so I moved out of my parent's house into a furnished room, and unemployed, and without other means of support, and through the influence of a friend in the Home Relief Administration, I was accepted as a relief recipient. So far so good. Though the procedure had been overwhelmingly humiliating and difficult for me to do, I stuck it out in order to achieve the goal of a seat at a table in the library, accepted and validated as a worker in the work I most wanted to do—writing. It was, however, late in the life of the social measures Roosevelt had instituted as the New Deal. At the time I filed my application, the Writer's Project was being closed down to new appointments, prior to its being shut down totally. That became clear soon after I had started the whole unpleasant maneuver; but once on the rolls, receiving my nine-dollar check every two weeks, out of which I discovered I could manage to pay my twelve dollar a month room rent, and with the supplementary aid of dinners at the homes of friends, a boyfriend to take me to the movies, and hand-me-down clothing from my sisters, the possibility presented itself of struggling on independently as a writer after all, and that I might, on my own, take a place at a table in the reading room of the library to read and to write anything I pleased, if I could overcome the discomforting aura of unworthiness and shame that being a relief recipient placed upon me, like a persistent indigestion of the system, a biliousness of the whole personality.

I was very political then (a member of the Young Communist League) and I told myself that my qualms stemmed from incorrect class values—a self-imposed petit bourgeois censorship which I must struggle to overcome. It's true that my family found my new style shockingly repugnant. Self-help was a strong element in the Jewish immigrant experience and I had been generously fed on it. There was a family Thanksgiving dinner just about that time with everybody trying hard to overlook the disgrace I had brought upon them; but in the nature of family parties, where the very intensity that is trying to hide itself inevitably bursts to the surface in a passionate explosion, my brother released his disgust as we were saying goodbye at the steps of my oldest sister's little attached house in Jackson Heights. "I never thought I would live to see the day that a member of my family would choose to go on relief," he said, and barely made it to the curb to vomit up my sister's excellent, rich, and lovingly prepared turkey dinner. My mother rushed to hold his head, a service my brother repulsed, and she managed at the same time to turn to me too with a glance to assure me that she was not a party to my brother's censure, however much she sympathized with him and failed to understand my motives. She was a wonder at supporting all her children simultaneously, an art which won her everybody's anger—and everybody's love.

I felt myself a criminal. Nothing so criminal as failure and uselessness.

The little stories I had gone back to writing were being turned down wherever I sent them. I had only done a couple, and I soon stopped, too disheartened to go on, and got another job as a typist-clerk and went off relief.

I married soon after that, to a union official with a salary good enough for both of us to live on modestly. I would be lying if I didn't admit that I married as a way out of a dilemma, and as a way into some kind of success. At least, getting married was a form of success for a woman. Sneakily, I also dreamed of using marriage as a way of starting again. I stayed at home, letting my husband support me, and I began a novel on a subject that had come to me through him. Just before we met, he had an almost fatal bout with tuberculosis, an illness that had killed his father. When we married, the disease had been successfully arrested, though he was deeply marked by his close call with death. A girl he had fallen in love with during his stay in the sanitarium was not as lucky as he, and she died just before we met. When we became lovers he gave me her diary to read. She had written it during the last year of her life when they were in love, and planning to marry, and hope and despair ruled her in equal amounts. It was not a writer's diary, but I was seized by it to the point where it entered my consciousness begging to have its life restored at my hand—or at least marked in some way. There was enough in the diary to stand as a model and not so much as to tie my hands in making up most of the story.

Writing the book was hard work and I was filled with the old doubts—making the work harder to pursue. Anyway in a few months, after completing a couple of chapters, I was forced to stop. The union had cut back on its staff. My husband's salary was halved and he was asked to relocate in another city. In the jumble of these pressures to move and the need to bring in some money, I lost touch with my grasp of the novel. When we relocated I took on some part-time office work at the union. I abandoned the novel. Anyway, I told myself, it wasn't any good.

Picking Up More Pieces
STARTING OVER

I t's odd. I always thought of myself as the youngest, the youngest of my family, of my crowd, of my friends—always tagging along on sufferance, running to keep up, being taken care of, paid for, ferried around, straining to reach what others grabbed for easily, on tiptoe to see what the others saw, hurrying, hurrying to grow up, rushing into the tandem harness of marriage, babies, kids raised with all the proper, adult touchstones—tender loving care by way of Gesell and Spock and the local PTA—then the rush toward divorce and remarriage and another baby and more Spock and the local PTA; and suddenly I was older than everybody, I was the oldest woman in the world, as if everything that had happened to me had gone on while my back was turned for a second, turned away from my true self, and now without even noticing I was on the downslide of the small span of time given to me for my own use, though I was unaware that I had ever passed the peak or of arriving at this undistinguished point where I was now located.

Do all women who give over a chunk of their lives to nurturing suffer this same shock? A lot of contemporary writing has dived into these waters and come up shaking the subject of women's liberation like a dog a rag, with a puppies' exuberance that a really good new thing has been fished up. But the complications of this subject are immense. Some feminist separatists argue that a woman mustn't marry if she wishes to live her life for herself and as herself. Some also argue that she should refuse to bear children. These are political stances, and it seems foolish to contend that such painful questions are possible to answer with yes or no checks in little boxes.

Whether or not to marry, whether or not to bear children are not cerebral decisions. They are irreconcilably tangled up with elements of emotion, eroticism, and duty, or of those related lusts, success and power. Traditionally women have been making their way in the world for a long time now through the activity we call "love," and alas for most women the pursuit and the winning of a man is still her prize and her major reward. "Love" is the intimate field of a woman's landscape, her kitchen garden, her designated plot of ground on which she is freely permitted to do her best or her worst; it is her means to fame, fortune, and to what life has to offer, whether she takes as her model Isadora Duncan, Charlotte Brontë, Marilyn Monroe, or her girlfriends down the block. Life, history, and literature overflow with the stories of women whose sole mark upon their times was made by way of their sexual ties or passionate friendships with powerful men; women who became stars because of the reflected light of their brilliant connections, the love goddesses of female mythology, bathed in an intriguing glow of physical beauty, gossip, and erotic excitement. These are the folk heroines, not the quiet, good, humble helpmeets, uncelebrated at their deaths for their loyal service to their husbands.

I would be lying if I described the horizon of my marriages and my motherhood as nothing but bleakness. If, as feminists argue, I had been *programmed* to need monogamous, romantic love and children of my own flesh, I did seem to genuinely *need* them, however artificial the stimulus. Whether or not I was plugged into a false notion of love by way of social and ideological conduits, I still couldn't have operated at all without love at the base of my days, and would have disrupted whatever else I was doing to seize and secure love first. I don't know whether any study has yet been made that disproves the universal appetite and need for love and for procreation. In my mid-twenties I was mysteriously overwhelmed by such an uncontrollable appetite to bear a child. When they came, my children were a wonder to me; I was as fascinated by them as by anything else that surrounded me, more so than by most things.

Was I happy then as a wife and mother? Yes, sometimes. Happy, busy, hard-working, eager to nurture, and feeling myself favored to be wrapped in protective layers of love, care, and need. I was just as often wildly angry at being shut behind this role I had been assigned—this wife and mother mask—that I was desperate to break out of. I hated housework though I loved a clean house. I was often depressed. I didn't know where to place my hatred—against myself, or the children, and the man I loved. I was ungovernably unhappy in ways I myself couldn't entirely comprehend. See-saw. Like other women, I struck the best balance I could. It was a real world of difficulties we inhabited.

There are some women whose careers march along a straight, well-marked line, contiguous and logical, as most men's careers do. Some of these also have happy marriages, children, and a warm family life. They are the lucky few. Most women endure a series of clashing, parallel lives which interrupt, attack, and sometimes demolish one another. It is as if a woman's life were a journey on a train subject to repeated halts, switching of lines, back-tracking, layovers, shuntings to sidings. Danger signals keep on blinking. Each start is stopped; then a new start, then another stop; the condition of the track is bad, getting worse through disuse; there are smashed wrecks outside the windows, all along the way.

When a woman marries she endangers her work; children enhance the danger, and to her marriage as well, in one of the many oblique contradictions a woman's life is subject to. She has already endangered her independence, her life lived for herself, in her own name and in her own interest, when she elects love, marriage, and a family. If she moves resolutely to protect her independence *and* her family life, she endangers the whole show and is likely to end divorced with custody of the children and a job that grants her time off to stay at home when the kids are sick. Women with private incomes are the luckiest of all—free to buy not happiness but baby-sitters, cooks, and housekeepers, and armed with the means to deflect a husband's misery caused by an entire family riding on his back alone. Unless of course he is bewitched by the old ideals of masculinity and control. And so we come full circle again. We hope that this is no longer the way love and marriage works for young couples; but that's the way it was for my generation when we married.

I married the first time at twenty-two, and the second time at thirty-four. Each time I knew in my bones that beyond romantic love hovered drastic possibilities, not the least of which was that love itself could be an illusion. Like other women I clung to another illusion—that since the best rules of the game had been met—love and good faith—I would be clever enough to keep all the balls in the air at once and as a reward for my special case, *my* fate would work out better. In fact, it worked out exactly as for many other women.

The men I married also had trouble getting started. Perhaps that's an inevitable condition for anyone with insufficient income to pick and choose at will among an assortment of professions. My first husband had been sent into a factory in his teens. With his father dead, a mother also working in a factory, and a younger sister to be supported until she was old enough to go on the same route, what else was there for him to do? He was happy, almost, to become ill and put factory work behind him. In a sense tuberculosis saved him from the deadly rigidity of that track. He educated himself in the sanitarium. He became a radical and went back into the factory as a militant unionist, in time becoming a union official. But with the reaction against the thirties' militancy that swamped the country after the Second World War, his union was attacked as a Communist organization, and in the retrenchment that followed, he had to go back to the cutting board as a worker. We had two babies by that time, and there seemed no other recourse. Again illness saved him. He contracted a sickness which had not yet been diagnosed by medicine as viral pneumonia. Given his history of tuberculosis, the doctors made the natural mistake of seeing this lung infection as a relapse. To be cured by rest, he went away, alone, to a farmhouse in the country for a couple of months, and had a wonderful time reading, fishing, and taking pictures. Taking pictures was what he really wanted to do. Ironically it was with the help of the brother who had so discouraged me as a writer that he was staked to all the expensive equipment necessary to begin to do photography. The rest was up to him. It was a struggle, but he made it, becoming a very good photographer who would come to live comfortably from his chosen and loved profession.

My second husband had always wanted to be a writer, but economic necessity put him behind a sink as a dishwasher in a cafeteria while he was still in his teens. Because he spoke Spanish and English perfectly he was able to work his way out of dishwashing and bus-boying into the office of censorship, where he read overseas mail at the start of the Second World War. He enlisted in the Navy soon after; when he was discharged he went to Black Mountain College for a while under the GI Bill of Rights, and began to write full time. When we married he had had a part-time job as the movie reviewer for *The Daily Worker*, but on the very day we did marry he lost that job and with my two little children to help support, he wasted no time but quickly got another job on the belt-line of an electronics plant and then a second one at night selling in a store. That was horribly hard, physically, and stultifying in every way. He applied for work as a bilingual typist for a pharmaceutical firm. He got that, and rose so rapidly that by the time he left twelve years later he was in line for the top of the top. He was then assistant to the vice-president of the international division of one of the largest drug companies in the world. But what he wanted to do was write. Making time that he tore free of the job and of family activities, he had pushed and driven himself to write a novel. As soon as it was published, he quit to become a full-time writer. He had stashed away enough money to keep us going for a year (there was a third child now), but in an economic sense, we were pretty much back where we started before the good-paying days in the pharmaceutical firm.

Throughout my husbands' locating of themselves, I was mostly having babies and taking care of them, though I worked at odd jobs in between. At the beginning of the war, just before the babies, one of my old friends suggested that I help edit a special legislative bulletin published by the Lawyers Guild, and I did that for a year. Then another friend called me in to help her edit the cultural section of *The Daily Worker.* I told her I didn't know how, but she said, "Of course you do," so I did it. My friends referred to me as "a writer." When they used that term I became uneasy, as if I were about to be caught out in a transparent lie or in an illegal impersonation. Another friend, editing one of the radical magazines, asked me to review books. I did creditably enough. By that time, I was a dues-paying member of the Newspaper Guild. That made me a writer, didn't it? Then, the establishment of even this modest career threatened to come to an end as the men returned from the service and claimed their old posts. We women were let go, of course. But I seemed to have been launched into some sort of hack editorial work and I soon got another job as one of the editors of the house organ of the International Workers Order. My work constituted a kind of profession, if not a career, when I started having babies.

Between the two sets of children and the two marriages, I worked again, but this time at anything I could get that was close enough to home to supervise lunches, or at part-time jobs that allowed me to juggle home and work. I worked as a dentist's secretary, office worker, fund-raiser, and publicist for the local YMHA; I did reviews, manuscript typing, free-lance editing, anything that paid some money. By the time my third child was nine years old, and my husband had published his first novel and quit his job and it was imperative that I go back to work, my work history was a mass of impossible stuff to organize into anything seemly enough for an employment agency to glance at twice. Going out to look for work was a bewildering assignment. Worst of all, I had become partially deaf.

It's difficult to convey to normal hearing people what partial deafness is like. Perhaps a metaphor will help. Today, here in Maine, a heavy snowfall is creating a hushed, white-blanketed world outside my window. I used to imagine that the deaf existed in such a white silence, but I was wrong. To be deaf is to live with constant, painfully confusing racketing noise—the kind of noise generally called deafening. At least that's the way it is with me.

I became deaf suddenly, when I was forty-five, as the result of an illness which started innocently enough with what I assumed to be a bad headache. I dosed myself with aspirin, but the pain didn't yield. It mounted. It was 1960. An extraordinary session of the United Nations had brought to New York a stellar cast of world personalities (it was the session when Nikita Khrushchev banged his shoe in appreciation of Fidel Castro's style at the podium), and I attributed the pain in my head to over-excitement, too much TV watching (I was glued to the set for every minute I could snatch from my household duties), and the ingenuity needed to keep my six-year-old youngest son occupied elsewhere while I monopolized *his* set. When the pain persisted through a night and another day, I shifted the blame to some dental work I had undergone a few days earlier, then I blamed it on menopause, and added phenobarbital to the aspirin. Accompanying the pain was a mass of noise. Industrial production at its most sound-polluting could have produced no greater noise—not steel, papermaking, construction sites, boiler factories, nineteenth-century cotton mills, not nature either in a combined roaring of winds and sea. This was in addition to that mild old malady: "a ringing in one's ears." My ears hummed, rang, harbored sirens and the harsh clangor of bells, and of metal struck again and again in a maddening vibration.

On the third day I was taken to the hospital by ambulance. The doctors x-rayed my head, tapped my spine, and monitored my brain by encephalogram. When all else failed they requested me to bring the tips of my fingers together with my eyes closed. I did my best. They came up only with conjectures as answers. They hinted at brain tumor and then fled to the other extreme, and talked of psychosomatic illness. After the first massive injections of pain killer, which made me physically ill, plunged me into nightmare dreams and left the pain untouched, the doctors did nothing, because they had no idea what they could do, apart from insisting that I stay in bed, where I certainly had to be since I couldn't remain upright without falling over. The disease finally got itself named as an aseptic encephalitis (whatever that is) and I was eventually sent home to lie in bed for more weeks of similar pain. Slowly, in infinitesimal gradations of relief, the pain diminished, though the noises persisted. It must have been at least a year after the illness was cured before I understood that the irritability, exhaustion, and misanthropy I would come away with from attending any social occasion was directly caused by my inability to hear what was being said. For an even longer time than that I went on denying the truth of my own senses, or lack of them. I didn't want to be deaf. I didn't want to be deaf so badly that I hoped to make my disability go away by refusing to admit its existence. How could I be going deaf before I had even gotten around to starting to do my own work?

Sudden blindness or the loss of limbs is clearly a tragedy; sudden deafness is a joke. Deafness is always good for a laugh. Say "hearing aid," and your listener will smile. Think of the silent movies and the old lady or gentleman with an enormous ear trumpet. Deafness *is* funny; there's comedy in the malady—mishearing works as an oblique, witty comment on the absurdities of a given style or manner when the key word is mangled into something that fits better by not fitting at all. But hearing people laugh at the deaf for another reason. I remember how nervous the deaf made me when I could hear. We're all afraid of deafness, as we're all afraid of age and death. To be deaf, in our imaginings, is to be old, senile, helpless, withdrawn, isolated, and, finally, dumb.

The deaf are idiotic. Look how they listen with intense fixity; see how they smile and nod at the wrong signals; listen to how oddly they speak, too softly or too loudly or too much, or not at all, but intently stare at our lips as we talk, with a look on their faces of being helpless, frightened, and lost. It's perfectly obvious deafie hasn't understood a word.

What can we do about it? Our way of speaking is perfectly okay, nobody else has any trouble with it. If we weren't heard the first time, are we likely to be the next? We try again and turn up the volume of our speech; finally we lapse into uncomfortable silence, give up, turn our backs, and talk to somebody else. We resent being forced to think about communication when all we had in mind was chatter, banter, a polite exchange or the pleasure of spreading our plumes for another's admiration. Now we must consider the deaf listener and deal with senses foreign to us— visual expressiveness, touch, vibration, acting out, care in moving our lips (at least) and in not turning our heads aside or covering our mouths with our hands or in getting too far away. Worst of all, we are forced to evaluate whether what we have to say is worth saying at all. As quickly as possible we turn to another hearing friend and with a snort of laughter report that "she's deaf as a post," glad to put the encounter behind us.

I was dismayed to cross that line from the "normal" to a world of the shunned, the partially deaf, the hard-of-hearing, a phrase whose closed-in connotations I loathed.

Yet I did exist in a different world, an "unworldly" place that had already identified itself unmistakeably.

During the period when I was recovering from the encephalitis, I woke in the middle of the night to the sound of music. Annoyed that someone had left a radio or record player or the TV turned on, I went about our large apartment looking for the source, to turn it off. I then had two teen-age children and our six-year-old youngster at home; one of them might have left something droning on; but all was dark, everybody was quietly asleep, no electronic gadget was working. I could not explain the distant, wierd music gaining and fading as I moved about.

I opened a window out to the street. Perhaps a thoughtless neighbor was playing an instrument in the middle of the night. Though the music changed, swelling into organ-like chords as I leaned out over the still street, all neighboring windows in the apartment houses were dark: only the stair-wells and elevator shafts were lit up and down my block. Now the strings began to lead, and celestial harmonies of high tuneless voices seemed to be chanting my name in a kind of parody of a sacred mass. Who was playing this stupid trick on me? I returned through the rooms of the apartment, enraged and frightened now, searching for the source. All was normal. My three children and my husband slept.

I hadn't lit any lights; New York City street lamps made the apartment bright enough to see by. I was scaring myself—I saw myself as a madwoman in a long trailing night-gown stalking barefoot through an apartment in the half-dark, searching for voices and music that couldn't be located.

In that second of still fear, the music abruptly ceased, changing as if by the click of a switch to a generalized bass roaring followed by the high note of a continuous siren. Roars and sirens were the noises I was already familiar with as emanating from my own head. Was this eerie music coming from my head as well? So it seemed.

The experience stunned me, because it was the first. In time I came to accept hearing celestial music, voices, the sustained pitiful wailing of a child, the clangor of metal struck against metal, sirens, boilers, pneumatic drills—the whole gamut of the hell of noise mysteriously manufactured in my own skull. In exchange, certain external, real sounds were lost to me—doorbells, the ring of the telephone, clock chimes. If a speaker mumbled, I heard the mumble but not a syllable of speech. Certain musical tones were beyond the range of my lost hearing. These blows seemed to come gradually, or perhaps I admitted to them gradually. I sat through a production of *Don Giovanni* in a rage against the orchestra, singers, and above all the audience, for putting up with a performance in which every other note was flat, and it wasn't until the audience rose in a standing ovation that I realized the fault must be in my ears—that I could no longer hear music without distortion of the melodic line since certain ranges of notes were too high or too low for me to hear at all. I could enjoy this shattered music only by replacing what was lost from memory, reconstructing "Là ci darem la mano" from the past time when I could hear all the notes. I said goodbye to piano music in concert. Goodbye flute, bassoon, beloved cello, goodbye guitar. Alone in the house I tried turning the volume up high enough to hear the lows, but then the highs blasted me out of my mind.

I tried to relearn listening. I discovered the power of

vibrations on a park bench by way of the wooden back of the seat I shared with two strange men whose conversation was communicated through my shoulder blades in an entirely new, rumbling language. I invented lip-reading for myself, and read, as well, eyes, eyebrows, hand gestures, body squirmings, and the brilliantly communicative signs that accompany and dramatize speech. I worked at the art of missing nine-tenths of a conversation and somehow still coming in with a sensible line of dialogue. I learned about patience and impatience with myself and others. At bottom, however exhausting the effort to stay in touch, I didn't want to shut out any part of living, or of human contact. I wanted to stay in the worldly world.

If insanity is a state of mind in which the imagined and the real lose definition, then all the deaf and partly deaf must be somewhat insane. I understand Joan of Arc and her voices. Nothing but middle-ear infection? Didn't I entertain voices? I developed a new perspective on Beethoven—at least the Harry Bauer film version depicting the dramatic agony of going deaf—and the sound track I had smiled at as melodramatic exaggeration in my youth, I recognized now as unadorned literal description.

Do I sound proud of being deaf? In some weird way, I must admit I am. We speak often of putting ourselves in the other guy's place, though we can't actually do that. To be handicapped, or to be old or poor or black or a woman, if we aren't one of these ourselves, is to embrace a mere concept which we surround with empathy, coolness, hostility, shame, guilt, or conscious help—depending upon our social point of view. But to know what the experience *feels* like is quite impossible short of living it out. So who needs it? Who needs to be shoved out into one of the harshly punitive categories set up by our society? I don't know if I needed it, but I discovered I could use the new learning. There's enormous loss in becoming any kind of outsider; I don't believe that pain, poverty, failure, or helplessness are good for anybody; but there's important knowledge to be salvaged out of every agony, and deafness too has yielded its arcane secrets of the mysteries of sound.

With deafness, I became a new, highly sensitive instrument. I discovered that sound is as much direction as volume and that without the first the hearer is lost, helpless, terrorized by danger. Not to know *where* a sound is coming from is almost worse than not hearing the dangerous sound at all. Hearing aids make this condition worse. Before I was fitted for two cunning hearing devices which are so unobtrusive that nobody is aware that I use them, I heard sounds, when I heard them at all, as coming from my right (my better ear); but with hearing aids all noises assault from behind, entering one's consciousness through the little apertures of the device tucked back of the ears. Sounds are otherwise altered as well. The human voice is an extraordinarily individuated instrument, marvelously colored and toned in its own fashion; but with hearing aids a harsh metallic tint removes all warmth—turns soft shading to neon. The natural human ear is a remarkable filter tuned to pluck conversation out of any bewildering cacophony of noise, but hearing aids beef everything up to an unbearable confusion. If a waiter drops a spoon in a noisy restaurant, there's an explosion through the hearing aids; while if he discreetly murmurs an offer to refill my coffee cup, I can only guess at the proposal. (One says "yes" to murmurs at one's peril.)

But all sounds are precious—even the lousy ones—for to lose one (snores, coughs, police sirens, even the savage whistling of the wind magnified through the aids) is to lose all. Even if heard imperfectly—exaggerated, mechanized, tormenting, falsified—let them still be heard.

Whenever deafness comes, nevertheless, it comes at a bad time. For me, it came when I first began to look for work again. I hadn't yet admitted it to myself, or to any need for hearing aids. I walked around partially deaf, telling myself I was fine, adding that handicap to my other problems as I tried to reenter the working world, a world where everything, sound, sight, meaning—the entire scene and the whole scenario—had been switched on me while my back was turned to home and family. Why, even the type-writers were utterly different from the ones I had been used to, bewitched into live, electrified monsters that responded to my nervousness like edgy animals to a bad trainer. I couldn't pass the simplest typist-clerk tests.

My first trips to employment offices left me suicidal. I was totally out of sync. It was at that point that I became the oldest woman on earth. Children presided over all the desks, all decisions, all opportunities. They spoke a new language, mostly gibberish to me, when I could hear them at all. Being deaf was a torment. They were a generation of mumblers, mutterers, and murmurers. And I myself seemed incapable of hitting a right note. I over-dressed; I was under-trained for the aptitude and intelligence tests that bristled with concepts I had never encountered in my long-ago schooling. I was terrified that the physical examinations required would reveal my deafness, or worse diseases, unknown even to me. I heard things hilariously wrong. I stood up when others were called and didn't answer to my own name since it was inevitably mispronounced. Told to sit down and wait, I would mishear and walk off into neighboring rooms. Once, in a posh employment agency on Fifth Avenue, I walked right out the front door by mistake, and like a lunatic toy set in motion and out of control, I just kept going, laughing hysterically as I went. I had been waiting for what seemed to be a real lead this time, but I couldn't bring myself to go back.

Any eighteen-year-old fresh out of high school was earning ninety dollars a week in 1963. Surely I could command one hundred somewhere? The terrible depression years of annihilating joblessness came back to annihilate me once more. To exorcise their curse, I would wear my best clothes, the costumes for my former role as wife of a corporation executive. The more mature personnel managers (thirty-year-olds) placed the costume, if not the woman, and suggested volunteer work, kindly proferring the names of charitable organizations that could use my services, without pay, of course. When I actually was granted an on-site job interview, I spread my wings and took off in a manifestation so dazzlingly beyond the requirements of the mean little job I was applying for that I couldn't be hustled out of the office fast enough for the comfort of the threatened department head I was supposed to be coming in to assist as a stenographer or typist.

It should have struck me as funny; it *was* funny; but I couldn't laugh. I remember coming home one late winter afternoon, walking along the edge of the subway platform, thinking, do it, do it. It would solve everything to jump.

A friend got me some work as an artist's representative. I hustled to sell the designs of a woman of my age whose work, first-rate once, had been by-passed by a younger group of design innovators, and her portfolio, which I lugged all over Manhattan to show to advertising directors with a great fake display of enthusiasm, had the clear delineaments of failure written all over its tired samples. I suffered agonies of discomfort. I wasn't happy about the product I was selling. Finally I wasn't making any money. And in the advertising business too! I went back to the employment agencies.

Politics was playing a part in my present difficulties. Of those dozens of jobs I had had before mothering became my central occupation, the important ones had been in organizations cited on the Attorney General's list of subversive groups. My work background should have placed me at the top of the FBI's most wanted list, except that I was nobody, and had held very lowly posts in the disfavored organizations I have already mentioned, as well as the places where I had reviewed books, *Masses and Mainstream* and *The Guardian*; or in the defensive, hurriedly assembled outfits set up to counterattack, like "The Committee to Defend the Peace Advocates"; and in a variety of disgraced, because "Communist-dominated," unions, like the Fur

Workers and Shoe Workers, in the days before they cleared themselves of such charges.

In those organizations, I had written, edited, addressed envelopes, typed, taken dictation, trundled mailings to the post office, made coffee, run the office, raised funds, arranged the annual dinner and anything else that had needed to be done. In the process of carrying on those activities in which I had whole-heartedly believed, I was often dismayed by the daily bad practice of my fellow "idealists." I had spent a lot of my energies raving and ranting at my comrades. I fought against glaring inequities (old left males were awful to their women comrades), and against bad ideology (national and international); but I went on stubbornly clinging to the validity of the proposition that humanity's happiness would be shaped under the guiding hands of world socialism. Those of us who so believed were surrounded with an aura of criminality. Anyone who has sat beside me in a plane knows that I'm an abject coward, not made of the brave stuff needed to be an illegal (even when I was arrested in the early seventies for anti-draft activity I was well within my constitutional right to petition the government); but in my attempts to find a job in the early sixties, I felt it necessary to totally suppress that earlier work background, as if mine were the record of a paroled criminal rather than the lawful and even lauded activity of a participant in the New Deal and anti-fascist American society of the thirties and forties.

It may be hard to believe, especially by the generation that saw the heroes of the sixties' anti-war and student rebellions, and the heroes of the black liberation movement, and the heroines of the women's liberation movement go on to become the popular and political media stars of the seventies, but an utter decimation of the old left took place under the withering spirit of Joe McCarthyism. It's true that the causes of part of that decimation were internal, brought on the old movement by itself, quite beyond the pressures of any outside evil. There were evils enough within the old left (particularly stemming from its venal and stupid adherence to Soviet Communism) to have killed it off for me without the aid of Joe McCarthy. If anything, McCarthyism kept me a party member long past the time when I had reached a profound disagreement with party philosophy. I stayed, out of a sense of solidarity with rank and file comrades whom I felt I would be cowardly in abandoning—such as the hundreds of thousands of foreign-born workers in the multi-national International Workers Orders, whose modest savings in life insurance and burial benefits mostly went down the drain in a shameful attack by a powerful democratic government on a powerless and useful people's organization.

Though I was once a dues-paying member of a party that considered itself the vanguard political arm of the world, I am not now nor ever was a political theorist. I admit to a vast general ignorance of things physical, technological, mythical, religious, and political-social. It wasn't an esoteric political formula that led me to socialist beliefs, along with hundreds of thousands of other Americans in the thirties, but a longing for a messianic response to the bitterly hard problems of my youth, problems which paled before the hardships others were suffering.

There is a moment in the Passover seder celebration which I particularly love—the invisible visitation of Elijah the prophet at the feast. (The seder is a ritual meal commemorating the freeing of the Jews from bondage, accompanied by prayer, song, wine, and the retelling of the history of the flight out of Egypt. Christians know it, of course, as the Last Supper.) When I was little, it was a transcendent moment to be delegated as the youngest child to open the door for Elijah to enter. I believed in Elijah, as I believed in the entire amazing story. I had no doubt that he slid past me, an unseen wonder and mystery, delivering on a gust of air intermingled with the neighbors' savory odors of chicken soup and honey cake his exquisitely kind promise of the coming of the Messiah. I welcomed him as a messenger bringing vouchers of peace and plenty to come, not only for us expectant at our family holiday table, but for all the world beyond. I kept my eyes riveted upon the surface of the wine poured into an ornate glass specially prepared for Elijah to drink from. There! An infinitesimal ripple. He had taken his sip. Now he was invisibly leaving, as he had come, off to the millions of other seders awaiting him. I worried about him. How could he manage such distances and so much wine? And shut the door on him regretfully, while keeping it open to hope. I still, yes, believe in the possibility of a good life for every person on earth. What I can no longer come up with are pat formulas to make it possible.

But the immediate practical problem I was faced with in reentering the job market was to bury my political past and wipe away my past job history. I needed to come to the employment agencies disguised as an unskilled housewife. There came a day when having looked for weeks without success, and having just been turned down for a miserable job as a typist to a research assistant (salary eighty dollars a week), I returned to my apartment and stood in my kitchen and howled my humiliated heart out. I was crying not only for the crummy job which I coveted, but that my life could have assumed such a shape that I would covet such a crummy job. The script of my future I had written in my youthful daydreams had never allowed for this debacle. What had happened to me? What the hell was I doing here, sobbing my brains out, in a kitchen in Washington Heights, my kids at school, my husband away at a writer's colony finishing his second book, and I cast as a red-eyed slob of a woman nearing fifty, deaf, and too dumb to be hired for a lousy typist's job at eighty dollars a week?

What my situation forced upon me was a confrontation between my assumed self and my *self*, that part of me I reserved for me alone. But our selves are made real through the tangible. My family was tangible—the man I loved, my three children. There was nothing else that arched from my sense of what I was to other real accomplishment. At an age when I should have passed the peak of my powers and amassed a solid body of work behind me, I could count up *love, one husband, three children.*

There were people close to me who considered that by quitting a position as a corporate executive, my husband had destroyed that too; that he had wiped out what had been built—the security and beauty of family life and love. In fact, in breaking apart the formal dance patterns of correct middle-class husbandry, he had set us all free. He had done the unthinkable—given up a good job, the best prospects, a steadily increasing salary, stock options, retirement benefits, life insurance, medical and hospital insurance, the whole neat package complete with excellent lunches, good clothes, dinners at the best restaurants, theater, opera, concert and ballet attendance at its easiest with a word dropped to his secretary and the tab picked up by the company—all the comforts and rewards that accrue to the man who knows how to play the game.

So what if the life he really wanted to lead was daily almost devoured by corporate life? Or if we had to drag customers along to our company-paid entertainments? With luck the customers were charming; often they were exotic Far Easterners who were interesting even when they were boring. Only a fool would give all that up, others said. It was as senselessly irresponsible and risky as jumping off a bridge. Risky, yes; senseless and irresponsible, no. In practical life, nothing succeeds like success, and as he succeeded in his new life as a writer, the charges against him were dropped. Such leaps are frightening to others; then exhilarating if perfected, like that of the young man who carefully planned and carried out the seemingly senseless feat of climbing the face of the World Trade Center one hundred and one stories into the air. *I am here,* such acts proclaim. *I, I am, I make myself felt, I have something special to do, I must do it, I will do it, I do it,* and in the doing they free not only something indefinable in themselves but in us who merely watch.

But there's danger in cashing in vicariously on another's accomplishment, and especially for women. José called from the McDowell Colony just as I finished crying. He was winding up his work. Could I arrange to leave the children for the weekend and spend his final days at the Colony with him? He would rent a car, reserve a room at the town inn, and we would drive back together. I jumped at the opportunity to put the red-eyed slob woman aside. I wasn't that woman after all. I too could touch the glamorous life of the artist in pristine New Hampshire, introduced by my husband, the writer, to his colleagues at the Colony, slog through the snowy paths to the charming studio where he had worked, read the names of the greats inscribed on a wooden plaque, those who had used this studio before Jose; I could sit in that hallowed space quietly reading while Jose finished the last pages to be typed. But disquiet gnawed at me through that happy weekend. It squirmed for attention, demanding to be interpreted. Apart from love, apart from happiness, apart from the true pleasure I derived from Jose's accomplishments, wasn't I making a fraudulent claim to the artist's life through him, because I didn't dare make a serious stab at winning it for myself by my own efforts?

There is a kind of woman who speaks of her husband's achievement as her own.

"We were nominated for the National Book Award," I have heard a friend say, though she had had nothing to do with the work.

"We made 'New and Recommended' " in the *Times*, a novelist's wife had called to report the night before, though the book was no collaboration.

"We're going to Greece for the winter. It's the best place for us to work." But *her* work consisted of looking enchanting and finding good little cheap restaurants to dine in.

Was I then this kind of parasite—a species that I despised as much as I pitied and understood?

It was a realization that pulled me up sharply. Whatever I was, I made the decision to stop the nonsense and get a job immediately. I looked for one close to home, where I could keep half an eye on our youngest son. There was an ad in the Sunday *Times* for a secretarial position with a long-term research project at Columbia-Presbyterian Medical Center, only a few blocks from where we were then living. I lied about my formal education, toned down my credentials, dressed quietly, hardly spoke at all beyond reassuring murmurs, and got a job at one hundred dollars a week. Huge victory! The work consisted mainly of using up a segment of the enormous grant the project had to spend yearly in order to be re-funded. This particular aspect of affluent flatulence was new to me—and amusing. It was a refreshment to be out in the real world. I brought home stories of the bureaucratic craziness running rampant in the project, and of the technological wonders of today's medicine, and gossip about "the girls" in the office. But in a fairly short time, the novelty was absorbed in the empty, spongy routine, and what I had built up into a smashing success in my deprived state retreated into the depressing reality of dumb, useless, and wasteful make-work.

But then life took off again, rising free as a gas balloon in a children's story. We went to Spain, using our last savings, on the theory that we could live there cheaply and work at writing, between us earning enough money to keep going. The old twenties' dream revisited. By the time we arrived in 1964, Spain was no longer the poor artist's haven; prices had risen sharply and in eight months, we were practically out of money.

Busted, our future blankly uncertain, we sat at a table in our favorite café in the Plaza de San Juan de Dios along the port of the city of Cadiz, where the clock chimed the opening bars of Manuel de Falla's *Fire Music* instead of the hours, sipping *cafe con leche* and deciding that no, Jose must not go back to his job at the pharmaceutical house which was now offering more pay, headquarters in Geneva, and sub rosa promises that he might even be given time off to write. We decided no, no, no; and to celebrate our bold choice for personal freedom, we took a bus to Jerez de la

58

Frontera. Naturally we visited the great sherry-producing house of Domecque. Naturally we emerged drunk and happy. We hired a horse-drawn carriage. There we were, Jose and I and our eleven-year-old son Rafael, our insides sloshed with every possible gradation of a magnificent scale of sherry wines sampled in the hospitable Domecque cellars, making our measured way through the narrow, white-walled, flower-splashed lanes of the town which formed a perfect gallery for the delightful clop of the horses' hoofs and the strong smells of the animals and excrement mingled with the sharp sea flavors of the mid-day meals being prepared in all the little restaurants along the way in the siesta heaviness of the sun-drenched, winey, vibrating air. Happiness is a strange bird, starting into flight when it is least expected.

Happy times. And sickeningly frightening times too. Our money situation was desperate. We'd solve it somehow.

We returned home in 1965, and again, saved by a friend I was precipitated back into my old profession. Our old friend, Warren Miller, the novelist, had taken up an offer to be literary editor of *The Nation*. He wanted me to come along as his assistant. Of course I said yes. Yes, yes, yes.

Picking Up the Last Piece
STARTING LATE

I was fifty years old when I began again as a magazine editor. Naturally I lied about my age—not to my friend Warren, who knew the truth about me anyway—but to personnel. For good measure I threw in a college degree that I didn't have. I felt I needed to lie to be hired in the first place and to be paid the salary that the work should command. Though I was hired, the salary was lowered, in spite of my bogus claim to a degree.

Perhaps because I was replacing a man, or for blunt economic reasons, management had changed the classification of the job. Once in, I very soon started a fuss about that, insisting that I be placed in an editorial slot and not a technical one, which automatically meant more money. I was again a dues-paying member of the Newspaper Guild, and even if the Union wasn't exactly overjoyed at taking up my defense, I was nevertheless bouyed by the connection. I amazed and slightly displeased my friend Warren. He hadn't counted on my causing trouble in my own interests;

but only on my being a great help to him. He forgave me because he was naturally generous, and more so because my crusade never impinged on my zest for the work itself. If anything, it gave the work an extra push. I tried harder, not to please in the old agreeable, self-effacing, female way, but in the cause of making the pages more interesting. I taught myself to think differently. I was among colleagues, mostly male, whose legitimate demands upon me did not include any nurturing, tending, protective caring. I wasn't a mate or a mother to anybody at the publication. All my fellow workers could ask of me was that I do my job as well as they did theirs. Anyway, I wanted to do my job *better* than they did theirs.

I was intent upon that, though tensely wound up in a contradictory web of reactions. I carried a sense of being an imposter, ignorant and unsure, teetering on the tiny shelf of prestige allotted me in the professional world. Yet even while I saw myself in this shaky position I was aware of straining upward to climb to the next level of achievement. I strove constantly to prove myself, yet I resented that I felt I had to do so. Surely everybody should recognize instantly how good I was? One moment I despised myself for being unrealistic (there wasn't any reason that I should be accepted on faith); the next moment I was in an irrational rage at some minor humiliation, however much I covered up in the company of my colleagues. I veered wildly in my self-evaluation. One day I was furious at non-recognition; the following day I humbled myself to a point where I was ready to pay for the privilege of being allowed to work on the publication at all. My notch as a kind of assistant-secretary to my friend Warren maddened me. How dared anybody set up these low standards? Because I was a woman? Because I typed and took dictation? Because I listened more than I spoke? I veered also between loving gratitude toward Warren for giving me this last chance to return to my work and what amounted to jealous hatred of his poised, superior position above me. So what if he was an established novelist who had proved himself over and over again and had *earned* his position? I was really just as good, deep down. Anybody with a modicum of insight should be able to recognize that.

How appallingly unreasonable I was; and what an unmanageably greedy ambition I seemed to be harboring. Where were these drives coming from? I had kept ambition and self-esteem under wraps for so long a time that I failed to recognize them as given portions of my earlier makeup.

In spite of this turbulent flow of underground emotions, I was happy in the exacting daily labor of my job. The work itself was wonderfully invigorating and satisfying; it filled me to the brim. I rode the subway to and from the office reading manuscripts, periodicals, galleys, books—so that every moment might be utilized. My agreeable, female manner was too ingrained a stain on my personality for me to abandon it altogether, but under its gentle camouflage I pushed hard to produce a section that would reflect my strong opinions as to what the back pages should be for readers. There were times I despaired of myself, of my colleagues, my contributors, and of the limitations of reader response; but mostly I reveled in the lucky moment I had fallen upon. It was the best of times to be involved in our kind of periodical; an active questioning consumed almost the whole of the intellectual and media community. I had come on staff in the fall of 1965 when all the old forms began to be burst wide open. There seemed to be being born every day an endless variety of new ways to pour human molds. It was a vibrant, violent period of exciting change. Few of us emerged from that time the same persons we had been; and we could feel ourselves changing every day. It was a time to become bold in one's personal craziness.

Secretly I thought of the back pages as "my" section. I understood, of course, that they were not, but a part of the communal effort of the magazine involving Warren, the managing editor, the editor-in-chief, the publisher, an advertising manager, copy-editor and production person, as well as printers, subscribers, and readers, My distorted, almost demented passion to claim as "mine" what was so patently an ensemble effort was a form of love for the work, a responsibility I set for myself that should need no apology, but because of the old condemnations leveled at ambitious women, I was uncomfortable with my new self-appointed command. The old terminology worried me—over-controlling, pushy, ball-breaking, aggressive, castrating, bitch. Why, I even coveted the job of my friend Warren, whom I dearly loved. I was set to bite the hands that fed me, growling and impatient with being fed. I wanted to become a wolfish animal, just like the other successful people, doing my own hunting, bringing in my own food. Even so, a great part of me pulled back from these coarse strivings, into the shelter of my former ways.

There's an old saying that warns those who wish for things to beware—they may get their wish. The spring before we had begun work on *The Nation*, Warren Miller had had an operation to remove a malignancy on the lung. Though we were told that the surgery had been successful and the cancer entirely removed, we didn't securely believe in what we were told. If he was out of danger, why cobalt treatments? On the plus side, he seemed well, happy, and active and particularly so in the fall when we started to work as Literary Editor and assistant-secretary, respectively. It took only a few months before it became obvious to me that his condition was hopeless. By early December he could no longer work. He died in April of 1966. He was a witty, generous, playful companion, intellectually spirited and joyous; he was something of a snob who affected harmless mannerisms far removed from his immigrant father's background, paradoxically co-existing alongside the strongest socially compassionate views. He was an understanding, loyal, and voraciously interested friend; a very good writer; a very good editor; an enchantingly attractive man. He was Jose's closest friend as well as my colleague; and his death left an enormous hole in our lives that has never been filled. His death also left me with the job I had coveted.

I have always liked to think that Warren consciously bequeathed the work to me. Actually it wasn't his to hand over.

To some extent I won the prize I sought by default. (I was there.) To some extent I won it by hard work and good enough performance. But the surprise was that once having won and secured the place I coveted, I didn't find myself settling back into the quiet state of satisfaction I had expected of myself. Instead I found myself boarding once again that new-old train of my desire to be a story-teller. Undoubtedly all the books coming across my desk must have played a part in my longings. Here were all these books being written. Too many to account for by genius. Some of them (among which were highly acclaimed works) were so bad that it didn't seem possible that I could do worse—no matter how badly I did. Good fiction is always an encouragement to aim as high; what had never occurred to me before was that it was possible to aim low. Perhaps it was simply that I had reached a point where there was no way to put myself off any longer, and any excuse would do. What I know is that I became obsessed with the idea of really tackling a novel.

This account of how at long last I started to do what I really wanted to do is not the full story of my life, though by its length it may seem to be. I have tried to produce the large markers that set me moving down certain paths. Warren's death was one of these. Not that I never before had been faced with the death of someone dear. Of course I had, and had been exposed to the intense grief that accompanies loss. But Warren's death was more like the shock of a total arrest. Death and personal mortality moved in on me as an urgent presence—not only loss was at work—but gain again. Death entered my conscious life to stay forever, as a permanent companion. Warren, in the form in which I knew and loved him, had disappeared. His physical existence could be considered to have had no more substantive importance than an onion's, set to grow its season, yield its crop and its juices, and dissolve into new matter. A man had ceased to exist as a unique working force, impinging on continuing time and action. That's how it happens, I noted, and can happen to anybody, to you, yourself, in a second, and with everything you have always wanted to do left undone. Think about that.

I thought about it. That was another gift from Warren, and the first large marker.

The second came to me during a run-of-the-mill husband and wife fight about money. I was then working at the magazine but not yet at a full senior editor's salary. It was one of the periods when we were very pressed for money. I don't remember the details of the quarrel. We're both good fighters and things can get very hot between us. I'm sure we threw off equally awful accusations, but I naturally remember only Jose's—which was to charge me with being insufficiently concerned with his career as a writer. What I remember vividly too is the rage that seized me. I wanted to kill him, and did my best verbally. I told him that he was damn right, I didn't care if he never wrote another word, that his writing was entirely his to worry about, it was his business and not anybody else's in the world and above all it wasn't mine. Not mine. Absolutely not mine.

Having said the unthinkable, I experienced a moment of pure, joyous clarity. It was true. It was true, what I had said. His writing belonged to him. It was true for him, true for anybody and everybody, and most important, true for me. True for me. Whether I wrote or not was entirely *my* responsibility. Nobody else's fault, if I never wrote a line. My responsibility, my freedom, my choice, my risk, my madness, my work. My work.

And the last large marker made its appearance during a luncheon with Christina Stead. She was visiting in New York from England where she had lived most of her life. We had been in correspondence about an article she was resisting doing for me, and I had invited her to lunch at a little Italian place in Greenwich Village close to my office where we could eat well and I might persuade her to do the piece. I was an admirer, and had been since the late thirties and early forties when she had published *House of All Nations* and *The Man Who Loved Children* and *For Love Alone*. (But I'm an admirer of everything this marvelous writer has produced.) It was our first meeting—a formal one between a respectful book editor and a distinguished and powerful novelist. I don't know how I expected her to be, but she was a wonder to me in ways I couldn't have anticipated.

Her husband of many years had recently died. She was somewhat at sea emotionally and practically. She was traveling, visiting old friends in this country where she had also lived for a number of years, and meeting with her publisher about a book they were hesitant to publish because, as she told me, "they say nobody's interested in the thirties." After a short time here she planned to go on to Australia where she had been born and had first started to write as a young woman. She was in her seventies when we met for our lunch. I was experiencing some difficulty in following her conversation, not only because the pitch of her voice was too low for my hearing aids to pick up, though I had turned the volume high, but also because she moved her lips differently, holding them taut in English fashion. I listened with all my other skills to feel for what she *was*, underneath what she was saying.

What I discerned was a person of extraordinary presence, with a sense of herself so quietly powerful and sure that my preconception of a commanding, creative character had to be erased as quite simply beside the point. I had for so long fantasized "the serious woman artist" (which was the kind I wanted to be) as a glamorous creature beyond reach, certainly beyond *my* reach, that the real thing, sitting so solidly and simply across the table from me, conversing without a trace of bullshit, had to be taken in slowly to be absorbed as someone to emulate. Suddenly the formula appeared easy. One just became one's self.

Toward the end of our lunch, Christina Stead turned the conversation from her work to mine.

"And what are *you* working on?" she said.

"I'm an editor," I said, thinking she had misunderstood.

"But a writer, too, aren't you? Do you write fiction?"

I flung myself into my usual song and dance—disclaiming any part of the territory of creation, while really sniveling and crawling for signs of outer encouragement to begin. She interrupted. Her words were distinct with irritation and emphasis—no problem to hear her clearly.

"You musn't talk nonsense," she said, "about writing. You're too intelligent for that. Just sit down and write the book you mean to write. That's the way it's done. You'll either succeed in handling your material, or you'll fail. If you fail, do it again until you get it right. Of course, there's more to it than that, as you know. But the details are nonsense until you sit down to work."

Her words stayed with me. And at last I did sit down to work—though it was some months later. I gave up being a high-class lady editor on a high-class magazine. I gave up work that I really did love doing on the magazine, gave up the infinitesimal measure of prestige my post carried in the literary world, gave up a good salary (for a woman), gave up the strictures and the securities of the spot I had wormed my way into, where if I had stayed quietly put until retirement (which at age fifty-four is coming up fast behind), I would have been modestly set for the rest of my days. What had dazzled me most about my position was that it stood for worldly proof that I had come a long way from where I had begun, but what took the gloss off the thin coat of glamour was the knowledge that this vehicle, however comfortable, wasn't taking me where I really wanted to go. I wanted to be on my way as a story-teller. Even though it was very late. I wanted to make a start on what I had always wanted to do.

I came to rest at last in a room of my own. It happened to be a broken-down cabin on a property Jose and I bought on the coast of Maine that included an old farmhouse on the inland side of the road, complete with barn, and two out-buildings, plus a tiny beach house sitting on a pie-slice of waterfront, the whole in a state of alarming decripitude. We bought the package for $10,000 ($5,000 down and the rest on mortgage) through the Author's League, willed to the organization by two women writers who had owned it. We were lucky and we knew it. My typewriter was balanced on a rickety table (left by the previous writers along with some other lovely infirm stuff scattered through the buildings) and that was balanced on the uneven, rotting floor where I too balanced on an equally rickety chair, yet I had never before felt myself so solidly entrenched. Not that I wasn't terrified of the desperately risky effort I was about to embark upon. It was just that I knew there was no turning back. The challenge must be met; the worst that would happen is that I would fail.

This history has a happy ending. Reader, I wrote my novel. Of course, I failed my material in some ways. But the novel was published; a section appeared in *The New Yorker*: it was awarded a Houghton Mifflin Literary Fellowship; reviewers reviewed it (more favorably than unfavorably); and strangers bought it in bookshops and wrote me letters saying, "Thank you for writing this book," thus becoming friends and granting me the greatest gratification a writer receives. Later, the same book appeared in paperback, looking in its new jacket like a different book; then it appeared in England, again in a new look, and in time it was transformed in Holland from *How She Died* to *Hoe Ze Dood Ging*—a metamorphosis that so pleased me it made forever worthwhile the whole chancy venture. I had become a story-teller, for real, at last.

BOOK TWO

Starting Early
THREE AT EIGHTEEN

Rafael Yglesias
PUBLISHED NOVELIST

I had tried to start as an adolescent and I failed. I had given up: or outside forces had been too destructive for me to contend with might be another way of putting it. Either way, it would seem that my own early agonizing experience should have qualified me to recognize the syndrome when it hit again, this time as an adolescent turmoil affecting my youngest son. Given my history, my response could only have been, one would think, "I understand." But that's not the way things work out.

A totally gung-ho kid, big man on campus, heavy competitor and frequent winner at the posh private school he attended in Riverdale, my son turned overnight into a brooding, unreachable fifteen-year-old crazy who was refusing to continue his schooling so that he could write a novel that would re-create the reality of his situation as he was living it. Not really overnight. There had been disquieting earlier signals which I had ignored—hoping they would go away. He was playing hooky a lot. So had I. He was lying a lot. So had I. There was agony clearly visible in every nervous inch of his tormented body and soul. I knew that agony well. Nevertheless, I said and did all the wrong things, and so did his father. We threw our weight around, leaned on him, came at him from all sides as coarsely as the villains he was pretending to believe we were—all because our hearts were twisted into an anguish of apprehension for him. What would become of him? He would ruin himself. We went through a nightmare experience with him.

He was intelligent, gifted, handsome, charming; he had been properly coddled, granted all the usual luxuries necessary to a middle-class, urban kid. Admittedly, his father and I had sent out some ambiguous signals. Parents want everything from their children. We want them wild, bold, sweet, undemanding, successful, striving, modest, just like ourselves, independent while securely tied to the family, rebellious, conformist, happy, beautiful, original. We had also mixed them up a bit about what was what in the world with our loose talk at the dinner table. Aberrant social attitudes flew about at mealtimes like great, exotic butterflies. But the kids weren't supposed to take that stuff seriously, for God's sake; didn't they have any common sense.

They took us seriously—not only our views, but the way we had lived our lives and the choices we had made. Our children took off, each in his and her own way. My daughter, the eldest, went to Mississippi the summer of 1964, to help secure voting and civil rights for blacks. That was her shadow-line—her crossing into adulthood. She never returned to us as a child; she went on to explore her own difficult, original paths. My middle son helped seize Columbia buildings the spring of 1968. My youngest son lit out for the territory *he* wanted to explore, the wilderness of his inner self. At fifteen, he made the decision to become his own person. He was through with waiting. He literally felt that it would kill him to go on pretending to be a schoolboy, an apprentice waiting upon permission to enter his own life

only after earning the going symbolic entrance fee—a diploma. Why not communicate the truth of what he knew
now? Wasn't that as real and as valuable as anything else?

We fought him every step of the way. It was amazing to
witness how that fifteen-year-old kid wouldn't bend. He
dropped out. He ran away. He wrote his novel. It was good,
and it was bought, and when it was published, he was seventeen—exactly the age I would have been if I had pushed
through my will against all disappointments and traumas.
He did what he did for himself alone, but his action brought
me, as well, an unbidden surprising gift—one of the great
gratifications of my life. A circle had been joined for me in
a consolation I had never hoped for. A child of mine had
done what I had failed to do.

That part of the story belongs to me; the rest belongs to
Rafe. And his story melds with those of the other early
starters that follow. Here is Rafe, talking for himself:

"I decided I wanted to be a writer at about age eight and
a half or nine. I didn't even know what it meant to be a
writer, even though my father was one, but I knew I wanted
to be an artist of some kind. A writer, musician, actor,
artist—something in the arts. The key word was "great."
Only great artists counted with me. I thought that I was
supposed to be a great artist. As if an outside force decreed
it. Perhaps my parents were responsible for that. Other kids
were *supposed* to go to college, to get into a solid profession, to marry and raise a family. I didn't feel those expectations for me. I was supposed to read, to go to concerts, to
go to the theater. I suffered through high art at a very
young age, willing myself to comprehend and enjoy it, because that was the road to becoming an artist.

"That sounds arrogant, and it is arrogant, but I wasn't
arrogant about anything else. I never felt I was *supposed* to
become President of the United States or Mickey Mantle.
I never felt that I could do everything better than anybody.
I only felt that way about art. I remember going to see

Shakespeare in the Park, *Hamlet*, when I was twelve or thirteen. I wanted to be on that stage playing Hamlet, I thought I could play Hamlet better than the actor up there. I felt I understood the playwright's intention better than that actor did. It was the *writing* that interested me. When I read *Great Expectations* and *Crime and Punishment* as a kid, I didn't think I could do better than Dickens or Dostoevsky—but they were what one aimed for, I hoped to do as well. They were great writers and that was what I was heading for—the way other kids were heading for business, or medicine, or the law.

"I don't see starting as happening at a particular point. It's true that one day I just began. But that's not the way it is. I started long before I started, back there as a kid of eight and a half or nine.

"Writing is a skill but before that, it's a way of looking at the world. I saw the world in the way that a writer must. There are lots of ways to explain this. When I discovered, let's say, the evil in a person I was more *interested* in it than shocked by it. I was more observer than a personality being acted upon. In writing, not the reality of one's life is expressed, but the story of it described so that it becomes more real than the reality. That's what I mean about starting long before I actually began. A way of feeling, a way of looking.

"I don't believe that you're born talented. Your life develops your talent—what's fed into your life. To some extent I don't know the answers to how I got started. I was stubborn about my own importance and about having my own way. I began to hate school. I began to feel that everybody was dumb—all wrong about everything. The things that most interested me in school—history and English— were becoming terribly disappointing—way below my interest in the subjects. It was as if these subjects were being handled like hobbies. Adolescence isn't a good age for hobbies. It's a very dramatic age. Everything you do you do for the first time. Everything is a climax, the first time you have a twenty dollar bill to spend, the first time you screw, the first time you take a cab, go to a movie alone. These become moments of great drama. But school was a hobby, a pastime. I was also living through a period in history that came on like great drama. The late sixties. Everybody was being bold around me. It was pointless for me to listen to people telling me, 'finish school and then do what you want to do later.' I couldn't do it. I reached a point where I literally couldn't get my body into a classroom. It wouldn't go. Lives of great men (I don't know about great women) proved me right, anyway: they were wild, undisciplined, arrogant, possibly insane youngsters. Balzac, whose work I loved, became a model. Balzac had decided he would become a writer at any cost.

"I was constantly fiddling with the possibility of writing a novel. I made two, three, four, five separate starts, and dozens of short story starts. Pathetically bad stuff. I knew that I was through with school, that I couldn't go on living that life, so I put myself in a position where I would bomb out, I put myself in a position where there would be no way to continue at that school. I cut classes, failed courses, didn't turn in papers—broke all the rules. After I bombed out, though, I couldn't help seeing myself as a complete failure. With my parent's permission, I moved to Maine to live with my older sister and brother-in-law and their little baby, and I enrolled in the local high school up there. Going to that school made me feel as if my life was in suspension, as if I weren't really living it anymore. I was no longer pursuing what is everybody's notion of success. I began my novel then.

"I knew the minute I wrote the first paragraph that it was different from the other stuff I had written. That knowledge kept me going all through the fall while I attended that ridiculous school and worked on the book. Because I felt the novel was true, and that it would solve all my problems, that I knew what I was now, a novelist. At Christmas time when my parents came to visit, I thought I was presenting them with an excellent plan for the conduct of my life. I would quit school, live with my sister, work as a carpenter, and begin adult life. What I kept from them was the fact that I was writing a novel, and without that information, my plan, I see now, didn't really make sense for them. But I didn't want my novel, my work, to become part of what I saw as a sordid argument, to be used as a weapon in the argument either by them or by me. I didn't want to hear, 'No, you can't leave school because your novel isn't any good,' and I didn't want to be arguing the opposite. It made the novel, the most important thing in my life, a weapon in an argument that had nothing to do with the quality of my work.

"We had a terrible fight. So terrible that I felt I would never feel close to my parents again. They refused me permission to stop going to school. My mother, maybe because she's of another generation, maybe because of McCarthyism and her past history kept talking about the law, as if the law was going to clap us all in jail if I quit school. I was underage of course for leaving school. I was fifteen. When my parents' visit was over, I had hardened myself to going my own way whatever happened. I knew that I would cut school and drop out. I felt it was the only way to earn the world's respect, but what it earned was disciplining and calls back and forth to New York. My parents yanked me back home to the city, but by that time half the book was finished. When I arrived in New York, I presented my parents with the book, but without any terms. Just, 'Here it is. What do you think of it?' Their opinion meant a lot to me. Because whatever arguments we had, my appreciation of my parents as critics was unbounded.

"They took it very seriously. They talked to me not as if I were a bright young boy who had done something precocious, but they talked to me for the first time as if I were an independent adult. Except about going to school. They insisted I had to go to school. They praised the book, but I was in the same spot I had been in. I pretended to go along with them. I felt different though. Their admiration proved that it was unnecessary to continue school, but I didn't want to mix up the two things. It was very important to me to remove my book as a weapon in this continuing argument.

"I made my plans to run away. I packed a small bag of clothing, took my typewriter, and about $200 I had stolen in bits from my parents. I arranged to take a 6:45 A.M. bus to Pittsburgh where I had friends living. My parents were asleep when I left the house. I left a note on the kitchen table saying that I had gone to school early. I had agreed to enroll in a neighborhood public high school. And I left another note saying I was on my way to live my own life in the mailbox downstairs in the apartment house for them to pick up later. I left just before dawn. It felt good. I was excited. I worried about being picked up by the police: though I didn't really think my parents would do that to me, I thought it might happen. You begin to think in movie terms when you do something like running away. I began to feel like a fugitive. It was all somewhat ridiculous. At the same time I felt a real self-respect coming up in me.

"Running away to Pittsburgh was idiotic in every way. I wasn't doing what runaways are supposed to do. I knew my sister knew where I was and that my parents must know that I was safe. I didn't look for a job. I just worked on my book and enjoyed my situation, especially being with adults, even if they were only eighteen-year-old kids. They were college kids, sharing an apartment, pretending to be grown-ups. So I joined the pretense. My older brother called me on the telephone and for the first time talked to me as if I were an adult. Then I got a letter from my parents giving me permission to come home and finish my novel without returning to school. I came back and went to work at it. I never had any more fears because I trusted their judgment. One way or another now my life would work out.

"I was aware that I faced a tremendous risk of failure if I

dropped out of school. But there's no guarantee against failure for anybody, unless you measure success as money and security, then the very rich are secure against failure. And of course that's so, at least that's what society keeps saying—that success is money. That meant that the measure of success was not going to be how good my book was but whether it sold to a publisher. The question put to me was never 'Are you going to write a good book?' but 'How are you going to live?'

"If I had to starve to death I would have done it to become a great artist. That was the theory that appealed to me. But these were just ideas to accompany the drive to become an artist. You cannot lay an ambush for artistic success—you can't plan it out like a career in medicine. Most kids in school are kept in line by the challenge to maintain a certain academic level. I'd already done that. I went to one of the best high schools in the United States and got A's. How much longer was I supposed to go on doing that? I had two alternatives. I could stay at school and hope to flower into an artist one day, or I could leave school and try to become an artist right away. The risk at fifteen is total failure, and at fifteen that would mean you'd become a bum. In the end I didn't see any difference between being a bum and being a student.

"Anybody's life is unsafe at any speed. I guess that I knew that when I was younger. I felt that my life wasn't valuable unless I took the chance to make it valuable. If I failed, it would have been a nightmare, but it worked, so it's a success. If I had blown it and had to go back to school a year later, it would have been a miserable humiliation. As soon as the publisher took a contract on my book, I was a hero— if they had turned it down, I would have been a loser. I don't know what I would have done if it hadn't worked, but I counted on it working.

"It's easy to be fifteen years old and stop going to school and write a novel. It was much, much easier than going to school. Easier to do something that interested me and that I did alone. After I was accepted by my parents, it was nice to wake up and see me and New York as two independent existences, instead of seeing myself as a shnook going to school—another schoolboy. Instead of being a cog in the machine, I was the machine. I was able to get up in the morning and do what my father did. We were two writers in New York. What scared and upset me was the way people had reacted at first—as if I had gone crazy.

"When I began to write I didn't think my book would be published, in a commonsense way of thinking, but in dramatic moments I daydreamed. I projected myself into a reality where it was published. I imagined then that publishing a book would be a passport to anything I wanted, but in fact the way it actually happened, publishing a book was a passport to keep going—another chance to fail, another opportunity to make an asshole of myself—or, with luck, to succeed. Because, you see, starting is continuing. The hard part is continuing.

"The shock was to discover that I felt then and I feel now that practically nobody really wanted me to succeed. It's like when you're a kid. When two little kids are friends and one gets a better Christmas present than the other, it's not uncommon for one to break the other's new toy. That's the kind of response I got. I think that was because I was young. I think that people hate prodigies. Their very existence proves something distasteful to others who are dissatisfied with their lives. It makes them see that they've blown their own lives.

"People react very personally to what I've done. 'My God,' they say, 'at seventeen I could hardly read.' Or, 'My God, I wish my son had done that.' Or, 'My God, I'm fifty-seven and I'm still struggling with my first novel.' That kind of reaction diminishes my accomplishment—because it makes the fact that a *youngster* wrote a book more important than the book itself. I don't want the issue to be my age—the work should be the issue. Either I'm a talented writer or I'm not. If I'm a talented writer I deserve respect for the work—not for my age."

"Now I'm going to be twenty-four. I've written and published four books in eight and a half years, I'm still not considered grown-up. The reality for me isn't sitting back and saying, 'How wonderful, I was seventeen and I published a novel,' or 'How wonderful, I'm twenty-four and I've just published four.' The reality is, I'm nothing yet, I have to keep working, keep trying. I've only just begun to do what I intend to do. When people spend most of their lives just surviving—and then decide to do what they have always wanted to do, that one act for them relieves the frustration of all the unsatisfying years. There are lots and lots of such people. For them, breaking out of the bind is a culmination, a crowning glory, an achievement. But for me, starting was a beginning.

"When I was seventeen and became a published writer I didn't feel different from everybody else. I didn't feel I was a freak. I felt I was home at last, that I was what I was supposed to be and that my life had begun—not that it had reached a climax. My first book was the first tiny step of a long march. Learning to write novels is serious work—it's like becoming a cardiologist—it takes just as long. It never made sense to me to think in terms of having another profession while writing. I had to become a novelist right away and work at that. That was my profession. A lot of people think you can become a writer at any old time. I think of writing as a lifetime thing. I meet young men my age now coming out of college with degrees, saying, 'When I get a chance I'm going to sit down and write my book, too.' I think that's nonsense. When they say, 'you had nerve starting so early,' I think, 'I didn't have any nerve.' I just wrote a book. That didn't take nerve. If there was courage involved it was in believing in myself. When it worked, it meant to me that I was what I thought I was. I was a writer—someone who could take what happens and make it new. Sure, as part of my motivation there was a vulgar desire for respect. The simple love and awe with which people watch Olivier perform or look at a Cezanne or read *Père Goriot*—as though these were gifts from a personless, omniscient God—I wanted to earn that. I'd like to think that some thirteen-year-old kid is staying up till three in the morning reading a book of mine with the same excitement I stayed up nights reading Dickens. Compared with that longing, high school paled. And when I get letters from readers saying, 'That's my life you've written about,' I feel good, because that's what I was after in my books about young people—to make our life valid. It was the validity of myself at fourteen and fifteen I was establishing by becoming a writer, but by extension doesn't it validate the real life of any adolescent?"

Barbara Parson
WOMAN CONSTRUCTION WORKER

Eighteen-year-old Barbara Parson's problem in starting
out in life was very different from that of a privileged, urban
youngster. She was born and grew up in a tiny coastal town
in New Hampshire, just south of the Maine border, and
has only been out of her state once, on a student trip to
Washington, D.C. Her mother and father or others in her
family have never gone even that far away from home. On
her mother's side, her people were among the first settlers
in the area. On her father's side, her family is also pre-
revolutonary. The Parsons emigrated from England,
farmed in Massachusetts for a generation, and moved to
New Hampshire in the 1800s. In both branches, there was
never any money; they are hard-working poor—lobster
fishermen, clammers, farm workers, carpenters, apple-
pickers, day laborers. The only job in the family above
manual labor belongs to her grandmother who was appointed the town mail-clerk about ten years ago when she
was forty years old. That was a good thing, because Bar-

bara's grandfather was incapacitated by a fall from a tractor when he was in his teens and hasn't ever been right in his head since. The grandmother, a cheerful, smiling woman with blackened, rotting teeth, supports herself and the old man. Barbara is close to these grandparents, but not to her father's mother, who married again after Barbara's grandfather died and moved more than a hundred miles away—too far to visit.

Barbara's mother and father married young. "They think I don't know that they married because Mom was pregnant with me. Not that they wouldn't have married anyway. They say they were in love," she adds, as if she doubts it.

Barbara's mother and father married when they were sixteen and eighteen. They were in their early thirties when Barbara graduated from high school at the age of seventeen, and without warning, erupted into a wild creature they barely recognized. She had always been a very good child.

Barbara is an American beauty—unusually tall, strong, graceful, blond, blue-eyed, fair-skinned, with a delightful smile—brilliant yet shy. She considers her complexion rotten, because she breaks out now and then in a couple of pimples, but her appearance isn't of paramount concern to her. She wears her good looks lightly, dresses in jeans and tops, combs her long hair simply, pushes it behind her ears when it falls in her face. She looks smashing, whatever she wears—clean, wind-blown, sexy. In the same way, she doesn't consider herself smart, though she was an honor student at the substandard village school she attended. "I never got to the new district high school. They didn't finish it in time." She didn't go on to college after graduation, though her parents wanted her to.

"What am I slaving for all these years if it isn't to make things a little better for my kids, better than we had it when we were kids?" her father demands to know. He and Barbara look alike. He is a handsome Nordic type whose beauty emerges in his daughter more strikingly because of the surprise of her height and the strength and womanly grace of her body. He reports a hard life. "I've been working since I was eleven years old—helping on lobster boats, clamming, digging worms, I did anything, I lugged bags of seaweed up from the beach loading onto trucks, I don't know what for but someone was willing to pay me to do it, I did it. I tended the village dump, me and my brother, like a couple of work horses, not producing a thing, just shoveling that trash around. When I couldn't get work here, I went up into Maine, picking berries, picking potatoes. I worked in the chicken houses and if you can stand that you can stand anything.

"When I began in construction I was nothing but an unskilled laborer. I worked my way up to be a skilled carpenter, and if I'm not making a fortune at least I'm getting by. I owe for everything I have—my car, my house, my furniture. But I've got my home as long as I keep working. I work for them, for my family, to give them a decent life. And their mother works just as hard as I do. Sure I would have liked to come home to a hot meal evenings instead of to a note, "Open this can, open that can, there's bread in the box" with the wife out taking care of some other goddamn family. But you can't kick if the wife is working to help support the kids. You gripe and you gripe, but you haven't got the right. The truth is I couldn't make it alone. I couldn't earn enough to keep us going without the wife working. Maybe we did wrong. Out working leaving our kids to knock around too much between their grandmother and relatives, her sister, my sister, but we thought we were doing good doing the best we could for them. I wanted something better for my daughter, for all of them."

Barbara is the oldest of three children. Her mother and father are semi-literate, with the equivalent of a sixth-grade education. Barbara's mother is a nurse's aide who hires out as a private practical nurse. The parent's lives consist of work, family, TV; the surprise is that they have developed so much intelligence and independence of mind.

Barbara says of them, "They did good. They're good parents. I know that. I disappointed them a lot when I graduated. But I couldn't help it. I couldn't stand any more going to school. When I thought about going to school, just to keep on going to school, especially some new place away from home, I'd get cold and scared. Any kind of school—college, secretarial, home-making, or nursing—I'd get sick thinking about it. Or working in an office, going in and learning as you worked. It made me feel sick and scared to just think about working in an office.

"In high school, when it came time to choose what vocational training we preferred, they told us we didn't have to choose what girls are supposed to like—secretarial, sewing and home-making, weaving and that stuff—that we could go into the workshops even if we were girls. I loved that kind of work, the work my father did—and I despised sewing and that stuff, so I went into the shop. Just me and one other girl. I was good at shop. In my last year in school, they sent two of us, a guy and me, to work at a shipyard where they were building wooden boats in the old way and they taught me finish work because that was lighter for a woman to do. That was the happiest time of my life, working at the yard. But I never dreamed that I could work at that kind of work in a regular way. You know?"

In the last month before she graduated, she took up with a bunch of new friends, a crowd that hung around with an older woman in the town, Evelyn Wilson, divorced, in her thirties, whose four kids had been awarded to the custody of her former husband. The gang would gather at Evelyn Wilson's big house every night for beer parties—pot, country music, rock, dancing, making out.

"My parents acted like they were jealous of Evelyn Wilson. I didn't care about *her*. I didn't even like her. When I fell in love with Cliff, Evelyn's was just a place to go to be with him. She told us we could use a little old camp on her land. It was heaven for the two of us, except when the other kids would come around bothering us, or they'd rev up their motors just to let us know they knew what we were doing, when they'd leave. You know. I didn't like that. But my folks talked about Evelyn Wilson as if she was, you know, a whore. My mother would yell at me that I'd better not come home crying to them I was pregnant. I wasn't going to get *pregnant*. That older generation didn't know what they were doing, the way we do."

The boy she fell in love with was a high-school dropout. He drank, wasn't working, had no training. "He liked cars," Barbara told me. "He liked fooling with cars."

"He sure knew how to smash them up," Barbara's mother told me, "driving under the influence. He's totaled more cars. Then he thinks he's doing something because he salvages a couple of parts. He's crazy."

Barbara and her parents began to fight all the time. They threatened her with not attending her graduation unless she stopped running with the crowd and stopped going to Evelyn Wilson's and stopped seeing Cliff Robertson. They said if she wasn't going on to college or vocational school, she'd better think about getting herself a job as soon as she graduated. If she was going to act like a bum, they weren't going to support her.

She hated housework, but she arranged for some day work cleaning houses right after she graduated.

Were her parents ashamed of her for choosing such work?

"Work is practically a religion with my mother and father. Doesn't matter what kind of work. The important thing is to keep on working, get a job and keep on at it. They despise anybody who goes on relief, unless they're very old and sick, they think it's disgusting to take surplus food, food stamps, all that stuff. They'd die first. Sure, they were disappointed that I started working cleaning house. I know I disappointed them. I'd cry and get mad thinking about how I'd disappointed them. Sometimes I felt I couldn't stand it, that I was going to go crazy with all my problems. They wouldn't let me alone about anything, making me think about things I didn't want to think about. I couldn't stand to think about what I was going to become."

She dreamed about becoming a veterinarian. "That's what I really would have loved to do—take care of animals." But the educational qualifications loomed like a mountain she had no notion how to scale. Easier to clean the houses of vacationing summer residents. She tried to pick employers who had babies—and pets—because that made the work more bearable. Except for bathrooms (she wouldn't touch the toilet bowls) she was good at housework. She was strong, fast, cheerful; she hardly ever broke anything; the people she worked for liked her. She could have arranged for as much day work as she could handle; but she chose to work only a couple of half-days a week—enough to satisfy her parents.

"I lived for the nights with Cliff. I told myself that I didn't care about anything else. I just wanted to be with him." Her wide, blue eyes manage a look both shy and sexy.

"Then right after I graduated, this freaky thing happened. There were a couple of really dumb kids, only about fifteen years old, kids who hung around Evelyn Wilson's. They were into popping pills, stealing whatever they found in the medicine chests, even what their sick old grandparents were taking, sleeping pills, tranquilizers, pain killers—they took birth control pills, they didn't know what they were taking, and to top it all they drank a lot at Evelyn Wilson's one Saturday night. They didn't have the sense to know they were sick and to get home to a bed. They had started off to an old boarded-up house up the road they were using to stash the stuff in. They had ripped open a window of the house a couple of weeks before. One made it inside. He was found out cold on the floor. The other kid flopped out on the porch, his foot had gone right through a rotting board.

"A couple of other kids looking to get something from the stash found them. They came running to tell us at

Evelyn Wilson's. They said at the hospital if we hadn't gotten the kids in so quick they would have died. We got them into cars and drove like crazy all the way to the big hospital, in the middle of the night. They made a big thing of it there, took down all our names, examined us, it was disgusting, and then got in touch with our local police and our parents and the whole thing got really blown up. They said the blood tests showed high alcohol content and proof of sexual activity. How can blood tests show that?

"My mother acted just like I was a criminal. My mother's an awful screamer. You'd think she'd break something in her body the way she screams at us. I ran away to Evelyn Wilson's house to get away from it. Evelyn said I could camp out on her place. Cliff would come to the camp every night, and leave just before daybreak. I guess what I was doing got my mother and father crazy. My father threatened Cliff when they met at the store. He shook his fist in his face and said, 'I'll kill you if you don't stay away from my daughter.' Cliff told his folks and they got the sheriff on my father for threatening. That's a crime, you know. And he did it. He did do it. He threatened. I told the sheriff he did it and that he had said that lots of times when they were screaming at me."

She looks at me defiantly: then her eyes suddenly flood with tears. She blinks them away and begins to speak again.

"My mother said I wasn't allowed to talk to my brother and my baby sister. Because I did what I did, because of telling on my father, I couldn't be in the family anymore and I couldn't see them. My brother and I figured out how to meet secretly, but there wasn't any way I could get to see my baby sister. My grandmother tried to help me, but she didn't understand anything. She thought my mother was all wrong. My mother really wasn't all wrong, and it would make me mad to hear my grandmother say she was. Because I really knew I didn't know what I was doing. Like my life was getting away from me.

"I love my baby sister so much. I felt so bad I felt like

killing myself sometimes except I was so mad at everybody. Then a couple of times my mom waited for me down the road where I was working and she yelled at me that I had ruined myself, that the whole town was talking about me saying I was nothing better than a whore. That's the way it is in our town. You can't do a thing without everybody knowing and talking. One day I walked past my Daddy at the filling station and he looked right through me like I wasn't even there."

She takes a deep breath, smiles a dazzling smile, and without transition, says, "So Cliff and I got married." Barbara wasn't thrilled about Cliff having no job, no high-school diploma, and no prospects, and it was a real worry that he drank so heavily and steadily. Her parents remained adamantly cold to them at first. Cliff's folks helped the young couple. His grandfather gave them a half acre of bottom land and his parents bought them a trailer to live in. After a couple of months Barbie's folks' anger cooled down, and though they still wouldn't allow Cliff in their house, they were eager for Barbie to visit alone.

"I should have told them, you can't do that to us. If my husband isn't welcome then I don't consider myself welcome." She makes herself grown-up and severe, but the look quickly disintegrates. "I was so lonesome for them, especially my brother and sister, I couldn't stay away. It was an awful time for me. When I look back on it now, I can't believe I went through all that, it seems like it was a dream or a story about somebody else, on a TV show.

"I was miserable. Whatever I tried to do turned out wrong. My mother let me keep my baby sister overnight one weekend and some of the guys came around with a couple of girls and Cliff got drunk and she told my mom, and my mom started screaming and we had a terrible fight. Just when I was trying so hard to be a good wife, thinking about how to solve Cliff's problems, taking care of the trailer, keeping it nice and trying to make real meals like my mom makes on Sundays when she's not out working, but instead of feeling good about it I just kept feeling madder and madder—at Cliff, at myself, at the whole world. Cliff would get a lousy job and then he'd lose it. He totaled two of our broken-down cars. Nothing stopped him drinking no matter what I said and he'd get ugly-acting when he drank. My skin kept breaking out. I hated the work I was doing—cleaning house—and Cliff had no respect for it either. 'You call that work—cleaning house—earning twelve, fifteen dollars a week?' That made me feel like I was nothing, when he said that.

"Nothing was any good anymore. I didn't care to run around with the crowd anymore. I thought Cliff and I ought to be getting somewhere, not running around with kids. I didn't know what to do. Finally, Cliff's daddy talked to a friend and he got Cliff a job at a garage. It was only a gas attendant's job, but they promised to let him work on cars when they were short of mechanics. That made Cliff feel better. I figured this was the time to work on his heavy drinking. I said, 'I'm not gonna sit alongside you drinking beer every night. Only Fridays and Saturdays, from now on.' He promised to try to stop. He tries. He has a real drinking problem—lots of the guys do, lots of his friends—that makes it harder."

"Then I did a fool thing—I bought a horse because I couldn't resist him. He was so beautiful and really cheap too. My father and I were talking again and he helped me build a corral near Cliff's grandfather's barn and Cliff's grandfather let us fix a stall for him so he could go in and out. He's beautiful. I love him. I love to ride him. I don't care how hard I have to work to keep him. After that, I bought a pony for my baby sister to ride because he was real cheap too. I already have two dogs and a cat living in the trailer. Cliff says I'm keeping a zoo. He says I should be an animal trainer or a breeder, but I don't know how to get started on that. I kept on dreaming about becoming a vet, but I knew I'd never do it, because of the money it would cost and all that studying—just like studying to be a doctor.

"I thought a lot about where I was in life. I was eighteen.

I felt so old and depressed. I didn't seem to be the right kind to make a good wife. Buying horses like that when we hardly had enough money to live on. And not knowing what I wanted to work at. When I thought about going on being married, I'd feel scared. I was going to turn out like my mom. My mom does everything she's supposed to but it makes her mad. Why else does she scream so much? I'm not like her, I'm more like my father, keeping things in, quiet. I don't even look like her, she's short and round—but I felt like I was going to end up just like her. That's why I didn't want to have a baby—and anyway, we couldn't afford it. And that's funny too, because I really love kids just the way I love animals. But I don't want to be like my mom. There wasn't anything to look forward to. Cleaning house for other people, acting ugly with Cliff and Cliff acting ugly with me, was that the way it was going to be?

"One day I stopped to talk to some guys I went to school with, working at a construction site putting up a big summer house. Me and one of them had worked at the shipyard together. I don't know how it all started, about me beginning to work. I can't remember it exactly. We were kidding around, I was bragging on how good I was, better'n him, just as good on that kind of work as anybody, and for fun I started to show them. I just picked up a brush and started putting on the finish. It was one of those natural finish houses, with the outside boards running vertical, easy as pie to put the finish on. They were short a man and first thing I knew the fellow in charge said I could help out. Maybe he was kidding, but I took him serious and went ahead. He teased about women's lib, but after he saw how I worked, he told me to come back the next day, that he'd pay me regular unskilled laborer's wages, four dollars to start. That was more than I earned doing day work, and anyway I loved to do this work. So that's what I do now, construction, eight hours a day, five days a week. I've been doing it four months now." She flashes her sweet, dazzling smile.

"It feels wonderful to be working on something real.

Okay, not every job is a breeze, some are nothing but headaches, one headache after the other. But when I drive my car past some of the houses I worked on, I feel real good. There was one old house we restored inside and out. I'm proud to have worked on that house. When I drive past it, I get a thrill just looking at it—the windows and the shutters so neat. People say, 'That won't last. You'll get sick of hard work, working in bad weather, it's too tough for a girl.' They don't know what tough is. Cleaning other people's toilets—that's tough. Yesterday I was up top shingling a roof and I could see over the trees to the water. The leaves were turning—all that beautiful color and the blue sky and the water darker than the sky. A painter would have wanted to be up there painting it. Every day I wake up feeling lucky. I just hope and pray nothing happens that they say women can't work at this kind of work any more.

"Cliff wasn't happy about me working a man's job. I told him lots of women are working in construction now. I'm not the only one. I was surprised to learn about that, and about the government saying they had to allow us. Cliff said to me why did his wife have to be the one to change the world. I'm not trying to change the world, I just want to work at what I like to work at.

"My mom doesn't know what to think. But I can see that my father's proud of me. I just know he is. I try to make them all understand that I'm the same Barbara I always was."

She pushes her long blond hair behind her ears, pulls her thin cotton top down over her flat hips.

"People say to me, 'Aren't you daring?' I'm not daring. I'm shy and timid. It's hard to explain. It's more natural for me to be working in construction, just the way I am. I had to push myself to do housework, going in and out of people's intimate lives, that's hard if you're shy. Or studying. That's hard, going to a new city, to a big college, first time you walk into a big classroom, nobody knows you—or into a big office or a bank—that's daring. I can't do those things.

Now I get up in the morning and feel good about going out on the job. And about earning good money. I don't know if it's helped me and Cliff or not. I don't know how we're going to end up. He keeps losing jobs, just like before, and he's got this drinking problem. But it's gotta be better for us if I feel better about myself."

David Fiske
FIRST CHAIR CELLIST

It's true that Barbara Parson never meant to change the world. But her actions *are* changing her world. Again without plotting or planning change, but simply by following the strong line of what he really wanted to do, David Fiske's attitude is subtly altering the world of music. And like Barbara, David too discovered that there were others out there doing and feeling the same, ready to join forces in what he experiences as a private upheaval.

"Musical prodigies start really young," David Fiske tells me. "I was old by the time I showed any talent. I was already in my teens."

His mother finds his modesty distasteful. She says that David showed musical talent from the day he was born. He thinks that's a preposterous statement. Mrs. Fiske is a woman of an almost too vivid personality, herself gifted in many directions—too many, perhaps, so that she has spread her talent thin. Music is only one of her talents. She dominated the household in which David grew up with one

older brother. His father is now dead, but alive he was a
large, commanding presence, if not within the home, then
for the power he represented in the outside world of business where he was vice-president and a member of the
board of a large corporation. They lived in a middle-class
to wealthy suburb north of New York City and the boys
were accustomed to getting whatever they wanted.

David Fiske is now in his late twenties, a large young
man more than six feet tall, broad and strong, with the
rangy, muscular body of a trained athlete rather than of a
musician. His face is fair, with down-slanted, sad eyes, a
prominent nose and a broad, noble forehead crowned with
lots of surprisingly dark hair and a matching beard and
mustache. The effect of the whole is angelic, a head drawn
by Blake, or a brother to William Morris. The calmness of
his face is belied by a body wracked with nervous tics.
David is constantly widening his eyes, jiggling his foot, bit-
ing the skin around his nails, giggling. He sweats profusely,
and ends a performance wringing wet.

When I asked him why he had chosen music (his
mother's field) over business (his father's), he looked surprised into blankness for a moment. Then he began to
speak in a rush, in a manner of communicating that is
characteristic of him. He often seems inarticulate because
of these pauses; but he dashes into hidden corners and pulls
out what apparently is a revelation to himself, as if he himself didn't know that he knew what he had just discovered.
"There was always music around. I must have been born to
music. I bet I was. She probably had the radio tuned to
Casals playing Bach in the labor room.

"My father was a great guy. He taught me all the important things—playing ball, swimming, driving a car—it isn't
his fault I'm a lousy driver. But he was always, you know,
remote. He didn't work in the house but in an outside office
in the city. My mother was always right there. She and the
record player and the piano. And my brother practicing.
My father was more of a mystery—removed. To this day I

really don't know what my father *did* for all that money he earned."

David's father died when David was in his late teens, suddenly, of a heart attack and left his wife and sons a great deal of money. The money is totally controlled by David's mother, until her death, though the will designated trusts in the sons' names. The mother can use the income, but not the capital of those trusts. The sons cannot touch them without the mother's permission.

David's mother had been badly trained as a musician by mediocre piano teachers, the only ones *her* parents could afford. But a prodigious energy and an innate theatrical sense carried her performances. When David was an infant, she was the moving force of a community amateur recital group; she had helped form a local symphonic orchestra and ballet troupe, and she spent a great deal of her daily time at the piano, practicing the Mozart sonatas and Chopin preludes she would perform locally. Later she turned her energies to amateur theatricals and musical comedy (she had a vibrant if untrained singing voice); but when David and his brother were small and she felt that her presence at home was indispensable, she burned up her excess energy at the piano. By the time David was ready to begin formal musical instruction, that instrument had been thoroughly usurped by his mother and older brother whose piano instruction had begun when he was five or six. Not that David wasn't good at the piano. He immediately showed a wonderful gift for faking the complicated music painstakingly being studied by his mother and older brother. It was fun for him. For his mother and brother, it was proof of a brilliance they saw was quite beyond *their* talents.

"He was born with a perfect ear," his mother says. There is, of course, no greater compliment from one musician to another.

David doesn't see his past that way. He sees himself as a very average player. He started his lessons in piano very much in the shadow of his mother and his older brother. "I never felt competitive with my brother," he tells me, "I loved him too much. I idolized him." After a couple of years at the piano it was his father who suggested that David switch to the cello. David had never heard the word before, or consciously seen the instrument. He was ten years old then.

As soon as he got his hands on a cello, he fell in love with the unwieldy, glowing hunk of wood which could yield such sweetness and sadness under the right, coaxing touch. "Not a sissy instrument. Something to grab hold of. And subdue. Too big for me to even carry around by myself. It was a big day for me when I went out for the first time with my cello to take a lesson. Just me and my cello. Big time."

He had been listening to all the greats in recordings on the family's expensive equipment long before he was old enough to attend symphonic and chamber music concerts. He heard what there was to aim for early on; and he aimed as true as he could, but he didn't particularly feel that he was succeeding.

"I kept going at it, but deep down I was depressed and discouraged. I didn't believe that I'd make it."

His memory of that period is blurred. He recalls the usual problem with changing teachers. His second teacher didn't approve of the method employed by the earlier one and set him way back in his training, to undo the harm the first teacher had presumably done. At thirteen years of age, David estimated his prospects as poor, but he kept plugging away. He had then been attending Juilliard on Saturdays for some time, his mother shlepping him and his cello in from the suburbs, week after week.

He had been a sickly child, subject to mysterious virus infections accompanied by fevers so high that he had a number of times suffered convulsions. According to his mother, he was a wonderfully self-sufficient child who would play quietly by himself for long hours; but his illnesses made her anxious about him and she tended to fuss over his physical well-being. By his adolescence, the infections had disappeared. He had grown very big, apparently physically strong, with the overgrown adolescent's clumsy unevenness of movement. He was a good student at the local junior high school he attended, and a celebrity as a performing cellist. His passionate interests ran to transport systems (he could plot any journey by public transit from the East to the West Coast and he was particularly intrigued by the New York City Transit System. "He was always trying to talk me into leaving the car behind and to try making it by bus and subway," his mother told me.

Playing ball, playing bridge and chess were his next vital interests, but when he thought about what he would be when he grew up, it was always music. No amount of discouragement changed that. His mother had set up an appointment for an audition with one of the great performer teachers of his instrument, who told his mother that David should forget music as a career. David was devastated, but he kept on.

"When I was fourteen I got lucky. I finally got a marvelous teacher. Also I was going to a music camp, full of wonderful people. It all began to come together for me. I really started to work. You can't get anywhere without putting in at least four hours work a day—some people need six or eight. I entered some competitions, and I won. I soloed with student orchestras. I came in at the top level in nationwide student competitions. I began to feel that I knew where I was going, knew where I wanted to go. I graduated from high school a bit of a celebrity. And I had been admitted to Juilliard. When I graduated, I was eighteen years old. Eighteen isn't young for a musician," he repeated, "it's an early starting profession, like dance. You make it early on or you don't make it at all. Even so, it was startling when one of my teachers at the summer music camp began to train me to audition for an opening with a major symphony orchestra. I worked. I really worked, but I didn't allow myself to believe that I'd get it. When I did, I couldn't resist it.

Stay on as a student at Juilliard, when I could play with a major symphony? Are you kidding? I was offered $12,000 a year—that was a lot of money ten years ago, and for an eighteen-year-old kid.

"I moved to the home city of the orchestra. I got my own apartment. It felt wonderful. To have gotten in like that. So easy. The older men and women in the orchestra were really good to me—helpful, kind—they gave me every break they could. It was all tremendously exciting. The music. The first time I played with the orchestra it was Beethoven's Seventh. Fantastic. And we were on TV too. My family could see me sitting there and performing.

"I was working well, living a grown-up life, saving money. I was in love with an older woman. It's true that I felt an outsider in that city. I don't know why. I was running into a problem with the army too. The whole country was rocking with protest. My older brother, still at college, was all involved. I was opposed to the Vietnam War, and anyway I wouldn't have wanted to go into the army. I wanted to keep on doing what I was doing. The symphony doctor came to my rescue. He reported that I had flat feet. I *do* have flat feet. Anyway, I was classified 4F. I was relieved, but I began to feel funny about being a musician then. Closed in, closed away. Ignorant. There was a lot of world out there I wasn't paying any attention to, a lot of knowledge I wasn't bothering with. You can't. You've got to keep at the music or you'll lose ground. At least that's the way it is for me. I was taking lessons and rehearsing and performing and recording as well as playing with a chamber group, soloing now and then, not with the symphony orchestra I played with, but with others.

"Then the boredom started to creep in. It gets horribly repetitive. Recording sessions—that wasn't making music—it was all technology—it was like making sex into a course in anatomy. Then sometime in the second year of my stay with the orchestra, another symphony called me in and offered me first chair. It was a terrific deal. Solos.

Chamber group. More money. It meant moving to a mid-western city, but that didn't bother me. I said, "Yes." There was a public blow-up about my case. The conductor of the orchestra I was leaving did a newspaper interview about me—he didn't name me, but everybody knew it was me. He complained about the harm done to young musicians when they're moved up too fast. I wasn't twenty yet and he kept referring to me as a teen-ager. He meant well. He had my future in mind, like a parent, I guess, but I resented him, I felt that he was just letting off steam because he was mad that his talent had been ripped off. I didn't think much about the point he was making. I mean if it was right for me or not. I was glad to go, to move on."

The new orchestra was made up of younger musicians— not quite as young as David was, but closer to his age. "I had a good time. The quartet was made up of first chair performers. They were good. There was a tie-in with the university. I taught cello. I was an assistant professor. I was earning $20,000 a year. I bought myself a brand-new Impala for $3500. That's what they cost then. Almost immediately I drove it into a bridge abutment and totaled it. I'm a terrible driver. I got $500 for the parts. I wasn't insured. I should have learned a lesson from that, but I don't think I did. I blew the $500 on something. I don't remember what.

"My father died then. Maybe it was before then. I get mixed up. My mother was very upset and going home got to be a drag. I didn't feel good about going home the way I used to, when Dad was alive. Mom sold the house my brother and I had been born in, and grew up in, where we shot for baskets with my father. When I thought about my father, I felt I had blown it, knowing him, I mean, and now it was all over and I'd never get to know him. It brought me and my brother closer. He had graduated from college and had moved into an apartment in New York with a bunch of guys. He was taking a graduate degree at Juilliard. I still idolized him. Even though he kept telling me I had shot ahead of him, it didn't feel that way to me. I thought he was a superb pianist. When my friends would criticize his performance, I couldn't believe it was happening. He seemed perfect to me.

"I love my mother. But we began to drive one another up the wall after my Dad died. She didn't seem to be herself anymore. There were new men. I couldn't stand them. I knew she was lonely, but they were such bozos. Then there was the money. She controlled it, but I felt it was mine. My father had left it to me. I guess I began to be a slob about money. I had gotten hooked on gambling, and I wasn't handling my money right." He pauses, smiles, smooths his beard. "To say the least."

The gambling began with poker and bridge, but it was the track that proved irresistible.

"The card playing began at once with my first orchestral job. There's a lot of wasted time in this profession. Sitting around. Waiting. Rehearsals, waiting for the conductor. Between numbers, back stage. Recording sessions. They say there's an affinity between mathematics and music. Maybe gambling is my mathematics. The card gambling was nothing. The track was something else. I spent a lot of money at the track. A lot of money pissed away . . ."

He broods for a minute, his vulnerable eyes suffused with guilt, pleading for understanding. Then he shrugs and smiles, "My mother thinks it was because I was too young. Excuses, excuses . . ."

He picks up his narrative, briskly. "Right about then I got a new offer—at a poker game, as a matter of fact. One of the guys I played with had been offered the opportunity to create a new quartet. He asked me in. I was highly recommended by the concert masters of the two symphonies I had played with. Anyway my friend knew my work. I had to audition for others. I did and got the post. Again I was glad to move on—this time to a small city in Michigan on the lake—nowheresville, about a hundred miles from a real city. I taught at the university—one hour a week. We did three concerts the first year—when we were still a string trio, because we ran into trouble forming the quartet. The second year we got going as a quartet. I had taken a cut in salary because I saw this as an opportunity to create music. In fact, that didn't happen. I want to say something with music. I want to say something with the cello—it's a dark, introverted, melancholy instrument—profound, thoughtful, emotional—it suits me—I can say what I want to with it. Once in a while I wonder why I didn't stay with the piano. Regretful, a little. With the piano you run the whole show yourself and the repertoire is not as limited as the cello's. But the fact is I'm married to the cello—it's my life companion.

"I'm not really drawn to composition. The last time I tried composing I was thirteen. I feel at home as an interpreter. There's a lifetime's work in mastering the repertory.

"Making music is what I'm after. That's why I took the offer, because of the quartet. It was the hardest work I had ever done. It took two years before we began to really blend. In three years we started to be good, and then we kept on getting better and better. We concertized, recorded—we were building a big reputation. We were on our way. And I began to get restless and unhappy. It's hard, co-existing as a quartet. The work is very hard, one gets fed up with criticism and totally tired of one another's company especially in isolated situations where there's no other life to fall back on. Too much time together. They were all older, everybody's always older, that's the trouble with starting young. You're always the youngest. They were in their late twenties and early thirties. By that time I was in my twenties too. When was I going to be considered grown-up? I kept trying to prove myself, to prove I had arrived. Had earned the right to make my own music. Chamber music exposes you—it's a transparent medium for the performer—very pure and simple, very demanding. You're out there alone and you're in there following. In every chamber group there's one dominating personality, and finally it comes down to the question of that personality. Can you live with it? Can you make *your* music with it?

All the tensions of the group center around this question of authority and clashing personalities—because it's a medium where you have to work separately and together. It's like marriage, I guess. You can dig and dig at rehearsal sessions, to get to the bottom. It's a terrible struggle. The tensions that build up are scary, and if you kept digging away, if you went deep enough you'd be setting off a nuclear war. You need a terrorist mentality for that kind of struggle. I wasn't willing to become a terrorist.

"After a couple of years, during one of our European tours, I found myself thinking more and more about leaving the quartet. I wanted to take my music to a higher point and I couldn't do that where I was. But it was terrifying to think about. I was deeply attached to the group, whatever difficulties there were. I couldn't leave then. I thought of alternatives—enlarging the group, letting out some of the tensions.

"What I was really not looking at head on was my deepest longing—to do my own music by myself, to become the soloist I had always wanted to be.

"So I quit the group, the job, the university, the whole shmear. In a way, you can say I'm starting over. Breaking into soloing isn't easy. And meanwhile you have to live and you have to go on performing. I joined with a group of musicians who have an entirely new approach. We're a small chamber orchestra, twenty-six members. We go without a conductor. We talk everything out—everybody's opinion is heard, everybody's opinion counts. When it comes to performance we play *together* because we're really listening to one another. Sure, rehearsals can be a real pain in the ass, dragging on for hours. The price of democracy. You want to be listened to, you have to listen. Our Carnegie debut was a smash. That was good. Because it's good to be doing music with others on terms closer to my own concepts, good to be recognized for it, good to know there are others struggling with the same concerns. For music. For musical conceptions.

"I quit the quartet at the end of the summer, after our

last performance on tour. There was a lot of pressure on me to stay, from my friends and my mother and brother. And from the group. I broke down and cried like a baby when I said goodbye to them. It was as hard as tearing away from family.

"Everybody thought I was taking an awful risk. I'm twenty-eight. Late to begin as a soloist. But I'm not beginning, I'm beginning again. I want to be what I want to be. I want to be my own man and get out and play my head off. I want to make *my* music, whatever it costs me, however hard it is to do. That's what I want."

BOOK THREE

Starting Anew
THE MIDDLE YEARS
THE FEMALE WAY

Suzanna Russell
STARTING ANEW
IN A DEEP RELATIONSHIP

Is there a male and a female way of starting? Barbara Parson's story seems to indicate that there's a difference in the way that men and women approach the question. For Barbara, what she wanted to become—a veterinarian, a carpenter—plunged her into a maelstrom in which vocation was only the merest whirling speck. Barbara didn't set her sights at "working at a man's job"; she preferred certain kinds of work—a desire that sprang from the most profound set of her nature. But what was for her a preference appeared to others as an attack on the heart of what society said she must be—a female, a category whose rigidities she hadn't had any say in.

She didn't say to herself, "Society is out to harm me by its rules as to how I'm supposed to appear in the world," but she felt the cruel strictures on her resisting flesh. She could not have articulated these sources of her unhappiness, nor make the intellectual political and social connections that a feminist or a sociologist might. Yet within the highly circumscribed conditions of her harsh world and the real limitations of her horizons, she recognized that her being existed in a painful discomfort. With a kind of blind courage she found a way of moving herself one step closer to the self the world would have denied. For Barbara, being is work, and in securing the kind of work that suited and pleased her nature, she slipped through the mesh of categories of what a "female" is supposed to be; she became the worker she wanted to be. She built things. She snatched a measure of success from the social disaster surrounding her.

She would be the last person to call herself a heroine, but in tackling the question of occupation for herself, she joined an army of women struggling to open up our society for all women. In this she's part of a sisterhood of heroines, whether or not they consciously take credit for their acts. In a sense, the stories of such women become one story, merging into a continuous battle to rescue the self from biological and social problems that remain dominant in the society. For it is still a woman's body that bears a child, and it is still overwhelmingly women who rear the children; most of the physical and practical details of democratic marriage and parenthood must still be worked out—but at least the myths have been blown. To the extent that male supremacy has been theoretically intellectually challenged, the struggle of women has been eased. But the conquest hasn't penetrated very deeply. A solid structure remains to be demolished and rebuilt bit by bit, by woman after woman. In the innovation young women bring to solving the puzzle of how to be wives and mothers, how to be women and how to be their own persons, they are some of our most extraordinary starters.

"I'm *not* a wife and mother," Suzanna insists. "Jon would never refer to himself as a husband and father," she says of her husband. "He's a historian. He's a teacher. He writes books—texts (and they're bringing us in some nice money)" she adds in an aside. "But that's the way he'd answer if you asked him who he is, what he does. Then if you pressed on and asked outright, 'Are you married?', he'd get around to telling you that he was married and has two children, a boy and a girl.

"But me, I'm always referred to as 'a working mother'— he's not a working father, but I'm a working mother, as if my working is an incident in my life, a hobby, and motherhood is my true existence. Neither classification applies. I'm myself, I'm not what I work at, and I'm not a wife and a mother. I'm a woman who chose to be married to a man I love and who chose to be the mother of two children, and who chose to be an early childhood teacher. Not a biological creature upon whom God and nature worked their will. I haven't chosen to have all the children I conceived. I had an abortion because the baby would have been born at a time when it would have been awful to have another child, when Jon and I were in trouble, and when I was in trouble, and that baby would have seen nothing but trouble.

"I can't think about what a wonderful child that aborted baby might have been. My two children are wonderful, so that one could have been too, probably. If you succumb to right-to-life thinking the logic carries you all the way to no contraception whatsoever. Every sperm and every egg is sacred and we women have to go back to uncontrolled biological destiny. I have to reject that. But I'd by lying if I said I sailed through the abortion I had. It bothered me. I hated having an abortion. I can't bear to think about it, or to really think about the child that was lost.

"What I learned from that experience was to be really careful about contraceptives, really responsible. It's harder in my case because I'm opposed to the pill, I don't like to take something that alters natural body functions, I don't like to fool around with nature. I tried an IUD for a while, but had trouble with it and had to have it taken out. It's a drag, contraception is. My mother swears by the diaphragm; that's what her generation used. I don't think we've made too much progress in the direction of a safe, easy contraceptive, in spite of all the excitement of the pill. It's still a problem.

"But I'd have an abortion again if I became pregnant. I don't want any more children. It's difficult enough as it is with two."

Suzanne is almost thirty. Her oldest child is nine years old, her youngest is four. She's been married for ten years to a man she met at the college they both attended, a small experimental college on the West Coast. She is a tall, slim, dark young woman with a mass of short curly hair. One visualizes her always in profile with the long line of her neck repeated in the elegant long legs and arms and stylized gestures of the hands—a piece of Eastern sculpture. She, herself, is unconscious of her effect on the watcher and simply moves and gestures without thought. She is serious, intense, and funny.

"Jon and I have been married a long time, but it feels like a minute. We're still in the earliest stages of working things out, though we've worked out a lot, given the medieval point where we started. In a way we're very different from one another, my husband and I, and in some ways we're very alike. He's outwardly calm and steady but things get to him deep down; I display all my tensions on the surface, and deep down I'm calm, steady. Even before we met we had done a lot of the same things. He went to Mississippi to work for black voter rights; I went to Chicago to work against discrimination in the schools and housing. We both returned potheads incidentally. We met then, started to live together, like slobs, the way everybody was doing then. I became a vegetarian; he loved meat too much to follow; we've both compromised on that.

"When we finished school we got into his VW bus and took off across country. It was great—that trip. We're great traveling companions. We fell in love with Vermont, almost settled there, but came back to Oregon. And I'm glad we did. We bought a little shack on thirty acres of woodland with a little money that had been settled on Jon by his parents. My parents were giving me trouble because I was pregnant and we had decided against marriage. Not because we weren't committed to one another, but because we were full of theories then—no formal, legal ties; no electricity or modern gadgets; wood heat—you know the routine. We did marry finally to satisfy our parents we said, but it satisfied something in us too. I was seven months pregnant." (She indicates an enormous bulge with her hands.) "I carry big. We went to the local justice of the peace, and then we came home with a bottle of wine and two glasses. It was lovely.

"But the rest was bullshit. I was going to make my own clothes, bake bread, can and preserve, press apples—except that I hated every part of that simple homemaker in the woods bit, everything but caring for my baby. She was gorgeous—a big, healthy, beautiful girl and she was the only thing that kept me going. I loved her. I nursed her. She was my life line to sanity. But I was miserable, stuck in the woods, with Jon away in town teaching. The loneliness and isolation were unbearable. I thought I was going crazy. I think I did go crazy. I became awful. I hardly spoke. I was in a rage. We had horrible fights all the time.

"We broke up the first year. I took the baby and went off to Europe to join a bunch of old school friends whose lives were just as messed up as mine. More. We rented a stone house in the south of France. It was heavenly—to be with other mothers and babies—and with other men. We'd do everything together, washing clothes, shopping, cooking, bathing the babies. I began to feel normal again, to feel the blood moving in me again, and I began to recognize that it wasn't my husband I hated, it was that life, that dismal life stuck in the woods alone all day with an infant. I remained in Europe for about six weeks, then I wrote Jon that I wanted to come home, and he came to the airport to meet us and it all seemed beautiful again, but as soon as we got back into that routine in the woods, all our troubles started again.

"I was trying to make him understand the dreariness, the emptiness, that it was suffocating, and that he had to listen to me, just as if I was telling him I had a fatal disease. I tried to make him understand that we had to work out our problems together; but he read what I was saying as an attack. On him. He'd accuse me of wanting to destroy him. He'd say I was trying to annihilate him, making him feel inadequate. I'd start crying like a lunatic, I remember banging my fists on the table, yelling, 'Why is it so hard?' I meant life, love. I knew that I loved my husband, wanted to live with him, wanted the baby, but there seemed to be no forms for us, no molds, no models to work from.

"I didn't want so much. I wanted to be busy and to feel good. Not to be miserable all the time. Not to be always fighting about money. And to feel like myself, not this mad, perfectly silent creature who would burst out into sobs and yells when I broke silence. I felt put-down all the time. Down, down, down on the lowest level of human life. Back there in the woods with nobody to talk to but an infant, doing nothing but dumb, heavy labor, spending my days waiting for my husband to come up the hill, going into a rage if he was fifteen minutes late, and into a major depression if it was longer than that. Did I believe that I owned him? Was that what love was about?

"It was very hard to communicate my feelings. To my husband it all sounded like complaints. Complaints about him not helping with the baby, complaints about money; to him it sounded like I was complaining about hard work, and about not having the comforts to which I was accustomed. And that was part of it, but mostly it was that I was disappearing. I felt that I was disappearing right out of existence.

"After a while I realized that if I was going to get anywhere with him, and work out questions of love and family and children, I'd have to be independent financially; but even that turned into a fight because I couldn't work and live back in the woods. So we broke up again. I rented my own little place close to town, just me and the baby. I got a job with a day-care center so the baby could be with me while I was earning some money. She was just two years old then. We both loved her very much; there wasn't any doubt about that. Jon couldn't bear not to see her every few days. So we saw quite a lot of one another during that separation. He'd come pick us up at the center, even though I had my own car, and we'd go off in two cars. Silly. Lovely.

"Jon kept the place in the woods and went about his usual routine, but he was at our place a lot. His work was getting more settled; he was doing well, promoted to associate professor, and he had begun working on a book. I was alone with the baby a lot. And even though I had initiated the move to separate, I'd go into a rage thinking of him working quietly at his place, or cruising into town for a little R and R at the bar, free as a bird, while I was stuck with the baby. I felt the loneliness like a punishment. Some nights I'd get terrified. There was a raccoon that would get into the garbage and make such a racket it sounded like a bear or an escaped maniac. I had friends down the road from me, and when I'd panic and call them they'd jump in their car and come over.

"My mother came to stay for a while, but she works and she lives on the East Coast. It was really a time I had to go through alone. Also I had the abortion then.

"It was a very hard time for me, but it was better than just going with what was expected of me. It wasn't so much that I was ambitious, though I was ambitious, I wanted to do worth-while work, something more than raising a family and being a wife, but it was more the desire to save my existence, to keep myself from fading away as a person. So Jon and I kept up these endless discussions about the husband's work and the wife's work (I had been trained in early childhood education) and about who should be responsible for the children, and who should change the diapers and take the laundry to the laundromat and shop and prepare dinner and do the dishes and I would get crazy, feeling that we were talking in the wrong language, but I didn't know *what* language to talk in, we needed to invent a new one to talk about what was bothering us. Most of the time I would be saying to him, 'No, that isn't what I mean,' and he'd be yelling 'Well, what do you mean, I can't figure out *what* it is you want,' and we'd be so frustrated, we'd end up screaming at one another and throwing things.

"In about six months, we got back together again. We had pounded out some aspects of our troubles. We bought a house outside of town but not deep in the woods, and we compromised on simple living. Jon was still sold on it, but I needed electricity. There was no way I was going to do without a washer-dryer and hot and cold running water. I didn't want to spend precious time just surviving. I was enjoying my work and my little girl meant everything to me, and I wanted to enjoy Jon, take pleasure in him, because that was the thing about us, we always had fun together and if it wasn't going to be any fun—"

Suzanne stops in exasperation. "I'm having the same difficulty talking about it with you," she said. "It all gets trivialized in these ridiculous details, but in fact it's the most important thing happening in the world today I think. Because it's going to change the way people live, the way they think, the way children grow up. My children have grown up cared for by their father—that makes them different— maybe that's why they're wonderful. Because they are wonderful.

"We fought and fought, Jon and I, but I'm glad we did because we won through to something important. We still fight. But basically we're pulling together. We're fighting attitudes outside us that could kill us, kill love. Not that it's easy. Some days I think the best thing to do is give up, just be a wife, I daydream about getting myself and Jon a wife somehow. It's too hard for both of us to be working and raising kids. Maybe a commune is the answer, but Jon hates communal living. I imagine I would too after a while. All I know is that it's very very hard and there's very very little help out there. Day-care centers, and you pay heavily for them. That's about it. Most of the money I earn goes back into the day-care center for my little boy.

"My daughter goes to public school now. Jon is making pretty good money and my salary isn't bad either, but we never have enough money. We pay a lot for baby-sitters too so that we can have time together at least once a week without the kids. It's very, very hard. It's almost as though the world were punishing us for having a family, making it as hard as possible to enjoy being married and having kids and having something for ourselves too. I go to all the conferences on new ways for the family, and I check out all the new ideas on child care, but there aren't any good answers, there aren't any really new structures to turn to, we have to invent them. And the same goes for how to be with one another as mothers and fathers and husbands and wives.

"I remember the first time I left Jon, I ran into one of the women in my feminist group at the supermarket. Someone had told her Jon and I had split. She began to dance up and down yelling, 'Hooray, hooray, you did it, congratulations.' Then she advised me to get everything I could out of Jon in child support, and that I should sue for that piece of property his family had given him. 'It's yours,' she said. 'It's half yours, community property law, get as much as you can,' she said as if my aim was to *defeat* Jon, to triumph over him in some way. But that didn't interest me, winning in that old way. What I wanted to win was love and friendship, family, gratification in my work, some fun in life and the dignity of being equals in the marriage, as people and as mother and father of our children. That's our aim and if we haven't entirely succeeded, at least we're working on it, and if we succeed, maybe it will be easier for others after us."

Teddy King
STARTING FROM SCRATCH

For a young black woman, inventing one's true life is even harder. When I met Teddy King, she appeared so assured and smooth, it was hard to believe that she was born of poor working-class parents in Harlem. She has the intensely black skin coloration that seems polished, a tall, exquisitely graceful figure; and she was dressed with high fashion dash—a flowing, layered look; soft, expensive leather boots; long strings of perfectly matched amber beads. Her hair is close cropped into a tight little cap of fuzzy blackness. Her face is enchanting, enormous black eyes, a cat-shaped lower jaw, a tiny nose with wide nostrils, thickly cushioned lips. She is in charge of a complicated cooperative venture in a rural setting outside a Massachusetts city which brings together the handwork of impoverished locals for sale. It has grown from its beginnings as a small roadside cottage a few years ago into seven or eight buildings comprising workshops in leather, ceramics, quilting, dress design, weaving, sewing, crocheting and related crafts; a bakery; a large structure in which products are displayed and sold; huge gardens which grow the produce sold at a separate stand; an ice-cream parlor; and the grounds include as well a tiny chapel for meditation and prayer. Teddy has a staff, but she is the engine which keeps the project chugging on.

When I asked her how she started the project, she corrects my question.

"You have to go further back than this," she says. "When you're born a Harlem nigger, you have to start from scratch. I was born in Harlem, lived in a dozen different streets, all of them in Harlem. My mother went crazy when I was a little girl. They put her away, and my father raised me. That sounds rotten, but it was nice. He's a wonderful man. He's still alive, almost ninety years old, and he does for himself in the apartment in the housing development near 125th Street that I moved him into almost ten years ago. He worked until he was seventy-six years old. Then he quit and started collecting social security. Because he worked so long, lying about his age, he had trouble with his union benefits, but he's doing all right, with his little bit of retirement money, Medicare, and the rest. I try to send him money whenever I can. He was an old man when I was born. When I was an adolescent I hated him for being so black and old and poor. Black, poor, and old—that was the worst in the world to me.

"I went to George Washington High School and I met all kinds of people there. My best friends were white and Jewish. There were a couple of other blacks in our crowd, but more mixed than me, one had a white father and the other a white mother who was Jewish. I'm black black black, all the way through, no matter how deep you poke. You can't hardly get my kind no more.

"I first began to feel like somebody with my high-school crowd. I was looking to them to copy *them*, but they were looking to *me* to copy me. They made me feel that being me was okay—more than okay, it was a good way to be.

They thought I was smart and funny. They'd copy the way I talked, while I was trying to lose it. One of my friends, she's my closest friend, still is, even copied the way I walked. She loved it, she said. And I was just *walking*, you know. She really did a number about me being so beautiful and moving so gracefully and that encouraged me to go along with her to the tryouts for the school musical. Wound up with me getting a speaking, singing, dancing part and my friend barely making the chorus. I couldn't believe it. Then I tagged along with her to the new dance group where she was taking modern dance lessons and then we went together to Martha Graham. My friend is a better dancer than I am, she always was, but I was black so I got moved along faster. Sometimes black is in your favor. Mostly not. That time, right away they gave me a scholarship. It scared me. 'Am I that good?' I wondered, and began to get rotten. Even when it's in your favor it's bad being special. I gave up when I was seventeen, I mean gave up thinking of being a professional dancer.

"When I was running with that mixed crowd in Washington Heights, we stayed out in Inwood Park past curfew one warm spring night, just kidding around like we always did. The cops came in their little kiddie car to drive us out and instead of moving us along with the white kids, they singled out me and a black fellow and took us down to the station house. My white friends stood around like window store dummies, while the cops shoved the two of us into the police car. I'll never forget how that felt.

"They told me later they were too stunned to think, but as soon as they got their heads together, my close friend quick called her daddy who's a lawyer. He came right down to the precinct and got us out. But we had been there almost an hour and they had fingerprinted me, and they had taken my bag and dumped everything out on the desk. It was just luck that they didn't find a joint on me. My friend wanted me to come home to her house, but I wanted to be alone, I didn't want anybody looking at me, seeing how I felt. Her father insisted on driving me home and I could feel how nervous he was driving through Harlem streets and after he drew up in front of my house, he could hardly sit still. I closed the door of the car. He took off like a shot. In my room I cried and banged things around like a crazy woman. I thought I was going crazy like my mother had. They were going to search me back in the station house. In another minute they would have had the matron in and I would have had to strip. And they could have put me away if I had a single joint on me. It made me crazy to think about.

"When I got out of high school I thrashed around doing a lot of different things. I was selling hand-knit Irish wool sweaters at Lord and Taylor, and I developed some neat ways of stealing—not only for me, but I fanned out, spreading it around for all my friends. I'd have a friend come in, buy a sweater, pay for one, I'd pack two, then she'd return the first one, get her money back—after a while I didn't let any money pass our hands, I'd just fuss with the sales slips and make it look like a real transaction. One day I thought 'Harlem Nigger' and that I could be sent up for what I was doing, and I quit the job.

"Then I did some fashion modeling—I even made it to the *New York Times* a couple of times. But I got sick of shlepping to cattle calls and go sees. Those casting photographers were always holding light meters up to my face to check out the lighting problems. I was too black. Then if they'd use me it would be for African fabrics or Peruvian ponchos. I quit that, and worked for a chain of movie houses as a relief cashier and saw all the movies I wanted to. I took courses at City in fashion and film. I made some clothes, crocheted stuff, worked with leather—some of it was smashing: a friend got some orders from Bendel's, but I lost interest. Then all the political stuff got really hot and it shook me up.

"Sure, I had marched for civil rights and peace with my high-school crowd. I was in school when the three civil rights' workers were lynched in Mississippi. I felt different about that than my friends did. I felt myself pulling away from the way they felt. I knew they shot all three, but first they beat the black kid to a pulp. Always a little something extra for us. And all the fuss was about those two white boys; you hardly heard anything about the black who was killed. When black power began I thought, 'Right on,' but then it got to be too much for me. My best friend was white, the girl I had gone to school with; and my next dearest friend was a white woman too, someone I got to know at Harkness Pavilion where my friend's doctor put me in semi-private for some kind of cleaning out. This older woman was in the next bed recovering from a new kind of hysterectomy where they didn't even cut her open, just sucked it out. We became good friends. She's a real neat lady. I learned a lot from her. She's been more of an education to me than I got anywhere else. I learned what to read from her. She's older than I am, married, three kids; pretty rich and she has a big job with a foundation; but she never pulls a busy signal on me, she always has time for me. And the men I was attracted to were mostly white men. In my school crowd the boy I loved was mostly white.

"I made a lot of mistakes. I took off for Europe without a penny, hitching and scrounging, following that guy I was in love with. I had my fare over, and my fare back, and that was it. I suffered and suffered over that boy I had gone to school with. He didn't love me. Then he went guru and took off for Pakistan or Turkey or someplace and I gave up on him and stayed in Europe. I fell in love with a tall, gorgeous, sun-God of a man, a European, and I lived with him for a couple of years. I had a baby with him. He was heavy into drugs, and they nailed him and put him away for possession and dealing. I waited for him for two years, standing by, doing what I could for him; and when he came out it was the same dumb story all over again. Worse. He came out a mess. He didn't love me except in a crazy, stingy way. He was too messed up in himself to love anybody else. He didn't love his baby either, and she's hard not to love. She didn't make him feel different about everything the way she did me—different about the whole world and about myself.

"I came back to the United States with my baby. My old school friend was waiting for me at the airport. It was beautiful to know that somebody loved me enough to welcome me back; I fell into her arms with my baby. She had married a guy I really liked and she had a baby just about the same age as mine, a big blond, blue-eyed husky boy and our two babies looked terrific together, Kim so delicate and coffee-colored next to him. I didn't stay with my friend long, but she helped me a lot, taking care of Kim while I was in the hospital being repaired.

"It was then I met my new friend. She got me a job as a clerk at her foundation and I tried to work and live in New York, but that is a hard road to travel when you're raising a child. I moved in with my father. He gave up his room to me and the baby and he slept in the kitchen on a cot. I was reading a lot, staying home nights with the baby, reading books my friend steered my way. I got hooked on the history of slavery and of blacks in America, and then I got hooked on the holocaust, on the extermination of the Jews. I read everything I could understand to read on those two subjects, and I keep up with everything that's being written.

"I feel connected to those happenings in a deep way. It's like if you cut me open, instead of a cancer or a rotten appendix or whatever sickness I have inside, that's what the doctors would find and have to cut out. And in another way I also feel like those happenings make me strong. Because they help me understand. Okay to the world I'm a Harlem nigger with interchangeable parts. Like I know if someone starts yammering about niggers living like animals, living off the government, living off their taxes, living like leaches on decent people, they're talking about me even if I never have lived off the government or off anybody's taxes, but just because I'm black they mean me. They killed those

Jews, just because they were Jews, just like they keep col-
oreds and blacks herded in South Africa, just on the basis
of color. Interchangeable parts. That's me. I'm sexier. I
dance better. I'm looser, dumber, I smell, I've got syphilis.
My skin is black, I'm a Harlem nigger. And I'll always be to
people who think like that. That destroys a person.

"That's what I mean about starting from scratch. From
way deep inside. I moved to Massachusetts, where my
friend helped get me an office job at the Black Studies
program of the university. I studied making myself over. To
become what I *was*, instead of what the world said I was.

"Right away I had a setback because I fell in love with
the head of the Black Studies program. That was a bad
scene all around. He fucked me over just the way he was
fucking over whitey and the establishment and academia
and the foundations that he knew how to shake more grants
out of than fleas out of a dog. And he was brilliant too. It
was wrong of him to waste himself like that. He wasted me
too. I know what was driving him. He figured, why not?
Blacks had always been fucked over, all through history, so
why shouldn't he return a share of what he had gotten? But
he was spoiling something good. Black Studies is important. I don't care that most academics are doing it too,
white academics, ripping off the students, ripping off
knowledge, ripping off the universities and the government, ripping off women. He ripped me off as a woman
and as a black woman and I expected better of him *because*
he was black. So in a way I was thinking the same way as I
was trying to stop thinking. Assigning him interchangeable
parts too.

"When you talk about your life it comes out very serious—deadly. I laugh a lot. I see the funny side of things. I
always did. No matter how many bad things were happening. I feel as if I'm giving a wrong impression, about the
way I am. Now at the Center too. It's a lot of fun. It's sweet.
I know that what we have here isn't the dominant kind of
thing in our society; I know it isn't all sweetness and light in
the world. But I'm glad we've built a little corner where it

does prevail. This is the way I'd like things to be in the world.

"When I see two old folks come in here, helping one another up the ramp, one maybe carrying the other's work because he's just a tiny bit stronger, it makes me laugh, but in a wonderful way, to see how they try to help one another. Do you know what I mean? That's the way I am. I'm a cripple, hobbling along, but while I can still hobble, I'll try to do some good, shake a couple of more grants out of the foundations, and Vista, run down to Boston and New York and get a few more orders for crocheted hats, design a few more shirts for the seamstress to sew up. All the shit I learned that seemed to add up to nothing. I love this work; my little girl has a good life here. People say to me, 'Don't they need your help in Harlem?' Sure. But I'm dragged down there. I'd go under. I do what I can here for others and if maybe one hundred, two hundred, three hundred white people up here see a Harlem nigger as a person for the first time in their lives, that's a change for the good, too."

Teddy King started a fine cooperative venture in Massachusetts, but her achievement goes beyond that, goes to the heart of her own vision of herself and to its establishment in the minds of others. She did indeed have to "start from scratch" re-creating an individual from a strong inner core of conviction that she could not and would not succumb to the crippling image our society imposed on her essential being from birth—the "Harlem nigger" image. Painstakingly (if haltingly) she remade herself to a different pattern, much as she would have pulled together patches of cloth to create a charming and useful object, if those were the only materials at hand. She doesn't consider herself unusual in any way, and perhaps she is not. "I just did what every poor black female born and raised in Harlem or anyplace else like that has to do. That's the way it is. If you want to survive, you have to get that picture out of your head and get down to what you really are. And I wanted to survive."

Minna Harwicke
MAKING THE BEST
OF BEING PUSHED TO START

For many women style sets the tone of their existence—
the sheen of their hair, the startling make-up effects, the
wit with which they dress, and the setting in which they
live and work. How do they arrive at this point, and what
does it mean in terms of becoming themselves? Minna Harwicke is such a woman, now in her forties, divorced,
mother of two, a successful entrepreneur in the public relations field on the West Coast. Her place of business is a
town house where she lives as well. She redecorated, leaving the Victorian detail of the original, contrasted with the
straight, severe lines and dead white of entirely modern
furnishings. Striking and astonishing modern art decorates
the walls, and there are occasional standing sculptures over
which she is as likely to toss a feather boa as a cowboy hat.
The room in which she has her office is flooded with sun-
shine and gorgeous plants; her desk, in an otherwise severe
room, is a large oak roll-top, and on it she keeps the latest

IBM Selectric. She's not traditionally beautiful, but striking, and immensely appealing. One thinks of her as having perfumed, sweet flesh. There is always something inimitably witty about her costume—today it is her shoes, whorey red patent leather slingback pumps worn with an otherwise severe black suit and man-tailored striped black and white shirt, beautifully cut to show off her sensationally full breasts. The hat is a touch of wit, too—a soft, floppy brimmed felt with a small red rose at the brim. She has large, very dark eyes, glistening with feeling. She says of herself that she was precipitated into independence. She didn't consciously seek it.

"It never occurred to me that a woman's final success could be anything more than marriage and children. To the right man, of course. And I had married the right man, when I was twenty. Big wedding, the perfect marriage, lovely apartment—I knocked myself out making everything beautiful—perfect. I never looked at the idea that I had a choice to be anything more than a housewife. A glorious housewife, naturally. Glamorous, sexy—a dream of a housewife. Everything I did was special—the look of the house, myself, the orderliness—fresh flowers, no sink full of dishes—I could prepare a gourmet meal at the drop of a fork. I never consciously wished for more than to be happy and content in the marriage. But my husband was *always* unhappy. I'm attracted to unhappy men. I always have been. I left home when I was nineteen. I walked out in a rage during a fight with my mother about my friendship with an older woman. She accused us of being lesbians. Actually I was having an affair with a married man (unhappy, of course) and I was using my friend as a cover. But I loved my woman friend, and it was disgusting to me that my mother should attack us that way. I left. I had no plans. But that's the way I do things. I jump first, then I look around and work it all out. My mother had never predicted anything good for me. I'm always going to come to a bad end as far as she's concerned. She hates it if I succeed and she sticks it in me if I fail. It's a no-win situation. I can do without it.

"I had a number of affairs before I married. Always with the same sort of men. I was attracted to men who are gifted, and who are sad. I have the power to make it all better. I'm still drawn to men like that; but now I know I can't or I won't make it all better—I won't sacrifice anything of my own to cure their unhappiness, even if I want to. I know it won't work. My husband had every reason to be happy—he was a success in his field, I loved him and would have done anything for him, we had two darling children, we had everything going for us, and he was always unhappy. My mission in life was to make him happy. If that included doing a dance on his file cabinets I would do it, and I have. I would have done anything to keep my marriage going; I told myself that I had the best possible marriage. I guess I thought if I repeated it and repeated it I'd believe it. Then one day, I dared to say to myself that I was unhappy. I remember the moment vividly. 'Your husband is young, talented, handsome,' I said to myself, 'how dare you be unhappy?' I felt very guilty.

"Being a housewife is hard work, and it's shitty work. My husband was doing very well in commercial photography and there was money for household help, so I got help, cleaning women and an au pair girl for the beach house; but he kept complaining about my spending so freely. One day he said, 'If you want help in the house, you'd better go to work to pay for it.' That made me furious. I had never had any real support from him, even the financial support was grudging—forget any other kind. I was ready to support him in every way. He was going through a crisis in his work, getting set to quit a connection which was lucrative and secure. He wanted to free-lance, to be his own man, do only what he liked doing. I urged him to do whatever he needed to, I never told him, 'No, we need the money, don't you dare risk our security.' Even though I knew it wouldn't work out for him, that it wasn't going to cure anything, he'd go on being just as unhappy as before. I didn't say that to him, but that's just the way it worked out.

"When I first thought about going back to work, I was in a panic. If I hadn't felt so strongly that he was pushing me to work, that he really wanted me to get out and earn some money, I never could have done it. Before I married I had worked at jobs that didn't amount to anything solid. I was a lousy student. Not that I don't know a lot, but then I felt ignorant and helpless. I had run the showroom for a furniture design place before I married. It was all a matter of style—developing a manner, a style that put the product over—I'm good at that. It's all in the presentation.

"My husband suggested that since he was going freelance, I could become his public relations agent. That was too scary to consider. I felt that if I did something wrong, he'd kill me. Or if somebody did something wrong to *me*, he'd kill *them*. I avoided becoming his agent, but through his contacts I became an agent for another man in his field, a competitor, but a friend. A friend of the family," she adds, arching her pencilled eyebrows. "On one of my first appointments with a corporation executive, the bastard broke the appointment. I came home disheartened and when I told my husband he threw a fit. I thought he was going to go out and kill that advertising manager. Under the guise of protecting me, he could have scotched my career before it even got off the ground.

"Because it turned out that I was good. I was really a success, and very quickly. Like magic, only not. I was putting a lot into it. My husband's reaction was crazy—all out of proportion. I was only a very minor success, I was hardly anywhere yet and he began to moan about being overshadowed by his wife's success. Maybe he was trying to build me up, maybe he meant it as a compliment or as a joke, but the effect on me was undermining. 'I feel like the husband in *A Star Is Born*,' he said to me. I didn't feel that as a compliment or a joke. It made me shut up about the good things happening to me because I was afraid my success would only upset him further, make him more unhappy, and the whole point in my going back to work was to make him happy.

"I didn't want to do shit work. I had been a housewife for eight years, but I decided to start as if I had been out in the field all along, as I had, in a way, through my husband. I started as if I belonged at the top, even though I started small, representing only one man, my husband's friend. I thought I'd better keep it controlled, because underneath all the bravado I felt I didn't know what I was doing. That's the way I start—I jump, then I see where I've landed. There's another image for the way I start. I go in as if it's blind man's bluff. I let it turn me around, get me into the game, and when the blindfold comes off I look around and see where I've landed and I take it from there. If I were to sit down and think about what I'm doing, plan my moves in advance, it would be too overwhelming, it would paralyze me. I have to do it without the idea that I'm doing it. That's how I got started again. I jumped in, without looking, without thinking.

"Getting out was marvelous in some ways—horribly scary in others. I remember catching sight of myself reflected in the window of a department store and I didn't recognize myself. I was wearing a smashing blue suit and a big hat and I was admiring an attractive young woman in the window when I realized it was me. It didn't seem like me because there was nothing in front of me, no stroller, no child, no protective other to put myself behind, just me out there, looking good.

"In other ways I was a wreck. I kept a body thermometer in the drawer next to our bed because I kept getting aches and pains—chills, fevers, it felt like flu. But I'd take my temperature and if it was normal and it generally was, I'd go out and see a client. I'd make myself go, no matter how sick I felt. I'd pop a librium in my mouth and go.

"There was so much I didn't know. Like how to set fees. One of my first conferences on an assignment I quoted the client $1000. The client said, $200. I was so shocked at how out of line I was that I literally went deaf. I couldn't hear anything being said. I thought I had ruined the career of the man I was representing. I excused myself, went to the ladies' room, took another tranquilizer, and came back and settled for $500. Another time, during an appointment with a top man on a major magazine, I was so nervous I went blind for a couple of minutes. The way you do when you look directly into a photographer's exploding flashbulb. I couldn't see anything.

"The crazy thing was I was having a lot of success. That was great. I began to feel good, strong, powerful, that's the way I feel when my work is going well. I feel satisfied about myself and that makes me feel sexy. I had lost almost any interest I had in sex with my husband, mostly because he had become so lukewarm. Work meant everything to him—anything else came a notch below that—me, the kids, love, sex, friends, were all less than work to him. I didn't understand then, the way I do now, the relationship for me between sex and work. When my work is going well, I feel like fucking." She laughs. "That's how I got into my first affair. The one that blew my marriage. The first man I represented, the family friend, was young, immensely talented—he's become one of the top men in the country—and he was sweet and handsome—and unhappy—so he met all the necessary qualifications for me to think I was in love with him. I was going to make it all better for him too. I guess also I was hungry for appreciation and hungry for some live sex, hot sex. I didn't mean to disturb my marriage in any way with that affair. In fact I began to enjoy sex with my husband much more while I had that other little thing going.

"He walked in on us unexpectedly. Barged into the studio. I think he deliberately set us up. He wanted out of the marriage, now he had an excuse. He ran. My marriage was over. Didn't take more than five minutes. He packed up and he left—that was it.

"Then I was really on my own. Me and the kids. I tried not to think, because if I did, I would think, 'I'm finished.' I kept going. I popped pills like mad to keep the panic down. I tried hard to make the right choices, not to leap at anything that came along, but to discriminate the way I always had. I knew I wanted my life to go on in the same style. It was *my* style; I had set the style of our marriage, not my husband, though he had collected the credit.

"I wanted to keep our home as it had been—just as lovely, orderly, fresh flowers every day, great dinners, wine, candles, good companions. I had had a very good woman working for me—a marvelous woman who would have been president of a major corporation or of the country if she hadn't been black and a woman—and I asked her to work for me full time as a live-in housekeeper. It was the luckiest thing in the world that she said yes. I couldn't have done what I've done without her. Her support, her advice, her friendship . . . She's a terrific worker, and we have the same standards—if there are to be white curtains at the windows then they have to be kept dazzlingly white. I never had to tell her a thing. She even sewed beautifully, made a lot of my clothes. More than anything else there was perfect continuity in the lives of the children—that was the greatest gift she gave me. Whatever happened, I was there or she was there for them. We had our quarrels once in a while, pretty fierce ones—how could we not quarrel—we were as close as sisters, I knew everything about her—she knew everything about me—we were as good as married. In a way, she was my wife—the wife every working woman needs—only I paid her and there wasn't any crap between us. After a fight, we'd clear the air; we never fought for good.

"Not that I didn't work like a dog. I'd come home so exhausted that in order to have some time with the kids, I'd take my bath with them, the three of us in one bathtub and after supper we'd all go to bed at the same time. After the separation when I went to my husband for a decent settlement or for specific needs he'd always come up with the same kind of response—'You don't have to live in this part of town. There are cheaper places to live.' Or, 'You don't have to use private doctors, you can take the kids to a clinic.' He wanted to make me feel like a scrub woman. Nobody was going to do that to me.

'I like to take risks. I'm glad I'm where I am, on my own, taking all the risks and all the credit, responsible for my own life, whatever it is. I'm in a funny kind of business, difficult to pin down—it's all up in the air—but it's good for me. If I have to deliver for a client, provide a camel, a belly dancer, set up a screening for a TV pilot, PR a rock group, arrange for rain for a film-maker, or an art opening, do the biggest party in the world in the biggest restaurant in the world in the tallest building in the world, I do it, if it means chartering a 747 or whatever. At one time or another everyone who needs something like that comes knocking on my door and I deliver. I'm proud of that, and of the way I live, and of the way my kids are doing, and of the way I am and the way I look.

"I could have collapsed on another man's hands, but I pulled myself together and made my own life. It may look loose and dangerous to others—(and it is)—I can fail, I can go broke—(and I have)—I can involve myself with the wrong men—(and I do)—but what's important is that there isn't any illusion, any falseness in my life—all the role crap is out. Women's lib came into itself at the same time that I was going through all the changes in my own attitudes, and the movement was a tremendous source of strength to me. Okay, sometimes the movement is really full of crap, but the important thing about feminism is that it's a support system. Even if what some of them write and have published is dreck, it's enormously valuable for someone like me whose awareness was zero. We need it all. Let it keep coming, brilliant or foolish, we can use it all. Later, we'll make decisions on who was right, who was wrong, which way to go. Now we need the freedom to explore.

"When my marriage became unhappy, I lost all feeling of sexuality. I missed it. I missed feeling hot for somebody. I was never hot then. For me sexuality and the sense of self is one. When my work is going well, I'm hot for everybody. I go in a constant state of lust. When all I was doing was giving out—to my husband, to my children, and to the house—all my spontaneity in sex dried up. I became bored, maybe with the habituality or the repression. Impulsive fulfillment, instant gratification became secondary to the needs of the children. You didn't grab it anytime of the day, anywhere in the house after the kids were there.

"I remember a fight with my husband. He complained, 'What happened to the girl who always wanted to fuck?' I came right back at him, 'What happened to the man who would make love to me?' It wasn't my idea of love that he would be jumping me at three in the morning. 'Either make love to me or no jumping,' I told him, 'husband or no.' I was last, after his work, and then it was I who had to be up at six in the morning—to take care of the babies. He could postpone his work, take a nap, if he wanted to, but there was no way to postpone my children's needs. I was very aware of the difference between his work and my work—as a housewife, I mean.

"If I were thirty-three today, I don't know that it would have gone any differently. There's a lot of awareness, now, but it's a surface thing in many ways. It's going to be a long time before men and women can live together equitably, each following his and her own needs. It's a surface awareness on the part of the men, I find, and even in many women there's a need to go on in the old way. A lot of women still want to feel needed; they think it's their most secure position. At least now, they have a choice—to make or not make breakfast or dinner—or whatever. Before, they *had* to. But some young women in their thirties are still caught in the old ways, trying to insure security with their boyfriends and on the job through serving. Even as short a time as four or five years ago, I felt incomplete because I was divorced, and I didn't have a primary relationship, where I was serving some man. Now I know there's nothing wrong with me because of that.

"That doesn't mean I don't need sex. I'm happiest in the beginning or the middle of an affair; when it ends I'm down, but I'm not destroyed. I used to be destroyed. I don't become less now when an affair ends, but I'm heightened while it's around. It's liberating to recognize that.

"My last affair taught me an interesting lesson. He considered himself a liberated man. He kept a copy of the Hite report beside his bed. He read it and learned from it and used what he learned because he's a man who wants to please women. Okay, I count that as liberation, and even the fact that he always did all the cooking. Mostly we were together at his place. It was great. Then I got needy. I was having trouble in my work and it took that form—emotional neediness. He reacted in the old way. What he saw was a demanding woman, and he ran. Even if it was a neurotic thing on my part, it's human to be neurotic sometime. It was a mark against him that he couldn't hang in there and see how I'd come out of it. That isn't liberation. He had been married for eighteen years and his history made him run away from my moment of need. I made a big mistake, I admit. I told him that I wanted to see more of him, to make our relationship a more dependable one, because that's what I needed at that moment. He saw eighteen years of wifely demands behind that, and ran.

"It didn't destroy me. I was sorry to end that affair, but it didn't destroy me. It would have five years ago. That's the difference for young women. My daughter will never have to deal with the things I dealt with. As a senior in high school she had a boyfriend who wanted to see her a lot—and she loved him a lot too—but her work came first. It was an intrinsic response for her. It is for me too now. You're a woman, but you do your work first, because it's important to you. Women have consistently put themselves second in the past—now the priorities are changed. I hope they stay that way."

It could be said of Minna Harwicke that she isn't a starter

at all. If she hadn't been nudged by her husband to get out and earn some money, might she not have gone on forever living the life of a lesser member of "a happy marriage," until it exploded in her face? Perhaps she never would have developed into the Minna Harwicke she now is if she hadn't been booted out of what she earlier had considered the safest berth in the world and the highest goal of a woman's life. But these questions are meaningless in the light of her personal triumph. She *was* pushed; and instead of falling apart she responded with an energetic and imaginative bounce back which turned disaster into success; in the process, her real self emerged.

Joanne Weiner
PLOTTING A CAREER
LIKE A MAN

There is something entirely new in the tone taken by
Joanne Weiner, an intelligent and well-organized person,
like many other women. What is strikingly different about
her is an approach to her life and to her career that we
have come to expect only from men. But there's nothing
apparently manly about this soft-voiced woman in her early
thirties who has just entered Yale to begin studying law.

Joanne Weiner also married early, straight out of college,
had a child three years later when she was twenty-three
and another child, two years after that, a boy and a girl,
and stopped at two. She married a psychiatrist and wanted
out of her marriage almost as soon as she had got in. "Marriage was an escape hatch for me though I'm not sure what
I was escaping from. Myself, I guess. Anyway my marriage
was a disaster from the very beginning.

"Some of our troubles must have come from my evaluation of psychiatry. I don't believe in it, so I guess that was
rough on him. I came not to believe in it. I don't want to

135

sound like Aimee Semple McPherson, or as if I maintain a Pollyannish view of life, but I do feel that one goes through life learning and moving on and getting stronger. That's what life *is*. I don't mean to say that really ill people shouldn't be helped or that they don't need help. But there's a tendency for people with normal problems—what I consider normal anxieties—to manipulate therapy. It all becomes a blaming kind of thing. My mother, my father, the kind of blaming that isn't useful. At least it isn't for me. I'd rather struggle and learn and do and grow strong while doing.

"But I don't think I could have become what I am without the feminist movement. That's a different kind of help. I joined a CR group, one of the first that was formed, and the support and friendship in that group was marvelous. I'm immensely grateful to the women's movement. I come from a small family, I have no sisters and I was never close to my mother. Learning to know women was a whole new thing—like discovering the other half of the human race. I gained enormous strength from other women. It isn't the politics of the feminist movement that has meant so much to me, though of course as a movement feminism is important to me, as much as the personal interactions. It would have been much harder for me, and taken me much longer to get where I'm at without it."

Joanne Weiner doesn't conceive of herself as rich ("My idea of enough money is not worrying about bills, and having a little house in the country," she tells me), though we are sitting in the living room of an expensive apartment overlooking Central Park in New York City. It is a large, airy room, quietly luxurious, furnished in traditional period style, the parqueted floors covered by Oriental rugs and the ample windows softly draped. We drink coffee served in fine china. Joanne is divorced. Only one of the two children who live with her is at home. He is a beautifully mannered child, and mother and son are warm and easy with one another. It is October, and the business Joanne conducts with her son before she turns to me has to do with a Halloween costume. He attends a private school as does her daughter. The perfectly kept, spacious apartment reflects a style initiated by Joanne but held together by a live-in housekeeper. Like many other women who reject the housewife role and are given or earn the money to replace themselves, Joanne revels in "her paid wife" and concedes that a career would have been inconceivably difficult without such a person.

Joanne is very attractive. She wears no make-up today and her straight, brown hair hangs loosely about her face. She is simply dressed in a soft wool skirt and sweater. Her dark, expressive eyes underline the quick, articulate, intelligent flow of her conversation. She often crosses her arms across her full breasts—a defensive, protective gesture, it might seem—or brushes her hair back from her face with both hands in a sweeping, cleaning gesture of beginning again.

What we are talking about specifically today is her new start as a law student at Yale, a particularly interesting development because so many women of her generation are doing the same. About twenty-five percent of the class she has entered are women, and this rise in numbers is reflected throughout all law schools in the country. Most of these are younger than Joanne, but some like her are in their thirties or more, returning to school to enter a solid profession, one traditionally closed to women until recently. Starting law school is not Joanne's first foray out into the world from wife and motherhood; she had been a successful editor and writer before her decision to quit a good job on a magazine and enter law school. Studying, learning come easily to her. She was an early admissions student at the college which she sailed through without really doing any work at all. Easily bored, she couldn't imagine at that time having the drive to work hard at anything. She drifted through, and married immediately upon graduating.

She didn't want to stay at home, and since working in publishing attracted her, she looked for and got a job in the publicity department of a large publishing house. She loved working. She worked steadily throughout the marriage and babies. "The great thing about a job wasn't so much the work, but the people. I loved being in an office, I loved being with people, and I loved the stability of earning my own money. I don't want to be dependent on anybody. I want to earn my own way."

She moved beyond publicity to writing and to editing. Her first book was published to some success, but she found the actual work of writing mostly unpleasant. "And I didn't value what I had done. I seemed to have the attitude that it had come too easily. If I could have done it, it must not have been worth doing. What I really love doing is editing. I like it better than writing. I enjoy text and line editing. There's something solid and satisfying in it for me. But I went on writing—writing with my left hand and editing with my right. I was now a full-time editor at the publishing house, but after a time my division of the firm was shut down. I actively sought another editing job while keeping my writing assignments. I did a regular column, regular reviewing for a newspaper, and articles for magazines. Then I landed a very good job on a fashion magazine.

"After my divorce, which was inevitable, I threw myself into work even more vigorously than before. I never worked so hard in my life. It was the greatest pleasure in my life, though I'm not a workaholic," she adds. "My friends, my children mean too much to me to bury myself in work.

"But I was dissatisfied. I thought of myself as 'clever and witty,' not serious. I knew that I was clever and witty enough to go on successfully as a writer and editor, but it was too easy. I wanted to get deeply into something solid; I wanted to become a more serious person. For a bit I was attracted to politics. I was doing some articles on politics and government, and of course politics is a very open field for women now, but a good look at that world turned me off. It wasn't for me—the wheeling and dealing bothered me.

"When I thought about going on the way I was going, I saw a long, dreary corridor down which I would be endlessly walking in the same way. I knew I could reach a level of competence in which I'd get to be an editor-in-chief of something, at age forty-five or fifty. I could see myself in ten to fifteen years automatically making it to the top editor's chair at Random House or *Time* Magazine, but I couldn't picture thirty to thirty-five years of pleasurable work in the process. I knew I didn't want to devote myself solely to being a writer. I don't want to be sitting alone in a room discontented, dreaming about stabbing Anatole Broyard, getting his job. Of course I mean to write and I am writing right now, I'm working on a novel that's almost finished. I don't think I'll ever give up writing, whatever I say against writing.

"But I had wanted to be a lawyer since I was a little girl. That had always been my answer to 'What do you want to be when you grow up?' I've always been attracted to law, I picked up any articles on the subject, read a lot of books on the subject, I always enjoyed talking to lawyers, I like the way they use their minds. There are solid qualities about the law. To read law is to learn something solid about the world. And it's a natural extension of editing and writing. It's dealing with words not as immutable objects but as the skin of living thought. For me the law is an intellectual extension of editing, but deeper, more serious; it's a clarification of reality.

"Once I made the decision to go into law I moved ahead. I applied to Columbia, NYU, Fordham, and Rutgers. I made the waiting list at Yale and Rutgers, and then Rutgers came through with an opening. But I didn't want to settle for second best. I thought, 'I'm not changing my life in my thirties and taking these risks to go to anything but the best! I want to go to Yale.' I decided to confront the Dean of

Admissions at Yale, see him myself. I guess I hoped to charm him into admitting me. I had to phone him for an appointment, but I couldn't do it alone. I called two of my close women friends, and they stood by me, each holding me by the arm, with me saying, 'I can't do it. I can't do it.' But I did do it. I made the phone call and set up the appointment. I didn't make Yale that year, in spite of the visit to the Dean, I applied again and had to go through another year of waiting. And then I did make Yale.

"I spend two nights a week in New Haven and the rest of the week at home with my children. I'll be going to school for three years. Nobody at Yale knows me. In the publishing world everybody knew me. I gave that up, the little smitch of power, fame, money that I had, and that was lovely to have. Sure, those matter to me. There's another big wild card thrown in here. What if I flunk out? What if I fail? But I know I won't. When I first started listening in class I didn't know what was going on some of the time, but I was sure that half the class didn't know either. I don't really think about flunking out. The chances of my failing are too slim to worry about. I know my level of competence and I know how the learning process works. Besides, the school doesn't let you flunk out.

"It's been good. It's exhilarating when you put it together, when you realize what you don't know and what you're learning. I can see some things very quickly—that's an extension of the editing too—I can find the main thought quickly, but perhaps I'm not as good at reaching the more subtle things, what's underneath. But that's coming, more and more. At first it was like climbing a sheer cliff using my fingernails—now it's an opening, an opening into solid knowledge—the whole world has opened out for me—it's all contained in the law—and solidly.

"What's hard is that there's very little time to throw away. I use eighty percent of my time now where I only used to use sixty-five to seventy percent. It's like having very little expendable income and worrying whenever you spend any of it. I figure my time very closely, working on the train, handling appointments very carefully. It drives me crazy if I have a wasted hour between appointments—that lousy wasted hour traipsing around Bendel's.

"I couldn't do what I'm doing if I were married or really committed to another person. I have my friends and my children—they're my great refreshment, and of course love and sex are in my life. I couldn't go cold turkey, I'm not the celibate type, but what's there is very pleasant and not demanding of my time or my emotions. It's planned, it's limited (once a week), it's fun and it's under control and that's what I need now. I'm glad to have it. We all know a number of terrific women—competent, successful, independent—who go around crying about love, love, if only they had love, life would be perfect for them, but that kind of love, all consuming, all fulfilling—if it exists—isn't on my present list of priorities.

"I've found more discovery of myself in studying law than in any love affair.

"I want to be independent financially too. I don't want to borrow. That's the main reason I'm continuing to write, working on a novel, mostly for the income. There's a lot of hard work in my life right now just to keep ahead financially. In time I know being a lawyer will pay off and that I'll earn good money. To some degree making more money was a motive in becoming a lawyer, yes. I haven't yet decided which branch of law I'll go into. I don't want to be a showbiz lawyer, that's for sure. I may go into publishing law. I have the experience and the information for that branch of law. Or I could teach law. And I'll certainly go on writing, perhaps differently. It's interesting to me to see how studying law has changed my writing, because it's done something different to my thinking. For example, learning the trick of proving that white is white immediately after proving that black is white. There's a fascination in that. People think of the law as a dry subject but it's so fascinating that any aspect of it proves to be not dry.

"The rewards are very different from the ones I enjoyed as a magazine editor and a writer—the openings and the pub parties, my by-line appearing regularly, the power I had at my desk, at my phone—though I'm glad to be rid of some of that. I no longer can stand to be brusque on the phone. But there was a lot of icing on that cake. There's no icing on this cake and I guess the question I had to ask myself was, 'How hooked are you on icing?' People say that I was too ambitious to stay where I was and be satisfied, but ambition is the wrong word for what women are doing now. It's more than ambition—and it's something else. It's true that I'm doing what I'm doing to get ahead, and to please myself, but I'm doing what I'm doing in the world, and that changes not only me, but the world too."

On the surface Joanne Weiner would appear to be the most feminine of women, but what is new in this new woman is the "male" coolness of her mind, exemplified in her approach to her career. There isn't a hint in her account of the hysterical thrashing about we have been trained to associate with the concept of "a woman on her own," the kind of woman we meet so often in contemporary novels. (The reader is sometimes left marveling that the heroine is able to get herself a cup of coffee without slashing her wrist with the spoon or scalding her child to death. The last accomplishment we would expect of her is an expertise in any sector of *work*.) But the measured consideration Joanne Weiner brings to the problems of moving ahead in a chosen career is the sort of trait we used to term "masculine," before the women's movement made us all more careful about our use of language. "Masculine" meant logical, thoughtful, rational, carefully reasoned and not distorted by inapplicable and irrelevant emotions. Joanne Weiner exemplifies the way those categories are being moved out of their circumscribed gender.

Diana Rhodes
MAKING THE BEST
OF HAVING TO START

Blocking out a career, the way a man does, may not be a "manly" trait after all. Certainly Diana Rhodes who displays a similar mind-set appears to be the most womanly of women, if womanly or manly have any meaning anymore beyond the basic biologic ones. Diana Rhodes, too, went back to school. But what is now a common occurrence for women was a more startling move when she did it as one of the first among her generation.

Diana Rhodes is now in her early fifties. She had quit college at eighteen to marry a man ten years older, a labor lawyer with political aspirations. They set up house in the small Pennsylvania city where they both had grown up. Diana hated the place, both for its physical ugliness and its social and cultural bleakness. But her husband Emmett's law practice was fairly well established there and so they settled in. Diana had been attending a small private college which was expensive for the time, and her ambitious parents, unhappy about her marriage to an older man with dubious political affiliations (he was a Democrat, they were loyal Republicans) refused to continue paying her tuition, and she was too shy to ask her husband if he would or could. Her schooling would have been interrupted in any event because within a few months Emmett was drafted into the army, and since World War II was in full swing, he went right into officer training after boot camp. He never left the country; he was sent South and Diana followed him from post to post. By the time he was mustered out, they had their first baby. Emmett never returned to his law practice; he went into the advertising business with some army buddies and they settled, not in the small Pennsylvania town where Diana's parents still lived, but in a larger city in the state.

It was a good period to have begun an agency. It did well, and they did well as a family. They had four children, two boys and two girls, a big rambling split-level house in a posh suburb; they owned two cars, a washer-dryer, a big freezer, all the usual gadgets *plus* a color TV before anybody else in town did. None of that meant anything especially wonderful to Diana. What mattered to her were her children, her family, her friends. She was devoted to taking care of the children; they interested her as profoundly as anything in her surroundings. It was a good life, she tells me—with many good friends, a rich social life; the worthwhile activities of Democratic party politics, the buying coop and the school board; and enjoying the many cultural events of the city.

Nonetheless when Diana was in her late thirties, and her oldest child was in high school and the youngest in grade school, she decided there wasn't enough to keep her busy all day at child rearing and she made the decision to go back to school to complete her college education. It was the period of the sixties and colleges were proudly announcing programs to help women return to school. But she immediately ran into a snag.

"If you decided to go back to school full time, you'd be

allowed to go during the day, but if you needed to go part time you had to go at night. I wanted to go part time during the day. The best time for me to be away from home was when the children were at school. I still had four children at home, and with me and my husband that was a big family. It took a lot of housekeeping to keep us going. Emmett brought home a good salary but with four kids, even with a good salary we had to watch our money, and apart from that, I didn't want my family neglected. I had put my best work into rearing a family; I didn't want that work spoiled. I fought like mad to be allowed to attend part time during the day. I wrote a letter to the president of the university. I even threatened to expose the program as fraudulent, because here they were making big statements about helping women but not when it came to taking our special problems into consideration. Anyway I won.

"They admitted me as a day student, and what's more three other schools made the same offer because I wrote letters to the newspapers. I battled that one out. They gave me full credit for whatever courses I took, and I was given a special dispensation that excused me from physical education. I was very proud of having won my battle to get in on my terms.

"I had tried once before to return to school, when I was twenty-one. I quit then because I was so embarrassed at being so much older than the other kids, but when I went back pushing forty, I wasn't the least bit embarrassed or uncomfortable. The only surprise was that I discovered I needed glasses, and that showed me more than anything else how it is for mothers and wives. You don't even notice when you need glasses.

"I loved school. I loved the work in class, and the homework. I had always loved going to school and it was wonderful to begin again to deal with something outside domestic life, reactivating my brain. I went to school three hours a day, three days a week. I did my homework in the evenings while the kids were doing their homework. I was studying for an undergraduate degree as an English major, but I had to take math courses. That was terrible because it was new math—a whole new thing and I had never been very good at math to begin with. But the rest was a dream—history, philosophy, western civilization—I even loved the bullshit courses—I attended all the lectures, I was never absent, my hand was always raised and I had something to say about everything. It wasn't a top university. The kids were run-of-the-mill, not very bright. I made no friends among them, they weren't very interesting, nor were the professors. I was older than a number of my professors. I may have been more of a threat in class than an oddity. But it was all terrifically invigorating. I was set up with myself. It was a good time for me.

"My women friends helped me a lot, did some of my shopping, gave my kids lunch. My family was proud of the effort I was making. My husband helped. My oldest daughter helped with the preparation of meals. Because after a year, I wanted to move faster and it was getting boring so I began some graduate courses for undergraduate credit with the approval of my professor and I took those at night.

"What I was doing was so unusual then that it was written up in the newspaper and I became a bit of a celebrity in our suburb. Our area is an old, established community with a high percentage of professionals and academics because of its proximity to the universities and academies. The local papers covered my graduation and did another story about that. My daughter graduated from high school at the same time that I graduated from college, so that seemed worth a story. And cum laude, too. Me, I mean." She smiles and displays an open, simple pride in her achievements that is very winning.

Our talk this afternoon is taking place in her office, a small busy spot in the almost frenetically busy suite of offices of the foundation she works for. Her phone rings often; her colleagues interrupt; she handles everything smoothly, lightly—with a quick, efficient hand.

"After my B.A.," she picks up on her story, "I applied for graduate school, and was admitted and I earned a teaching fellowship. Graduate school was more difficult than college courses, and I also had to teach two sections of Freshman English. It was exciting at first, but it soon became a drag. There were lots of papers to correct and I had to prepare my own papers for the courses I was taking. That on top of still having a sizeable family at home. I had completed my first year of graduate work. Then our settled world was knocked sky high.

"My husband was offered a fantastically better paying job than his partnership in the agency was yielding. It meant relocating. I resented a lot of what was happening, I hated to leave our community and our friends, uprooting the kids and breaking off my plans for myself. I could have said, 'No, I don't want to go' and my husband might have said, 'Okay, we won't go, then,' but I didn't feel that my wishes, what I wanted to do, had equal weight in the reality of our situation. The reality was that he was supporting us in excellent style; he would be putting our two sons and two daughters through college; he made our life. Also, in the back of my head there was a sneaking longing to forget about school and to get moving on some real work.

"But the relocation created an enormous interruption and break in my new life. I became completely reinvolved in the old domestic scene. Finding a new house, selling the old one, not satisfied with the new place and moving again, dealing with my children's real problems of new schools and new friends, spending good time thinking about drapes and blinds and wing chairs. One day I said to myself, 'Enough of this crap. I'm not going to expend myself in this house all day, I'm going to get a job.'

"The awful thing was that after all the schooling, I still had no marketable skills and no idea of what I wanted to do. I answered an ad as a special projects assistant in a religious publishing house, only it turned out to be the Hebrew religion. I felt like a fish out of water. I didn't know a thing about the Hebrew religion. And apart from the teaching, I had never worked in my life. I worked directly under the rabbi with material that was completely foreign and new to me. I figured I couldn't last more than six weeks. What was I doing there? And I also found that being in an office for eight hours a day was a lot more confining than I had imagined it would be. But getting a salary at the end of the week was sheer loveliness even though there wasn't any money pressure then. I loved the idea that the housekeeper I hired was being paid with the money I earned. After that I could indulge in a few extras for myself. It felt good.

"It turned out to be so interesting for me to be in that strange environment. I was finding very different values existed in the real world, very different from my preconceived notions. That was the most important thing I learned, to open my eyes and broaden out, but I also learned that I liked to work, that I was good at it, that I was successful at it and that I wanted to be more successful, and that intelligence combined with persistence and diligence could be well rewarded.

"And then the real crisis struck. My husband's job folded. He couldn't go back home to the agency he had pulled out of and there was nothing else available at his position and salary level in the city we had moved to. He tried looking around where we were but he really wanted to go home and to try again there. I was ready to go back home too, and to take our chances back among our friends, where we had many contacts. There was a business recession and there had been tremendous cut-backs in the advertising business, and that didn't help our situation any. For myself, what I knew by that time was that I really wanted to work, whatever was happening to my husband and to my family. I wanted to follow my own bent. Not that I loved them less or cared less what was happening to them, but I knew I could do both, or give them as much as they needed of me while I did what I wanted to.

"We returned to our old area and my husband quite

quickly landed a new job, not as well-paying and as glamorous as the one he had lost, but good enough. And I found work as a copy-editor close to home. It was work in a congenial and familiar set-up, but it was a boring job and there wasn't any future in it. The places open to women are severely limited, for all the talk about opening doors to women. Most women are in teaching, editing, agenting, direct mail, fund-raising. These are primarily women's fields—it's interesting that many men who work in these areas are gay. Maybe the field demands feminine talents. I worked at many different jobs before I settled on fund-raising as the best for me. I knew by that time that I was ambitious. I had a real go-getter father. I thought I had rejected him and his drives all my years, but he contributed a lot to my ambition. The parent-child claim is more complicated than one thinks at age eighteen. I learned that in my forties.

"I had worked my way up to a well-paying job in a non-profit membership group, when I was offered a job in an educational entertainment media organization. It meant traveling, much more responsibility and hard work, more money. I grabbed it. I've loved every minute of it. I earn more than my husband does now. I don't think he's as happy with me as he used to be when I was a housewife and not so independent. Maybe I imagine that. Last year he had an opportunity to take on a new job, but it would have meant relocating. He didn't even consider it seriously. He turned it down before discussing the problem with me. He knew that there was no way that I would leave what I was doing. Besides, I bring in more money than he does, so now the reality of our situation is changed, isn't it?

"I think being a woman has helped me to do a better job. There's a lot of detail in this kind of work that most men can't be bothered with. Women are used to detail—that's what housekeeping is, a mass of detail. And other womanly attributes come into play, nurturing, mothering, accommodating attributes. I see myself as an accommodating person." She smiles. "Perhaps my husband and my colleagues don't agree. An assertiveness training brochure came into my office and I took it in to my boss as a joke, asking if the organization would sponsor my enrolling in the course. He said, 'You don't need that. You're too assertive as it is.' " She laughs aloud. "You can't win."

"I'm fifty-two, and I'm pleased with where I am in my career. Not that I don't mean to move it along. I do. I've come a long way in the ten years since I graduated from school and I mean to keep on going. It's odd, though, how much value is placed on what I'm doing now and how no value was placed on the years I spent as a wife and mother. Things I had to do as a mother were harder and more important than what I do now. Child-rearing needs to be legitimized in a new ideological stance. Imagine what it would cost to produce the four human beings I've produced—there's almost no way to calculate the value to society. Child-rearing by the mother should be a legitimate profession in our society. It takes more intelligence and creativity than most. My children are my most important source of strength. Even in that dumb, old, cliché way: they'll be good to me in my old age. They give me a good, happy, secure feeling. Raising my children was the best work of my life, but society never credited me with that important work. I don't mean I would have wanted to go on staying at home forever. My child-rearing work was done by the time I went back to school. But I should have been awarded a B.A. for rearing my four children. *And* graduated cum laude."

Diana Rhodes so clearly defies and mingles our strict notions of what constitutes "masculine" or "feminine" traits, that for me her story symbolizes their dangerous uselessness. How "feminine" of her to designate her best work in the world as the years she spent being a wife and mother. Yet how coolly "masculine" to have plotted her rise in a man's world from unskilled housewife to her present considerable position of executive administration—marshaling her forces, gaining skills, taking her sights on reality and moving ahead with a steady, sure confidence and ensuing success. In this quietly assured woman is embedded a startling piece of news about our stereotyping of the nature of women.

Mabel Jerome
STARTING AGAIN
ON THE SEX SCENE

Starting again in terms of a career is a comparatively easy step compared with starting again in terms of being. And sexual being may be the most fundamental of the varied existences we embrace. What happens when a contented, middle-class woman for whom the gratifying contours of her life are happily expected to go on and on, forever and ever, faces the sudden, awful loss of her husband, her only lover? Mabel Jerome took the blow of her husband's fatal heart attack with the kind of numbing grief that was close to death for herself. "It was like being in a coma," she told me. "It was a terrible shock. I couldn't seem to absorb it. I really thought the shock would never wear away." Her husband was forty-four when he died, sitting behind the wheel of his trailer cab, waiting to go through a toll booth. Mabel was a few years younger. They had met in the small-town New Jersey high school they both had attended. They married the day after she graduated. He had been her first and only boyfriend all her life.

152

"I leaned on him in every way," she characterized herself for me. "I never had to think or act for myself." This is no exaggeration of the depth of her dependency, in spite of the fact that she had never been an inactive, passive lump in the marriage. The couple had three children, and in addition to functioning as a full-time mother and house-wife, Mabel had worked at home as a typist for a university publisher, and as town correspondent for a trio of local newspapers. She also prepared the reports of official town business. But none of that improved her evaluation of her-self: she continued to believe that whatever she was, she existed because of the vigorous initiative of her husband.

Every word she still uses to describe him is adulatory: handsome, vital, outgoing, good provider, the life of the party, smart, dedicated, civic-minded, a terrific dancer, loved by all—and much more of the same. She was secure in the sense that all she had to do in life was to sail along in his active wake to be happy for the rest of her days. She never worried about anything happening to him. He was a truck driver on the New Jersey to New York run, seldom taking on a long trip and thus seldom away from home for any stretch of time. He owned his own rig, a huge trailer-cab.

"He was a joiner," she tells me. He held an advanced first-aid license in the Red Cross and was captain of the town's first-aid squad. He was fire chief of his town's fire department, a special police officer and chancellor com-mander of the Knights of Pythias. He toyed with electoral ambitions and ran for positions of borough councilman and member of the board of education. He was happily gregar-ious, loved parties, dances, and going out. He kept their social life in constant movement. When Mabel speaks of this more than twenty-year period of her marriage, there is no hint of anything but happiness in her tones, in her facial expressions—every nuance expresses a fortunate life which she never consciously questioned in any aspect. They had worked hard of course: they had had financial successes but they had also experienced financial setbacks (at one point her husband had gone into business for himself and failed), but on the whole they had done well and had lived well.

It was not thinkable that all this had come to an end. Her children were grown and out of the house. Alone in her apartment in the terrible emptiness left by the departure of such an overwhelming presence as her husband's had been for her, she felt herself sinking into an apathy too strong to overcome. A woman friend drove her into saving herself.

"She would come over and make me get dressed, make me go out, bring me the want-ads, show me jobs to apply for. She yelled at me, 'You want to sit in your room and die?' After a long time I began to make an effort."

She began by getting a job outside the home as a technical typist for an academician at a nearby university. The university atmosphere intimidated her; but she forced herself to stick it out. She thought herself too dumb to do well in this restrictive air. She didn't like it, but she wasn't going to let it defeat her. She is a very capable woman who picks up new skills easily, and among the acknowledgments in a book by the professor she is proud to point to her name singled out for special praise in the preparation of the manuscript. But when an opportunity was offered, she was glad to quit and to move on to a media job as a technical typist, where she worked for nine months, when she was fired in a general cut-back.

She quickly replaced that with a job in a semi-government agency, and she was worked there since. Her official classification is clerk-typist. She describes her domain as a "one-girl office." She manages inventory control in a maintenance department. She is somewhat bored but values the security in this position, and means to stay in it until retirement when she will cash in on her benefits. "No gripes at all?" I prodded. She ventured the information that the classification system discriminates against women, rewarding men with higher pay for the same work done by women for less, but she isn't interested in taking up arms against inequities. She thinks the women's liberation movement is a good thing, and generally agrees with its aims, but she doesn't participate. No special reason. Other activities draw her more, that's all.

That took care of her occupation and her finances. But that was the least aspect of her life. For someone like Mabel for whom the ultimate fount of her energy was located in the "beloved other," it was an irrelevancy to be urged to find fulfillment in her "wonderful children," her "wonderful friends," her "good job, thank God." She enjoyed all that, but what was starving was a core that craved what it had lost—the trappings and prizes of her former life, the parties, the dancing, the shows and dinners and organized events, and the natural source from which all social sustenance sprang for her—a man to love and be loved by. What was terribly lost was sex.

Because she enjoyed dancing, and because so much of her happiness with her husband had been associated with "going dancing," she tried attending a singles dance with a couple of women friends. (She had already been put through the full distasteful course of the single woman in the crowd. She had been subtly cut out by the old crowd they had run with when her husband was alive. She had tolerated evenings spent with well-meaning guilt-ridden friends attempting to match-make, half-heartedly. Then everything stopped. She didn't brood or blame her friends. She knew it made for stiffness and tension for couples to have an extra woman around. It wasn't anybody's fault that pickings in available men were dishearteningly slim.) It was the same woman friend who had roused her into getting a job who now forced her to dress up and go out to a singles dance.

She had a miserable evening at the first try. She came home to cry, vowing never to go back. But she did, sampling a different club, another dance, a new group. She tried them all—meetings, lectures, encounter groups, amateur theater groups, sports groups, tours, whatever was around. "They're all disguised singles groups," she told me. "Not even disguised. Everyone who comes knows why they come. To meet somebody." Then she did meet someone she liked very much, and in a very short time, he came home with her and they were lovers. She came alive. She was happy. Though all comers to singles events are supposedly single, in practice it isn't always so. Mabel learned that her friend was married, soon after they became lovers.

"Just like 'Queen of the Stardust Ballroom,' " I said.

"Yes," she said. "I could have written that TV play myself. Or acted in it. Only I didn't kill myself or conveniently die off. I didn't even break off. I was happier with him than without him. We were together for a long time—for years. We went everywhere together. We went to all the singles affairs together. Everybody knew we were a couple. I was satisfied. It was almost as good as being married. He wasn't the man my husband was, but I loved him. We had a good time together. I guess he began to feel married to me too, because he began to cheat on me, just the way he was cheating on his wife with me. I got the word through the grapevine. He was dating another woman in the singles crowd. I couldn't take that. I confronted him with it. He didn't deny it. I guess he would have liked to keep everything going at once—all three of us. But I broke off with him. I'm not sure why. Maybe it just hurt too much. Maybe I didn't love him enough.

"I had to start again only this time around I knew a lot more. I had been through the whole scene. It was revolting, in a way, to be going back to the same old places, starting all over again. I thought, 'Why can't they be easier to come to, warmer and more human?' and then it occurred to me that I could run a better singles group than any I had been to. So I started one."

From any point of view, she seems an unlikely person to be doing so. Everything about her is too quiet for the role. She's a very sweet-looking woman, in her late forties or early fifties—hard to tell. In appearance and manner, she could be a member of any one of the many ethnic groups in our country; it's difficult to place her as coming from a particular background. What is typical about her is also oddly reassuring—how she fades into anonymity—a middling-prosperous-American-housewife-office-worker. She wears a wig so quiet in its effect, so discreetly and mousily brown and so modestly styled that I wondered why she bothered. "I'm too busy to fuss with my hair," she says. "I have too much to do to keep running to the beauty parlor. So I send my wigs." She has several.

She lives in one of the more posh retirement communities near Princeton. The development is planned to imitate a New England town; but of course it fails to be anything other than what it is, though it is one of the more pleasant communities of its kind. When the weather is good, it can seem a nice place to be; but when the weather turns unkind and the wind blows across the fake, self-consciously curved sidewalks on which hardly anybody ever walks, this haven may assume the chill of a sentence of exile; and loneliness transforms each separate little house with its lone occupant into a series of isolation cells. The development is spread out upon a broad, flat landscape bordered on one side by the New Jersey Turnpike. One must pass through a guarded gate to enter. Small private houses (a few divided into two separate apartments) sit back on neatly landscaped, petite lots. The landscaping will get better as the new trees grow a bit. A centrally located clubhouse provides quite lavishly outfitted rooms for diversified uses. There are facilities for all sorts of social gatherings—gala breakfasts, luncheons, and dinners in the dining room, which doubles as a large auditorium; there's a library, diversified arts and crafts, and for outdoor activities, there's tennis, golf, and an Olympic size swimming pool.

Mabel lived alone here at first. She says she doesn't know why she chose to live in a retirement community. "They make a big thing about how it's not really a retirement community and that people of all ages live here, couples, children are allowed to visit, all that, but let's face it, they're mostly old and retired. I was too young to be living in this place. I hoped it would be more of a community. I don't even mean single people. Just interesting *people*, nice people, couples, women—and sure, I wanted to meet an interesting single man. I thought I'd be less lonely here. But it was worse than ever. Hard to make friends. Maybe it takes time." She had been living in the community less than a year when I first met her.

I had heard about Mabel even before I met her, from other members of the retirement community because of a community sponsored singles cocktail party she had been instrumental in initiating. Everybody agreed it was a disaster. Approximately eighty-five women showed up to ten men.

A woman resident reported the event as "a total bust. Hundreds of women, all dressed to kill, and a pitiful handful of men walking around as if they were roosters in the henhouse. It was all the fault of that woman Mabel Jerome who runs some kind of singles club. She pressured the social director to hold the cocktail party. The men all clustered around her. The few men who came. God knows why, she's not *that* attractive. If you ask me the only reason that woman moved into our community was to build up her business, her singles club. I don't think management should allow that. It's not right. Every one of those men danced with her and never asked anybody else to dance. I hope they never hold another party like that one."

"I decided to stay out of the social life of the community after that flop," Mabel told me. "But I couldn't stick to it. They've got this twenty-eight-year-old professional social director running the events. What does a fellow his age know about the needs of people like us? Sure, I urged the meeting to vote for a singles cocktail party. I thought we could have some fun. The women got all upset because I was the center of male attention. The men knew me. They like me. I don't scare them. I'm a good dancer, I know how to listen, they like to talk to me. So it gets blown up into some kind of scandal. I don't know what's the matter with those women." None of this was said with any stridency by Mabel. She's always soft-voiced. She added, "I feel sorry for them. They don't seem to realize that they're dying sitting home by themselves. I started a dance group going—line dances, that kind of thing, so that they can keep their blood circulating at least. You don't need men for that kind of group—you can manage with only women. I do it for nothing, just to bring a little liveliness into their lives. I ran an ad, I'll show it to you, and you know that I didn't get a single response to that ad? Not one. I think these women are too high-class and uptight to admit they need human companionship."

I'm new in the area [her ad read], my name is Mabel and I am the hostess for the singles group. I am looking for new friends in the area (or nearby). Let's get together and enjoy life. Also if you need a ride to any of my singles affairs please call me after 5 P.M., weekdays or anytime on weekends. Or call me just to chat and get acquainted.

Another resident, a beautiful woman, recently widowed, who is also new to the community, told me, "Mabel's a sweet person. I like her. She has more life than most of the women here. But I'm not about to go in for her kind of activities. There's something cheap and tawdry about the singles club. I tried it once, really just because she asked me to. I'll never go again. It's not for me. I went with her in her car, and that meant that I couldn't go home when I wanted to, which was practically immediately after I arrived. I had to wait around until she could leave. That was three o'clock in the morning. People tell me I don't look it" (she doesn't by ten to fifteen years), "but I'm seventy years old. I can't take those late hours. Not to mention the kind of men and women who showed up there."

"Why is it so hard for people to believe that I just don't want them to be lonely?" Mabel asked. "Anymore than I want to be lonely myself."

There would seem to be no time for Mabel to be lonely. In addition to her full-time office job and her very active family life as daughter, mother, and grandmother, she is busily occupied every Friday, Saturday, and Sunday night with the singles club which she had been running for four years now.

On Friday and Saturday nights, the group gathers in the bar lounge of a bowling alley in a shopping center on New Jersey's Route 1. On Sunday nights the locale shifts to a night spot, also in a shopping center, on a similar highway. Both locales feature live music; there are drinks available (extra, paid for at the bar); and the Sunday nightclub entrance fee includes an Italian buffet—all one can eat.

Mabel furnishes other benefits to her clients: a dating service, which consists of the publication of a regular matchmaker brochure.

Other brochures, distributed at all affairs, are schedules of special events or flyers advertising weekend tours to Las Vegas, borscht belt resorts, or longer trips to Hawaii, Puerto Rico, and the Virgin Islands. Mabel has led some of these tours. Rap sessions are available for an extra one dollar an hour, scheduled in the lounge one hour before the usual Friday night festivities; and dancing lessons may be had (for an additional buck) on Sunday nights, prior to that night's festivities.

A final fillip announces parties for those couples who meet at the club and who plan to marry, complete with a rebate on the cost of the marriage license.

I accompanied Mabel to one of her Saturday night events. The back of her big, expensive car was taken up with shopping bags. She handled the car with the capable confidence I had quickly grown to expect of her. We drove along highways for about forty minutes—a journey in taste from the retirement community's pretentious gentility to the shopping center's pop sleaziness. The parking lot, dark and almost entirely empty of cars, was spread with the eerie miasma of after-hours shopping plazas. I helped her lug and unpack the heavy bags which held the paraphernalia of the club—stacks of brochures, flyers, coils of tickets, a metal money box, name tags, a small table lamp and a checkered oil cloth to cover the series of connected tables where all comers would stop on entering. It was now close to nine o'clock; but the lounge was dead, nobody at the bar except the bartender setting up. There were no musicians at the empty bandstand.

A paid ticket taker and a woman friend who sometimes helps Mabel arrived together, forming a welcoming committee behind the table, I becoming one of them, my job to hand a name tag and a pin to Mabel as she greeted and pinned each new arrival. The ticket taker collected passes and money, made change, and moved the patron down the line of smiling females. The first woman, Mabel's friend, recorded the arrival's name on a name tag. (Among the males, there were a suspiciously disproportionate number of John Smiths and Tom Joneses. The women were apparently giving their true names. *If I'm in it, I'm in it all the way*, seemed to be the women's attitudes.)

I was next on the receiving line, where Mabel had placed me, and where I was glad to be, safe from the discomforting possibility of being mistaken for a supplicant in this ritual of open desire. It was beyond my image of myself that I might be driven to this adventure; but I wasn't a woman alone, condemned to sexual and emotional solitude, aching for touch, talk, intimacy. In such a state, did I know what I might do?

The whole scene was giving me some trouble. I found it hard to handle an almost comical throwback to adolescent pain and uncertainty—an uncontrollable and sharply unpleasant response, and entirely unjustified by the facts of my life. I knew that I hadn't come here a lonely beggar, hot to attract a man, but the supposition on anybody else's part would be that that was exactly why I was there, and I couldn't throw off the apprehension that if I didn't attach someone to me promptly, I should have failed. Emotions which I would have sworn were long dead and buried rose in a hot flush to plague me—the desperate bravado and agony of teen-age exposure, and fear of rejection.

The music was another throwback—this time to a period in my late teens when I had worked as a ballroom dance instructor. Oddly this memory served to orient me into a better fit. I had worked this territory before, and it hadn't changed that much.

Mabel had become subtly altered; she glowed with a party excitement that contained something more than the usual hyped-up hostess jollity. Again I felt linked to a past experience. At nineteen, I had made the excuse for myself that at the height of the Depression the only job I could get was as a ballroom dance instructor; but I knew that it was sexual excitement I was really after in my ambivalent way. Sexual energy is called by many other names. But it was open sexual energy Mabel was contacting and dispensing with her greetings. The disparate personalities entering the lounge were bound into instant intimacy by a common taste, like gamblers craving the excitement of winning—and losing. That it was all open, laid out on the table, added to the excitment. It was clear that Mabel profoundly understood the scene she managed.

She pointed out a young woman in a mini-skirt who was on the dance floor, in perpetual motion, gyrating to the music as if she were in a fit. "Isn't she cute? She's a school-teacher. Would you believe it?" Later, in repose, having a drink at the bar, the schoolteacher could have been described as plain, straight, narrow, and flat; it was while dancing that all her charming zaniness came into play. She left with a handsome man in his late thirties or early forties whose clothes and aloof bearing made him suspect.

"Do you think he's married?" I asked Mabel

She answered flatly, "Only singles are invited." But added in a worried way, "I've been wondering about him. I wouldn't want my little schoolteacher to be hurt."

There is no screening process. The married man looking

for outside play is in little danger of exposure—unless his wife were to walk in, searching for similar excitement. Married women aren't frequenters of the scene, though Mabel offered the opinion that the singles scene was a natural source of extra-marital sex for both men and women, the easiest and laziest way to cruise.

A woman who arrived alone was so defiantly unattractive and unmade up for the part of luring female—mannishly cut hair, sloppily combed to one side, a dowdy, tailored suit—that I asked Mabel after she had greeted the woman as a regular, "Why do you suppose someone like that would come here?" For Mabel, her answer was sharp. Perhaps I was annoying her with my shallow analyses of every entrant. "Why shouldn't she come? It's better than sitting at home and staring at her four walls. She pays her entrance, sits at a table, has a drink, listens to the music, and watches the dancing. Maybe a man will ask her to dance, or start a conversation with her and she'll make friends with somebody—so what if it's another woman? A friend is a friend. Maybe she'll have some good luck in the games, find a companion. If she stays home and broods, alone, she'll just rot and die."

"What about gays?" I asked. "Do you suspect that that kind of cruising goes on?"

She shook her head, no, but the woman left with another woman, and my supposition could have been right or wrong. It was certainly uncharitably and conventionally prejudiced, since it was based solely on accepted notions of how a woman should look.

I asked Mabel if she had ever had a serious charge brought against a member—if an evening ever ended in ugliness and violence. She shook her head, no, with a murmured "Thank God. Of course they happen. They're bound to. It's the law of averages. Like driving a car, if you drive long enough you're bound to be in an accident. There was one time I was lucky to get out of alive, when I was doing the singles scene myself."

"Do you have a regular boyfriend now?"

She gestured vaguely, smiled mysteriously.

Our conversations took place sporadically, broken up into moments caught between her constant duties and activities. I asked if her mother was living, and when she nodded, I asked her to tell me what her mother thought of Mabel's role as a club hostess.

"She couldn't believe it, at first. *Nobody* could. My children, my friends. None of them could imagine me doing what I am doing. I was always so quiet. I'm still quiet. Still waters run deep. I brought the whole family to the club one night, even my mother, to see how I do it." Her pride in herself was manifest. "They couldn't believe it was me, handling the mike, keeping things running. They were amazed. They loved it. They said I was as smooth as a professional emcee."

I had not yet seen Mabel handling the mike, but she took to the mike at the first band break, to announce some of the special events coming up, to sell the other regular nights, and to generally greet and prod the members. The pitch was delivered in Mabel's usual conversational voice— soft, friendly, totally without the hysterically rapid huckster speech I had been expecting her to assume—and with genuine feeling for the plight of her club members.

"We have destroyed the word lonely—the terrible word lonely that the single knows so well. You don't have to be lonely anymore. Three nights a week we're always here for you, to share fun and life with you. Your weekends don't have to be lonely anymore. And who knows, tonight or tomorrow night or next weekend may be the last time you will ever find yourself alone again. So get in and mix . . ." in a long, easy flow of encouragement.

Her mike was hand-held, and she moved about freely, speaking and smiling directly into the half-shamed, half-angry faces of the women sitting alone at the little tables, softly scolding and encouraging them. "Don't sit there alone. Talk to somebody. Make a friend. Get up and go to the bar. Get up and ask somebody to dance. Later we're going to have a lot of fun with our games. Meanwhile, move around, get happy."

The evening was dwindling to a close. There were a couple of die-hard, lone men at the bar, and during the last few numbers by the band, a man who had danced with Mabel approached me. "You two girls have been working too hard all evening. You need a drink. What'll you have?"

Mabel said, "That's real sweet of you, John. But I can't leave the table right now."

He said he'd be glad to bring our drinks to the table. The lounge was emptying out rapidly. When the smiling fellow returned with our drinks, he kissed my hand. "Because you're married," he said, "I'm keeping this very formal."

Another woman I know, a widow who has covered the middle-aged New York singles scene for years now, off and on, says that there is a sophisticated sub-rosa system of circulating information among members. My friend was left a lot of money through the death of her husband, and she lives well, in a luxury apartment near Lincoln Center. She tries to keep the fact hidden because she knows news of it will be spread through the grapevine. She never permits a new man to pick her up at her apartment—not only because of reasons of safety—but because she doesn't want to be tagged as a woman of means.

The possible dangers in these encounters are not exaggerated. (Anyway isn't danger one of the deep hidden delights of the activity?) But sometimes a man gets out of hand, or is a con, and the thrilling lift of excitement takes a dive into horror. Women invent built-in safety devices into their first-time dates, such as a friend in the same building holding a key to the apartment, whose barging in without warning is triggered by a pre-set time-signal system. To sit in on the planning of one of these elaborate protective schemes is to be as intrigued and amused as by a who-done-it with a Marx Brothers touch of the absurd. The women laugh at themselves, but they know that their ad-

vance precautions may be the saving factor against calcu-
lated criminality or irrational savagery. Perhaps men have
similar awful experiences with women; but I've never heard
any reported.

What kills the men is rejection. Of the last two men to
leave the club, one was bitter on the subject. He was young,
and seemed highly presentable, but he looked fairly demented with frustration and anger at the new aggressive-
ness of women, granting them the privilege of turning
down a man like him.

"What do you women want, anyway?" he railed at me.
(Did he know that he was quoting Freud?) "Can somebody
tell me what the hell you women are looking for anyway?
Can anybody tell me? Would *you* turn me down? *Would*
you?"

I murmured something soothing, but he demanded an
exact response. "No, no, you don't get away with that. I
want you to give it to me straight. Look at me. Look, look
at me. Here I am. I'm offering myself. Are you turning me
down?"

His quieter friend stood by, watching our by-play. I
laughed uncomfortably, continued evasively expressing be-
wilderment that an attractive young man should have had
any difficulty with women.

"You're not answering me," he persisted. "I'm not a fool.
I know you're not answering me. You're just like the others."

I protested that I was too old for him. "You don't want
me. I'm a grandmother. You're a young man."

"I'm thirty-nine," he said, "and I don't care if you're a
great-grandmother. That's not the question. I'm asking you
a simple question. I'm saying, here I am, are you turning
me down?" His eyes became wild. Too much to drink? His
speech wasn't slurred.

I soothed and evaded, complimenting like mad as I
skirted what seemed like a real snare. He wanted me to
reject him so that he could hit me? Mabel also soothed.

"Come on, now, Bob. You know the ropes. You win some, you lose some. Tomorrow's another day. You'll be the one laughing tomorrow while somebody else cries. That's the way it goes."

Bob's friend took over. "That's right, Bob, let's cut our losses and say good-night like gentlemen." He took my hand, raising it to his lips in a courtly charade. "I picked that up from John," he said, referring to the man who had bought us drinks.

"What's with the hand kissing?" Mabel said. "I want a kiss on my lips." She stood up, leaned across the table, and offered her mouth. They kissed and he aped a response of fainting dead away on the floor, making aaahhing noises as he fell. "It's good to know I still have what it takes," Mabel said.

We lugged the reloaded shopping bags out to the car and stowed them away on the back seat. The night was very dark, windy and cold for May. The parking lot was entirely empty of cars—cold concrete in an enveloping black, silent mist. The scene evoked TV images of erupting violence—a figure in black would emerge to beat, rape, murder us.

"Aren't you scared when you do this alone?"

"You mean because of the money box?" Mabel said. "Sure I'm scared. The highway is deserted at this time of night. I lock the doors of the car and pray nothing will go wrong. Imagine if I had a breakdown. A nightmare. Thank God I never have. I take better care of my car than anything I own in life. You know what helps me? When I have to do something that seems too much for me I think to myself how my husband would have done it and then I do it his way. You never know what you can do until you do it. You never know what you've got inside until you let it out. I had a lot more than I ever realized."

She settled behind the wheel, fussed with her car keys, checked herself out in the rear view mirror and jiggled her wig into a more secure position. She was obviously pleased with herself, pleased with the way the evening had looked to a visitor who was going to write about it. Poised to start the car, she smiled at my shyly, with a hint of triumph.

When I checked on how things were going with her a couple of months later, she told me that she was getting married.

"Will you give up the singles club, when you're no longer single?" I asked.

"I don't like to leave them stranded," she said, after a pause. "All those lonely people. Anyway I like doing it— and it keeps me more independent. I've been running the club for five years now and it's going very well. Since I'm really started on it, why should I go backwards just because I'm getting married again? After all, it's not the first time I'm getting married. I know a little more now."

Mabel could be seen as another starter who was pushed, like Minna Harwicke. If bad luck had not dealt her the terrible blow of her husband's sudden death, she believes that she would have lived out her life to its presumed happy ending as the gratified partner of a man just right for her, who satisfied all her needs. Out there alone, after he died, in the no-life situation where she was expected to exist without love, without sex, without companionship—and even without a dancing partner—she resolved her problems brilliantly in the all-in-one solution of the singles club she established, winning not only the essential missing ingredients but also independence and a new sense of herself in the process.

Ronnie Rothstein
SEIZING
ONE'S SEXUAL FREEDOM,
ANOTHER WAY OF STARTING

Our society doesn't offer much in the way of unrestrained Dionysian bliss—the rituals of the singles scene, drink, drugs, suburban and urban orgy, swinging pornography and plain pornography—an occasional storm blown up, like Woodstock, to startle the community. The community, in the main, remains untouched, unrelentingly tight in its surface attitudes toward sexuality, fearful that relaxing the Old Testament moral strictures will let loose a terrible beast that will prowl beyond society's grasp to control. Tolstoy's "battle of the boudoir" goes on in each tight little bedroom, where two by two a private war is fought for the most fundamental freedom—the right to be one's self to the core of one's individual sexuality. Most of these battles are lost— on both sides, of course, since the only way to win this struggle is by ending winners all.

How odd that sexuality, the most basic of human experiences, has been largely unexplored except in negative terms: illegality, criminality, immorality, pathology, and commercialization. It is true that, along with other free-doms, sexual freedom must be an expansion of liberty and not a license to harm others—but our Judeo-Christian concepts of original sin and the fall from grace has set the whole subject wrong side up. (A contemporary Garden of Eden would have to show a handsome profit and a guarantee of a franchise in every major city before it could get itself going.) Like our political democratic freedoms that are equally rejected by autocratic thinking as anarchic and repellent to its sense of rigid order, sexual freedom would undoubtedly make for a more openly messy society. But who would trade our political and social messiness for others orderly repression? Yet, despots all, we lock away our immense sexual problems, and when they burst forth in terrible forms of retribution, instead of questioning our autocratic approach, we jail, judge, and imprison. There are nothing but losses in our methods.

In a jungle of ignorance about sexuality in general, our specific ignorance of homosexuality is especially wonderful. Consider the following letter (*bona fide*, though it reads like a Russell Baker parody) written by a Maine resident in Florida deploring the sorry sexual state both areas have arrived at. It carries the headline, "Perversion Should Not Be Publicized" and appeared in a local paper.

Dear Sir:

For many years I had thought California and South Florida had the corner on human weirdos especially when the queers of Fort Lauderdale start a club for homosexuals called Gays, Unlimited and are asking the public in general to join. However, in the last edition of your paper was a notice that there would be a meeting of the Feminist Lesbian Club or Society. I had long been of the belief that Maine was one of the more sensible of our states but it seems that I was wrong again. If perverts wish to do their thing in private, that is their constitutional right but perversion should not be publicized. Keep a watch on Dade County, Florida where the county passed a recent law allowing homos to do anything. Now the citizens are up in arms and the law will soon be changed and many politicians will be out of office.

The letter-writer was referring to legislation which re-moved discriminatory statutes barring homosexuals from public housing, employment, etc. Anita Bryant, the Florida orange queen who can be caught exuding healthy Ameri-can good feeling regularly on TV, had announced herself a holy warrior in the drive to undo this new leniency. She declared her children's right to grow up in a decent and safe atmosphere. Apparently Miss Bryant sincerely believes that all heterosexuals are upstanding citizens—excellent news, since all that remains to be done to secure a morally sound society is to round up the homosexuals. Anita Bryant's ludicrous theory was however endorsed in a public vote which backed her view.

For people like Anita Bryant and her supporters, includ-ing the letter-writer, homosexuality is, above all, a state of sexuality. They conjure a morbid vision of homosexuals in unrelenting, single-minded, perverse, sexual *activity*. In an ABC television special on the subject, a lesbian offered the startlingly sane perspective to the audience that lesbians didn't spend any more time, give or take an hour, in sexual activity than any other group in the population. "Every-body is always concerned with what we do in bed, as if we spend all our time in bed and all our energy on sex. That's not what it's about."

Some years ago, while teaching a course in creative writ-ing at Columbia University, a friend invited me to join her CR group. "Consciousness raising" is one of the tools used by the women's liberation movement to help women un-derstand the special, shared, social circumstances of their individual problems. It was an experience I wouldn't have missed for anything. Our group was made up primarily of active, professional women, some of whom were the wives of well-known men (among whom I counted myself), and we had special problems we shared within the larger prob-lems of other women. I thought of us as "the wives of." There were a number of younger single women; a couple of older, married women; a lone housewife and mother in her late thirties in the midst of changing her life by going back to school to establish a career, very concerned with her new accomplishments as well as with controlling these within a marriage she wished to hold intact. Finally, there was a lesbian couple.

The purpose of such groups is to examine, to discuss, to bring out into the light of reason and awareness what has been kept hidden and suppressed. Among the first questions we tackled was whether it would be fruitful for them or for us to admit a lesbian couple into a group of "straight" women. There was also argument against admitting "a couple," whether lesbian or not. No one else there had brought along a husband or a lover; why should a dispensation be made in their case? Because they're both women, and this was an essential difference, it was argued. But wouldn't the dispensation also create awkwardnesses so severe that the couple would uncontrollably hold back, or worse, feel compelled to put themselves on show? And finally, of what use were their insights to the rest of us, or our insights to them? Even if they struggled to be honest?

It was true that one of the lesbian women felt herself on display with us, because she viewed lesbianism as a political position in the feminist movement—as an example and an ideal for the rest of us women to reach toward as a measure of true liberation, and therefore did hold back and falsify her relationship to her lover, covering up the problems she and her lover were having—as bitter as any the rest of us were suffering with males. And it was true that her partner helped in the cover-up out of loyalty. But even that became an instructive lesson for us. Indeed every part of our contact with Ronnie and Connie was instructive. For me, this relationship became the litmus paper which I dipped into all my glib solutions to the problems of women—a test that invariably produced new shadings.

The vaudevillian names of the couple (Ronnie and Connie) and the fact that they were both fat women, was turned into a comic routine by Ronnie—with its inevitable tinge of despair. In the case of Ronnie, fat was endearing, as it is on a sub-adolescent girl. Connie's fat was solid, monumental, impressive—attractive as strength and solidity is. Straight women in the group were obviously attracted to Connie; they endowed her with favored mythic symbols of the feminist movement—earth mother, goddess, Amazon. The fact that she was a therapist added to her luster. She achieved an aura of "Come unto me, lean on me, I listen, I sustain, I nurture, I love." The other lesbian, Ronnie, was too down-to-earth, too much of a borscht-circuit comic realist about herself to lend herself to deification and myth-making. She eluded even this stereotype.

Ronnie is an artist and an art teacher. When I first came to know her, she and Connie were living in a town house in the Lower East Side of New York City. They were both then in their early forties. They had faultlessly renovated the 150-year-old building, and furnished it in lush, romantic excess. Their shared bedroom was an erotic dream bedroom—an oversized, lavishly cushioned bed, open woodburning fireplace, Victorian couches, soft chairs, Oriental rugs. The bedroom took the entire upper floor of the narrow house.

Inside, their house felt like a country house, though it sat on a city street so degenerated it was difficult for me to believe I was in New York, whose worst neighborhoods were no news to me. There was a shelter for alcoholics further east on the block, and from the spot where my car was parked to the locked iron gate guarding Ronnie and Connie's front door, I picked my way around piles of human rubbish embedded in piles of material rubbish. Men slept in filth, or lay abandoned in states that looked like comas. Other partially erect men approached for a handout in a staggering, decrepit dance, but they were too spaced out to be dangerous and were easily evaded. There was a noxious stench from the uncollected garbage, and from the piles of old clothing and parts of furniture and discarded gadgets; but the men smelled worse—urine, liquor, vomit, accumulated filth. To enter Ronnie and Connie's house from that direction was to be disoriented by the violently sudden contrast. It took a second to adjust—as from black night to full light.

They were accustomed to the horrified exclamations of first-time visitors. "You get used to it," Ronnie said flatly. "After a while you're not conscious of it anymore."

Our group was gathering at their house for a session, and it was for many of us the first time we had been there.

"But doesn't it scare you to death to come home alone? How about late at night?" one woman asked.

Connie shook her head. "They're not dangerous," she said. "They're out of it. They're in another world."

"But I notice your keep your street gate locked," another commented.

"That's just to keep them from flopping on our stoop," Ronnie said. "Come from the other direction if they bother you next time you visit." They refused to be ruffled by shocking surroundings. If we wanted to keep our illusions that such sights didn't exist, that was our problem, not theirs.

The large living room on the second floor also had an open fireplace, and since the day was cool, a lit fire brightened the room, already made brilliant by the sun pouring in through the old, small-paned windows. On the ample coffee table was a spread of fresh-ground, brewed coffee, little cakes, and dried and fresh fruit. Ronnie, graceful in a floor-length, vividly colored tent dress, moved about with large gestures, making people comfortable and serving; Connie was seated majestically on a high swivel chair—settled solidly yet spread widely—a Gertrude Stein effect. Until all the women arrived and we began to talk, a Mahler recording washed the room with the romantic anguish of "Das Lied von der Erde." They were a couple on stage, set up for us to view as an option we must consider, or admit ourselves bound by conventions that imprisoned us. An article in *Ms.* Magazine on the subject of separatism put the question in the form of a slogan: "No woman is truly free to be anything unless she is also free to be a lesbian."

True? Ronnie believes so. Yet she herself became a lesbian not by way of a persuasive theoretical position, but through more unmanageable forces—and less cerebrally arguable.

Ronnie was born in 1925 to a Brooklyn Jewish couple, eight years after her brother and about three years before her sister. She remembers her childhood in Brighton Beach as nothing but happy, happy, happy. Her father was a dress designer and there was enough money for Ronnie to be indulged in every way. "I was the original Jewish princess," she says. Her father had worked his way up, beginning as a machine operator in a shop. At one point he could have become very rich. A man who was later successful as the owner of one of New York's most prestigious Fifth Avenue department stores was then a fellow shop worker; he suggested that he and Ronnie's father go into business together, but her father refused. He thought the man's venture a risk. Ronnie tells that story as a typical example of her father's failure to seize an opportunity. She depicts him as somewhat helpless and ineffectual even though she acknowledges that he did well by his family and that when he died he left her the money that made it possible for her to achieve a measure of independence.

When she was young it was her mother who drew out her whole soul. "I wanted to be everything to my mother— her sister, her mother, her son, her daughter, her lover, her husband. If I could have been the air she breathed I would have been happy."

That sounds morbid, but the daily life Ronnie reports is serene. She loved living close to the beach. Her memories of her father and mother are beach images. In good weather, they began each day by crossing the wide avenue to the beach, robes covering their bathing suits, towels over their arms. They dropped their robes and towels on the sand and entered the water. Easily swimming side-stroke, face to face, between the jettys built out into the sea, her mother and father would converse. Ronnie always thought that they saved the secret things they wanted to tell one another to talk of then, while swimming between the jettys.

On Saturdays she loved to be allowed to leave first thing in the morning with her father to go to his shop in his car. Later in the day her mother and her younger sister would join them, having come into the city by subway, and they would all go out to a restaurant for lunch, and from there to the new show at the Roxy Theater, or the Capitol. Sunday was picnic day, and not necessarily on the public beach they used daily. They were adventurous; they found new spots.

Her mother was a *berye*, a Yiddish word which translates as a highly efficient housewife and something more; it carries the tone of self-pride as well as industry. She cooked, baked, sewed the clothes she dressed her girls in; when her house needed retouching, she painted the walls herself, put up the wallpaper, moved the furniture to new and better positions, waxed the floors once again. She was the kind of neighbor who became deeply involved in the lives of others. There were dozens of people who looked to her for help and to whom she responded with her energy, time, and money. There was "nothing she wouldn't have done" for her daughter. That meant Ronnie pretty much got whatever she wanted. (Quite early Ronnie showed talent as an artist and was taken to museums and to art instruction classes.) Though she played the role of the traditional, muted Jewish wife and mother, Ronnie's mother had her odd spots of independence. She smoked and offered a cigarette to adolescent Ronnie, with the inevitable warning, "Don't tell your father."

Ronnie thinks that her mother worried that Ronnie wasn't pretty enough, perhaps because she was always fat. Ronnie has a broad face framed by loose, brown hair that swings like a soft curtain with her expansive, vivid gestures. Her eyes are narrow, Kirghiz-slanted, heavily ringed, dark;

her mouth is fully and coarsely molded, but beautifully quick to react sensitively. A handsome face. Today she is handsomer than she was five years ago when I first met her; perhaps because she's happier—and slimmer.

In 1942, Ronnie was sixteen and a half, just graduated from high school. Instead of going on with her art schooling, she took a job in a field newly opened up to women because the draft was drawing off men into the armed services. She became a window display artist for a chain of women's specialty shops and later for a Fifth Avenue department store. She already had met the man she would marry, "I think mostly because my mother wanted me to marry him. I think she was worried that I couldn't get anybody else."

I asked how she and her husband met. "It was a World War II 1940's romance. We met as civil defense wardens. Nice touch?"

Ronnie has an unusually deep, husky voice for a woman. It is her only physical trait that could be described as "masculine." Its effect is to make anything she says carry a comic undertone, an indefinable gift that clowns work hard to achieve. No matter how serious her tragedies, if she tells them, one laughs. She brings her experiences close enough to make one gasp, then snatches them away with a quip. The joke is always on her, but it introduces distance into the tragedy that involves the listener in a greater closeness, but more bearably so. She loves to talk and will do so at great length when encouraged. She's always amusing and interesting—and also interested in others around her.

When she speaks of her former husband, it isn't possible to conjure up any picture of the man to whom she was married for so many years. It is as if some vital part of herself was withheld from the relationship. Her usually vivid talk fades out when she describes this section of her life—except for the trimmings, like the big wedding. "Formal dress. Sit-down meal. Full color glossy wedding pictures in a white leather album. Revolving colored lights."

She raises her arms, hands palm-outward in mock awe. She was not yet nineteen years of age when she married.

Her husband was in the business of wholesale optometric supplies—not exciting but well paying. Their life was busy, pleasant, active; Ronnie enjoyed it. "I hope you understand that I never had any problems about sex. My husband was a good lover. That part was perfect. So let's get that straight, okay?" It was an important detail to have straight, since one of the theories about homosexuality is that it is a response to sexual failure with the opposite sex.

The young couple had been married in June. In September Ronnie's mother died of a heart attack which struck without warning while she was shopping at the neighborhood five and ten. Ronnie's sister was at home when this happened. (Ronnie was living in Manhattan and at work.) Her mother had decided, on the moment, to run out to the five and ten nearby for something she needed, and had taken no pocketbook but just a couple of dollars in the pocket of her house-dress. When she collapsed, there was no immediate way to identify her. Ronnie's sister became alarmed at her long absence and went out to the street to see if she could spot her mother returning. A man she knew slightly was walking by. He stopped to tell Ronnie's sister that he thought he had seen their mother being taken away in an emergency ambulance, but he wasn't sure. It was this hysterical message that Ronnie received on the telephone. By the time she got out to Brooklyn and contacted the hospital her mother had been dead for some hours.

"It was my fault, right?" Ronnie says. "It *had* to be my fault. If I had been at home, taking care of my mother, it wouldn't have happened." She laughs. "Wonderful me, powerful me. A little thing like death? I can stop it if I'm given the chance. I can't tell you how I blamed myself. I kept telling myself that I should have been at home. I would have controlled everything. I would have gone with my mother to the five and dime. I would have got help instantly. She would have survived. I really used to think that I could control everything.

"You know how my father reacted to my mother's death?" She mimics her father: an outraged whine against fate, head back, gazing heavenward in accusation: " 'How could she *do* this to me?' " She shakes her head in disbelief. "It destroyed him. Not because of what happened to her, but because of what happened to him. He walked around the house for days, hollering, 'How could she *do* this to me?' So when you have that kind of a father, what can you do? I picked myself up and moved back home. I became my mother. I became his wife."

She and her husband gave up their apartment and moved into her father's house in Brooklyn. She quit her job, but she set up a studio on the sunporch where she could paint. She was the mama of the household, and most especially the staff on which her father leaned. Apparently he leaned heavily. "My father called me Anna (her mother's name) more than he called me Ronnie. I was his wife, his mother, his daughter, and I had to be his son, too, because of that whole piece about my brother. That's a piece I find it hard to talk about."

Her brother, eight years older, a handsome, bright, winning youngster, had mysteriously begun to go off the track mentally some years earlier. Ronnie has no theories to account for his history; her love for her brother is open and passionate, and the fearful identification she lives with is painful to probe. Her brother was another major reason that she returned home. "I was going to cure him, right? All-powerful, all-loving, all-controlling, wonderful me. Sure, sure."

Her brother was already deeply disturbed when their mother died; he grew steadily worse afterward. Ronnie's patience was thinner than she had counted on, and her disappointment with failure more acute. The family called upon all available medical help, but her brother's condition deteriorated steadily. From a childhood as a top-of-the-class gifted boy, he had become a vague, disoriented, depressed creature. The only work he could perform was that of a messenger. Ronnie took the brunt of the punishment of her brother's illness on herself. (As always her husband remains so shadowy as to be almost non-existent in the scene.)

She nurtured her younger sister and her father as her mother had; at the same time she was dependent on her father. She and her husband were struggling with severe money problems and her father was generously helpful. Then the wholesale optometry business failed altogether, and her husband became an automotive parts salesman. They waited four years to have the child she wanted. She "felt right" about becoming pregnant. Motherhood was "good," it was doing what she should be doing, doing what was expected of her. She was twenty-five when her first son was born. But after the birth, motherhood was a let-down; she felt as if she had accepted a false bill of goods.

Ronnie's description of the first sight of her son is a comic routine. She is lying in her hospital bed, admiring other mothers' pink-and-white pussycat infants being carried into the semi-private ward. Then her first-born is delivered into her arms. She is appalled by a tiny, screaming mass of red-faced misery, topped by a wild shock of black hair. "You never saw such a mouth. It was bigger than his whole head. The primal scream. Yelling! Wide open. He was screaming blue murder—mad at the whole world the minute he emerged into it."

The routine of baby care was stifling to Ronnie, but she had another child in five years. He too was a boy. The couple were still living with her father, partly because they needed his help financially, but mostly because the father continued to need Ronnie. Her sister, who was now a slight, slim, attractive young woman, married a man Ronnie is very fond of.

"I love them both," Ronnie told me, "though you might think us worlds apart. He's a body and fender man who is a real Stanley Kowalski character, except he's a lovely human being. They have one of the best marriages I know and they have wonderful kids. My sister's a darling. If I told you that she's a dealer for Las Vegas nights in temples and churches, you'd get an idea of her that would be wrong and right at the same time. We have entirely different life-attitudes, but we're good friends. I can count on her, and on them, for anything. They've always come through for me, and I'd do anything for them. And then my sister and I have our family sharing, we have exactly the same feelings about our brother, the same love, the same guilt, the same fears."

Her father married again, and when he did Ronnie and her husband and the two children moved at last to their own place, but no further than around the corner from her father, who still needed Ronnie, in spite of his new wife. He was generous with Ronnie, helped by buying her a car, and he paid for her continuing art instruction.

She had been married for sixteen years when she met a woman at the local Parents' Association who offered her a job as art counsellor at a summer camp. Ronnie was then thirty-six. She took the job without much enthusiasm. She said yes because it meant a free summer camp for her two boys where she would be on hand to keep watch. "Control, control," she says, mocking her illusions. "The way it worked was that our husbands came up for weekends. I took the job, thinking, 'Oh God, I'm going to have to spend a whole summer with this bunch of dull, middle-class women!' "

That was the summer she fell in love with Adele. Through her neighborhood school Parents' Association, Ronnie had been acquainted with Adele and a couple of the other women now at the camp. It had flitted across her consciousness that Adele and another woman might be lovers, but she had rejected the shadow of a thought. After all, weren't they just like herself—nice, middle-class women with good husbands, adequate incomes, and wonderful children? She wasn't attracted to Adele until she heard her sing. It was at a rehearsal early in the summer for a performance Adele was appearing in. Ronnie was producing the sets and the costumes. "I fell in love at that instant, only I didn't recognize it as anything but excitement at discovering that marvelous untrained voice she possessed and didn't know how the hell to use. She didn't know how to use herself in any way. I knocked myself out putting color into her for that performance, in the sets, in the costumes. I love performers. I love talent. I'm a sucker for two things—brilliant performance and good bone structure. Adele had the talent and nothing else. I taught Adele a lot that summer—and later on."

The summer went by in a strange muddle of lesbian affairs that Ronnie watched from the sidelines. Her suppositions had been correct, after all. By the close of the summer, Adele was freely confiding in her, and Ronnie was privy to the linking and unlinking going on between the group of women. Adele's affair with one of them was on the point of breaking up. And then one morning after they were back in the city, during a conversation about breaking off the affair, Adele said, "Ronnie, are you gay?"

Ronnie describes the scene to me. It was at Ronnie's apartment. All the children were at school, their husbands were at work, the two women were having a second cup of coffee.

"Adele said to me 'Are you gay, Ronnie?' and to my amazement I heard myself say, 'Yes.' I don't know where that 'yes' came from." She mimics herself looking about the room wildly. "What, 'yes'? Where did I find that 'yes'? Where did it come from? And the craziest thing about that yes out of nowhere was it was true. It was totally true.

"We got right into bed. We spent a lot of our time in bed. We had perfect freedom, all the daytime hours, no worries about covering up. We were all close friends, I mean as couples, Adele and I and our husbands. Our kids were best friends. That year was incredible. I had an inexhaustible supply of energy. I couldn't get enough of sex, Adele during the day, my husband at night, I was painting, I was active in a dozen different projects, I never had so much energy.

Adele and I worked together on a number of projects. I loved working with her, working for her. I loved using my talent to buttress hers. I was intoxicated with the whole scene, even our shared social life when the four of us would go out together, Adele and her husband and my husband and me and sometimes all the kids too for picnics or a city outing to a museum or zoo."

That was the same year that Ronnie's father died, as suddenly as her mother had. He was hit by an automobile as he crossed the street from his parked car to the opposite sidewalk. Ronnie's brother had had himself committed to Kings County Hospital just a short while before that, while Ronnie was still at the summer camp. She had received a call from the police at the camp to that effect. His depression had reached an unmanageable stage and he was making repeated attempts to kill himself.

"Only my brother would try to commit suicide with the end of a spoon! A *spoon!*" Ronnie laughs it up.

He was sent to Creedmore for treatment. Ronnie and her sister hoped to keep the news of their father's violent death from their brother, but he read about it in *The Daily News* while at the hospital. The conjunction of her father's death and her brother's commitment created ghastly problems for Ronnie. Her father had adamantly refused to recognize that his male heir was incompetent, and had persisted in naming his first-born son executor of a will leaving some $50,000. Other assets were also in the brother's name—stocks, safe deposit boxes, insurance policies.

"It was left to me to juggle that mess so as to protect him and ourselves. We had to get all that money off my brother's name, otherwise the state would have eaten it up. Suppose my brother got better? He'd have nothing left. It was too much to hope that he would ever be able to support himself. I had to maneuver first to get him *out* of the hospital so I could get power of attorney from him, then to get him back *in* the hospital, because he kept trying to kill himself. I kept reminding myself that I was doing the right

thing for him and for us but I felt horribly guilty and the
psychiatrists weren't helping me any. The phychiatrists laid
a real guilt trip on me about my brother. When it came
down to committing him again, after the money was secured, my sister said, 'I can't, Ronnie, I can't do it.' So I
had to do it. And I *did* do it. What else could I have done?"

She looked directly at me. "I'm exactly like him. Everything that happened to him could have happened to me.
It's a miracle it wasn't me instead of him."

"Is it possible," I said, "that you became a lesbian to
replace him?"

Her look hardened. "I don't know what you mean by
that."

I didn't quite know what I meant myself. One of the
half-baked theories afloat is that homosexuality is a personality response to a set of engulfing problems, not necessarily
sexual. I had been working to relate Ronnie's experience to
my own, attaching it by innumerable tiny threads of likenesses in a conscious effort to connect. Before I was born,
my mother had lost her fifth child, a male, a brother I
never saw. The account of this baby's death at eighteen
months of age during one of the devasting diphtheria epidemics which swept the slums of New York, haunted my
emotional ties to my mother. I never exactly understood
why. Vaguely I felt guilty and responsible in some way for
this loss, and that in some compensating miracle I was
meant to make up to her for the severe blow she had suffered. I knew that she had desperately wanted him to live
and as desperately wished me never to have been born
since she already had more children than she could care
for when she became pregnant, for the seventh and last
time in her life, with me.

It was not in my mother's nature to withhold love from a
child, and once I was born she loved me as well as any of
her other children—all of whom she loved well. When my
first son was born, I named him after her lost baby. My act
of tribute went against the grain of Jewish tradition, which

calls for naming after wise, much beloved, but above all long-lived predecessors. Nevertheless I named my first son after the dead baby as an offering to my mother. Here, here is your son returned to you, mama, was what I was trying to say. A foolish gesture, I understood ultimately. Now it occurred to me that perhaps in Ronnie's case, the removal of her brother as first-born son and heir of the family put an intolerable burden on her and in a loving gesture of compensation she was trying to become that son for them. Not a startlingly original idea. Any two-bit psychiatrist would have come up with the same. It angered her.

"I don't go for any of that," she said. "When I went into therapy the first thing I wanted to straighten out in *his* head was that I wasn't there to be cured of lesbianism. It isn't a sickness. I wasn't looking for a cure. What I needed to be cured of was being hung up on societal strictures—the notion that only heterosexuality is normal. So does the world."

Ronnie went into therapy after the breakup of her love affair with Adele. "She took another lover," Ronnie told me. "I was devastated."

"Because you loved her so much?"

"No. I don't know. Not love so much. It was an obsession. I wanted to mold her; I wanted her to become what she could become. When I heard her sing that first time, I can't explain it," she paused. She was sketching me as we talked and she stopped, gesturing toward the large sheet on which she was working. "It's like drawing, it was like starting a drawing when I first fell in love with her. She was a sketch, an outline that my love would fill in. Like a drawing with all the detail still to be done. It was my love that put in the detail. I made her, I created her in a way, I changed her. I tried to do everything for her, choose her clothes, her whole look. She became vivid because of me. I would have given up everything for her, I would have left my husband and children for her, but she didn't want that.

What she wanted was to keep a safe affair going alongside her marriage. That's why she had to ditch me and find another lover. I was getting out of hand."

Ronnie sold some of the stocks left to her by her father and went to Europe alone that summer. It was a marvelous trip in spite of her dreadful emotional state. She immersed herself in looking, looking, looking. Europe was a revelation. Though she was familiar with all the great works of art from reproductions, the originals in their magnificent settings made an entirely different impact. When she returned her paintings leaped into new strength. She began to teach, giving private lessons and classes at a neighborhood center.

I asked Ronnie about the money left by her father. "It more or less evaporated," she said. "I don't know where that money went. It was divided between me and my sister and a share put aside for my brother, so it wasn't that much. I sold some of the stocks for my first trip to Europe and I sold some more for the second trip. It was all over then with Adele, and I had already met Connie and we were in love. Maybe more on her part than on mine. It helped to have someone who felt strongly about me, after the blow of Adele."

"Was it Adele who wanted to break off?"

"No," Ronnie said. "No way. She would have been quite content to go on. I was the one who broke it off after she took another lover. It would have killed me to go on in a three-way thing. I'm jealous. Or I was. I've changed about that piece, but at that time I couldn't bear it."

"What about your husband?" I meant, *wasn't that a three-way thing*, but she heard my question as something else.

"You mean did he suspect?"

"Did he?" I altered my question.

"Sure. He'd have been a fool not to. He's not a fool. He confronted me once about Adele. I didn't tell him the truth. No way. I lied. I denied everything. It would have

been a disaster between me and Adele if I had done anything else. She wanted to stay married to her husband. I
had to keep things together to save what we had. It didn't
bother me to lie. But after I broke with Adele, and Connie
had come into the picture, I felt differently. Anyway Connie was pressing for me to leave him, to live with her
openly. She put enormous pressure on me. When I took
my second European trip, I set it up so that my son Victor
would meet me in Venice." (Victor is Ronnie's oldest son,
a designer-artist.) "I had given my itinerary to Connie and
every city I landed in, there was a letter from her waiting
for me at Poste Restante or American Express, sometimes
both. Love letters. My son Victor also had my itinerary,
and if he hit a city before I did, he'd pick up my mail. I was
terrified that he would open one of Connie's letters and
read it. I hadn't yet decided then how much I was going to
tell my children. I got very nervous about that, but when
we met in Venice he turned over a batch of unopened
letters from Connie. Victor and I had a marvelous time in
Venice. He was a joy to be with, and going to the galleries
together was wonderful."

When she returned from the trip, she had decided on an
honest understanding with her husband. They would stay
together, but Ronnie would also live somewhat separately.
He knew about Connie and, retroactively, about Adele
now. She had compromised with Connie's demands by
agreeing to spend her weekends at Connie's apartment,
and in a move toward individual autonomy Ronnie had
taken a studio for herself in an artist's complex—hand-
somely renovated buildings set up as living and studio areas
for working artists.

"There were all these pieces. The wife piece, the mother
piece, the artist piece, the lesbian piece. I was going to my
therapist, but that wasn't pulling it all together for me.
Then everything blew up."

Ronnie's husband resented her new way of life. "He's a
nice guy," Ronnie said. "He stood for a lot of bullshit from

me. But I'll never forgive him for what he did. He'd make a big deal about my leaving every weekend—not about the real content of what was happening, but about bullshit, about how the kids were suffering, not getting proper meals or attention—he'd do that number on me. Then one night at Connie's, very late, I got a call from him to come right home, that Victor needed me at once."

During a quarrel between father and son, her husband had told their son about his mother's affairs with Connie and with Adele. She found Victor in a state of shock and intense anger—as much at his father as at his mother. Ronnie's husband seemed very frightened at what he had done. Ronnie exploded—ordered her husband out of the house. He went. He moved into his mother's house a few blocks away, where he has continued to live till the present.

For a time Ronnie continued to live in her old house with her two boys, and she fit Connie into this picture as well as she could. Then she sold the house and moved into her studio with her youngest son, Billie. Victor went out on his own. With a childhood friend he set up a commercial art venture. The two youngesters, both in their early twenties, were fabulously successful. Victor seemed headed for easy stardom. Then Victor's closest friend and business partner was killed in an automobile accident while racing to the airport to join Victor in a big-deal Hollywood conference where they were to map out a campaign for a major film. Ronnie thinks that that ghastly blow out of the blue knocked Victor off base, but she believes it was a rocky base to begin with.

"Victor's a marvelous person. He's more gifted than anybody I've ever known. But he's crazy. He was always crazy. From the minute he was born and opened that big mouth and started screaming at the world, he's been crazy."

Victor will now have nothing to do with his mother, or as Ronnie is quick to point out, with any other member of his family (a not entirely accurate addition, because he does see his brother Billie from time to time). When I first met

Ronnie, at the time she was living with her son Billie and her lover, Connie, in the town house they had jointly bought, Victor had cut off all contact with his mother.

I tried to probe a possible connection between her open lesbianism and the violent negation on his part of the son-mother relationship. She won't have any part of that two-bit psychologizing either. She rejects facile concepts of cause and effect. "You're not the first to try to pin his state of being on me. No thanks. I'm not having any of that. I don't buy it. As if *I* did it. I'm not that powerful. I am not guilty of ruining my son's life because of my sexuality. *Nobody* is going to lay that guilt trip on me." She emphasizes her refusal with slow deliberate anger. She's angry with me for jabbing at a nerve that has been punished enough.

The friendship between Ronnie and her younger son, Billie, is solid. Billie had a hard time of it, living with Ronnie and Connie, but he expresses no resentment against his mother and the life she chose to lead. His problems in the lesbian household were not appreciably different from the troubles of any youngster in a second-marriage stepson situation. He felt that Connie didn't like him and that she showed it; so like any kid he didn't like her back. She exhibited common characteristics of the uncertain step-parent. According to Ronnie, she was either too cold or too intimate, disproportionately over-indulgent and unnecessarily disciplining by turns, jealous of the mother-son connection and resentfully contemptuous of it, along with being generally inexperienced in the raising of kids, but confident that she had all the answers. The added aura of her professionalism created more tensions. Connie is a therapist whose specialty is teen-age problems. A real live at-home subject was an irresistibly attractive challenge and irritant. Billie is twenty years old now. He's on his own, living with a friend.

The exquisitely appointed bedroom that Ronnie and Connie shared was disturbed by quarrels; in that perfect love-nest stage setting, sexual love had dried up between them. "Not only because of Billie. Not at all. Everything was wrong between us. Connie's a liar. She lies about herself, holds back. It's hard to explain. When I love a man I want him to be a man; when I love a woman I want my lover to be a woman, not a fake man. She didn't want me to love her woman to woman—physically or any other way. She doesn't know what loving a woman is about."

In the CR group, Ronnie covered up her unhappiness and carried on the Ronnie-Connie show of exemplary living for the "straight" women. When Connie was present in the group Ronnie hardly participated in the talk at all. On the other hand, Connie spoke a lot—mostly generalizations, a mix of expertise jargon and arcane wisdom presumably unavailable to those who were neither lesbians nor professional therapists. Both women avoided discussing the problems that were acutely upsetting them at that time. When Connie missed a meeting, Ronnie spoke freely of other phases of her life, of her former marriage, her children, her work, her problems about her work, her reluctance to show her paintings, the humiliation of *shlepping* a portfolio from gallery to gallery and the fear and loathing of rejection. She spoke eloquently against the commercialization that constituted an inevitable misuse of talent, and of the particular discrimination against women which made the whole scene that much more painful to survive. "You take your pick of bad alternatives if you're an artist of any kind, and if you're a woman artist, the alternatives are worse and worse, more and more narrowing and corrupting. There's no way out that I can see right now. Ballyhoo and exploitation—and you're lucky if you get that. Maybe you have to get really old to get beyond it. Louise Nevelson. That's beautiful. She's beautiful. I love her, the whole get-up, the costumes, the yard-long eyelashes. When I grow up I'm going to be Louise Nevelson." She laughs at herself.

She's a very good painter; but she wasn't working enough. She felt herself at a loose end, and the more unhappy because she was supposed to be feeling good—liberated. She was an active feminist, but she was also deeply involved in projects she disliked. "I was becoming a real estate lady." A below-ground apartment in the town house was under renovation for rental purposes. That would bring in some income. And she and Connie were building another house—a dream cottage on a tropical island in the Caribbean, as a vacation place. Their finances were as closely intertwined as the most together husband and wife might interlock them; their life together was a marriage, a husband and wifely thing, the very situation Ronnie had thought she was freeing herself from. "Every day I watched myself imprison myself more and more. We did it to one another. We were looking for safety. We were bargaining for a piece of security. I worked on the town house and became a real estate lady, making house beautifuls, nest-building. I thought I was obliged to cook well, you know, the whole shmear. But nothing helped. Connie was sick. She had an operation, there was that whole piece, nursing her. I did it gladly. Not gladly. No good. All the while we were dying on one another."

As in many failing marriages, their relationship kept going of its own momentum. To be a lesbian is to live a life no different in its outlines from the life led by others; lesbians are professionals, wage-earners, workers, home-owners, renters, social beings, family members, theater-goers, bridge players, ballet, opera, basketball buffs, or whatever else—to which they add a rich underground layer of "gay" life, the special community created by gays. This too made for problems. Connie was active in the politics of lesbianism. She lectured, participated in panel discussions, spoke on radio, appeared on TV. She specialized in educating the public about lesbian mothers—a subject on which Ronnie felt her to be a specious and untrustworthy witness, given Connie's record with Billie. Ronnie was torn between admiration for the good work Connie was performing in support of lesbian motherhood, and her private insights into Connie's failures. It made Ronnie uncomfortable that even this aspect of a bad marriage had entered the relationship, that she was acting the good wife, covering for Connie, and secretly criticizing her. It was a terrible thought that perhaps all relationships were alike. (Simone de Beauvoir makes the point in *The Second Sex* that to his wife, the great poet is just the man she lives with who invariably forgets to flush the toilet.) Ronnie knew that her profound reservations about Connie must be showing through, that Connie must be feeling subtly undermined by this attitude, that Connie must know that Ronnie thought her something of a phony.

The details of the quarrel that brought them to a final break is too complicated a story to reproduce. Lesbian relationships are like any others; some are monogamous; some last for life; some are stormy quick joinings quickly unjoined; some lesbians play the field; some cruise; some go in for a kind of adolescent adventure, trying anything but in the safety of their own crowd; some indulge in a mix of the above. All exist in a social ambiance which marks, condemns, and isolates. Lesbianism is designated a sin (crime against God) subject to penalties (crime against nature) and act against the social order (crime against the family based on heterosexual organization); and until recently lesbians were automatically considered to be mentally and psychologically ill. A most difficult situation, it would seem, in which to find happiness.

As a lesbian, Ronnie knew there was danger out there; what she never expected was to be threatened from inside the community. She and Connie parted in intense mutual bitterness and made a mess of extricating themselves from their knotty financial and legal ties. Because their union had no legal status, for mutual protection they were bound by legal documents involving their joint ownership of the properties in New York and in the Caribbean. Their separation became a nightmare of ill will, bad faith, jealousy (Ronnie's new lover was a woman Connie had also been in love with) and squabbling over money. In a typical lawyer's ploy, the blackmail of disclosure was threatened: Ronnie's new lover would be named in Connie's suit.

Ronnie's lover, Diane, is a professional of standing in her field. Diane neither hides her lesbianism nor proclaims it publicly. In her private and social life, she's a lesbian, and she counts on the sisterhood of the lesbian community not to blow her professional reputation. She's a feminist and a supporter of actions to remove discriminatory statutes against gays, but she isn't a lesbian politico. The threat of disclosure constituted a real problem that could undermine her professional and financial success. Nevertheless she assured Ronnie that she would stand by Ronnie and face the action if Ronnie wished her to. Ronnie did not. Throwing Diane to the rough winds of a legal action was not her concept of loving; she also had her own financial future at stake. Ronnie now was working as a teacher in a posh private prep school, and if the school was an unlikely institution to initiate a witch-hunt on the basis of Ronnie's private sexual activities, it was also unlikely that administration would stand up for a new teacher against blasts of public notoriety. The parent community too could be counted on to respond, in part, in an outcry for dismissal of an "immoral" element thriving in the midst of their adolescent children.

Dismayed and stunned, Ronnie turned the mess over to her lawyer who locked horns with Connie's lawyer and moved to seal all information. In time all problems were negotiated, without disclosure, and with a decent cutting of losses on both sides. Ronnie got what she wanted—no involvement in the real estate ventures and a minimum return on her initial investment in the property.

"Any losses were worth taking as long as they got me clear of the whole mess. I just didn't want to have anything more to do with it or with her."

"So what's so special about homosexual relationships," I asked, "if this kind of horror can happen? If homosexual isn't *better* than heterosexual—then what is it? A taste, a

sexual appetite, no different from preferring Bibb to ice-
berg?"

We were again on ground that is an irritation to her to
hear explored in that manner. "It's an option," she said,
shortly. "A human option. There's no freedom without the
freedom of this option."

It still seemed too painful to pursue as "a human option."
I suppose I was "hung up," as Ronnie would have said, on
the concept that homosexuality had to try harder, perform
better (wasn't it number two in the field?)—and extend
human happiness, or it failed as a human option. But what
if all this was nonsense, and homosexuality wasn't *doing*
anything. It was just being. Perhaps there aren't any answers or any questions about homosexuality. "What is the
answer?" Gertrude Stein is said to have asked herself on
her deathbed and answered, "What is the question?"

Ronnie lives alone now in her former studio in the artist's
complex. Her space is no homosexual love bower, but a
comfortable, working-living space, dominated by her paintings on the wall and the racks of stacked canvasses. On the
easel and about the room are a number of the oversized
portrait drawings she has been devoting herself to. They
are startling—a mix of realistic detail almost in the Durer
manner coupled to the blank, spaced-out dimension of pop
comic-strip blow-ups. Ronnie has done more than fifty of
these close-to-the-bone revelations of individuals, recog-
nizable likenesses which added to one another, and framed
and hung in groups of four, transcend the particular to
become anonymous portraits of "women."

This new technique absorbs and excites her. So does her
work with the young students at the private school where
she teaches. She has also continued to teach a group of
private students, mostly women, as she had been doing for
many years now.

Her new lover also absorbs and excites her. Her relationship with Diane is happier, looser, lighter than any she has
had before. Diane is very much "her own person." She is a

tall, slim, handsome woman in her early forties with the bone-structure and the outstanding accomplishments that Ronnie is a sucker for. Diane has never married or had any children. She has made her way in a field difficult for women to succeed in, and she enjoys her success and its rewards. She keeps an elegant New York City apartment, and Ronnie helped her design and decorate the lavish offices where she practices her profession. They don't live together.

"I like my plain studio," Ronnie told me. "I like living alone. And I love having Diane's place to luxuriate in. I spend a lot of weekends there. It's the best of both worlds for me. I want to hold on to that autonomy. I want to be alone. I want to be my own person and I want to let Diane be her own person. I don't want any more of that old clawing for security. It's wonderful not to feel that I *have* to do things for Diane or that she *has* to do things for me. All that bullshit of nest-building and propping one another up. We do what we want to do for one another—and that's a lot—and we get enormous pleasure from doing them. I don't want to give up everything for Diane—whatever that means. I don't want to control her life, the way I was obsessed with controlling Adele, and anybody else I ever loved. I don't even want to control *me*. That doesn't mean I just want to drift. I don't know where I want to go with my painting right now, that's why I'm concentrating on the drawings. It's got to be right, and about my life it's got to feel right too. I love Diane and admire her and enjoy her and want to be with her. We've gone to the Caribbean together and to Europe and it's been marvelous—the best. But there's Claire. She's very important to me too."

Ronnie and I were talking at dinner in a "gay" restaurant near Ronnie's studio. That is, it was gay if you knew that it was owned by a lesbian couple and that many of its clients were gay. If you didn't know, you would be struck only by its gaiety—a pleasant, country atmosphere, rough wood surfaces, a blackboard menu. Ronnie was well known here.

When we arrived she had been kissed in greeting, first by the owners, then by the waitress and a couple of diners, and in the course of our dinner and our talk, we were interrupted a number of times by kissing greetings from new arrivals. The food was country good—fresh and prepared with care for preserving its freshness, served with hearty country manners. Prices were cheap by New York City standards. A very attractive eating spot.

The diners were on the young side, dressed in prevailing unisex costumes—blue jeans and ponchos. Impossible to determine which were homosexuals, if one cared to. Still, surrounded by homespun simplicity, I felt the atmosphere charged with an electric promise of sexual license. All in my own head? The women who were greeting Ronnie so warmly fit no physical stereotype. Most were beautiful even by extreme macho chauvinist measure. But they differed, indefinably, from other women. Again, all in my own head? There was a deliberation in the careful way they acknowledged the introduction to me, an older women, obviously new to this scene. There *was* a promise in the greeting; but when I thought it over later, I characterized it as a promise of support, sisterhood, security. It had no direct sexual overtone. What it spoke to was the person. *Here*, it said, *we will try to recognize you as your self, okay? That's what we owe you, woman to woman.*

During the period when Ronnie and Connie had been on-stage in the East Village town house, one of my close friends in the consciousness raising group spent a night at their house. She was going through a bad time and was upset about an event in her own life and didn't want to be alone. She is a divorced woman in her forties, the mother of two teen-age children, daring in her professional life and in her sexuality—a woman who takes risks, and collects the rewards and pays the full punishments that go with risk-taking. Not a cloistered woman in any way. But it was a very strange night for her. She had been comfortably bedded down on the oversized living room couch, but she couldn't sleep. She found herself reacting with the exaggerated nerve ends of an adolescent to the vibrations of the house, alert to every creak of the old boards, first too hot, then shivering, unable to fall asleep yet exhausted, mysteriously excited, expectant, angry, inviting, and negating. Nobody disturbed her. She entertained vague fantasies about what was happening in the big bed in the lush bedroom above. She imagined she heard cries and gasps of love-making. Laughter. At her?

She jumped up and prowled about, clattering glasses, running water, making enough noise so that Ronnie came down to see if she was all right. She was glad to have Ronnie fuss over her, give her tea, and tuck her back into bed; but left alone, she was seized again by the same mysterious agitation. What did she want? What was she afraid of? She had no notion. She got up again, wandered about, again heard sounds from above. She was strangely angry—at herself? at them? She lost her breath, was sure she was having a heart attack, almost screamed aloud for help. Both women came down to soothe her. They took her upstairs and put her in their great, comforting bed. Immense Connie lay beside her, holding her hand. Ronnie sat on the sofa, making reasuring jokes. My friend cried like a child, lying in the bed of her imaginings, clinging to Connie's hand as if to a rock of security, the tears streaming from her eyes. At last she fell asleep. She ran from the house in the morning ashamed that she had displayed so much weakness and confusion, but the two women seemed to think there was nothing special about her behavior.

Contrary to popular lurid notions of homosexuals setting ambushes to ensnare innocent heterosexuals, it's impossible to imagine Ronnie seducing and corrupting, if for no other reason than that she is too vulnerable to rejection. In any event, there's no need. There are enough women available who want to love other women.

Claire, the other woman Ronnie started to tell me about, is particularly dear to Ronnie because they have everything in common—age, artistic pursuit, and a shared background of a long marriage and years of motherhood.

"Most people refuse to deal with how they relate to the idea of monogamy. In heterosexual *or* homosexual relationships. Why close oneself down to one relationship? Is that a real fulfillment? Is there anything real about monogamy? Is it a human need, or a hang-up that society has imposed on us? Virtue, and all that garbage. I want all my options open. I love Diane. And I love Claire. I feel closer to Claire than to anybody else. I can talk to her with perfect freedom about everything that's important to me and know that she'll understand—my work, my children. That doesn't take anything away from Diane. Diane loves Claire too, and Claire loves Diane. We have a great time together— the three of us. We're letting it play itself out, just letting it be. No rules of conduct. See where it goes. Some gays think they have an obligation to be exemplary family people, monogamous as hell, goodie goods out to prove that they're not sinners. I'm not out to prove anything. I feel free for the first time in my life, born again as me, not a daughter or a wife or a mother or anybody else's life-long partner—just me, myself."

BOOK FOUR

Starting Over
THE MIDDLE YEARS
THE MALE WAY

Jack Jasper
SWITCHING CAREERS
IN MID-STREAM

In the sense in which the word "starting" is being used, many women must start anew, painfully unmaking the personas they had been drilled into becoming—compliant, dependent, "feminine" personalities—and remaking themselves into individuals capable of functioning not only interdependently but independently. A different process is seen in adult men starting over. Whatever the difficulties embedded in the hard ground of becoming one's own man, it doesn't usually necessitate remaking a core of being.

Males and females may theoretically be born equal, but almost from the moment of birth the male is taught autonomy and the female dependency. Men move in a straighter line toward their hoped-for destinies than women do and when a man takes a risk, it doesn't generally endanger his whole life, but only a section of it—the career slice. When men change the direction of their activities, it's more a switching of a track than a whole new discovery. (There are great exceptions, of course. Like Ronnie, male homosexuals, if they open themselves to the full risks of their sexual preference, are remaking themselves, and so are male artists, saints, political and social revolutionaries—or others who dive head-first to swim against the mainstream.) But the stories told here haven't been of great heroines: they are mainstream women struggling to reshape the distortions superimposed on their natural selves by societal strictures. When we seek out men at a similar intelligence and performance level they are inevitably higher placed than the women, they are more likely to be functioning at the top level of wherever they aimed to be.

The differences between male and female starters is I think exemplified in two profiles of very dissimilar men whose careers nevertheless share the common characteristics of the self-made, successful businessman. Jack Jasper, now in his middle fifties, is a first-generation American of immigrant parents. He grew up in New York City and like many bright city boys, attended Townsend Harris, the honors high school of its day. His people were moderately poor, but an uncle who was a rung higher on the economic ladder helped financially so that Jack could go on to a tuition-free college. Jack's father ran a steadily failing retail clothing store in the neighborhood in which they lived.

Jack did well at school and graduated in 1941 at the age of nineteen. He had begun as a math major, but he decided early on that he had no special genius for math, and he switched to statistics as a better field for his talents. The switch had been prompted by practical considerations as well. There was work available for statisticians in the rapidly expanding government agencies then being established, and getting a well-paying job was an important consideration. But he was offered a teaching fellowship upon graduation, and he accepted it and went on to graduate school. His father tried to enlist him as some sort of advisory helper in his retail shop. Jack wanted no part of the store—that was definitely not for him; but he did point out to his father that in his studies he had come across a miraculous cure for what ailed the store—something called bank-ruptcy law—which he strongly advised him to file for.

When he began to teach he discovered that he not only loved it, but was phenomenally successful at it, so much so that he acquired tenure before he had completed his Ph.D. and even before he published. He took his Masters Degree in 1942, the year following his graduation: the Ph.D. took longer and was not completed until 1953. He had married in 1945, a pretty, dark, slim young woman who taught typing and business arithmetic in high school. By 1947, their first child was born; Jack's bride became a full-time mother and housewife and never returned to teaching. They later had two more children.

With a growing family to support, Jack taught in the evening as well as the day, and in summer school, and he worked in the registrar's office between sessions. The busier he was, the better, because teaching became less and less interesting to him the longer he did it. He found himself increasingly bored with teaching. He began to feel that there must be something else he could do with his life—something more rewarding.

"Teaching was becoming too automatic. I found myself repeating myself, and I was teaching techniques that I had personally never applied, had never tested outside of the classroom. There was a new man in my department who was very attractive, very bright. He was doing a lot of out-side consulting work. We shared car trips into the city to-gether. (We had moved out to the suburbs by that time.) I found I was enjoying conversations with my friend in the car more than anything I was doing in class. I felt that the luster of those conversations came from his worldly con-tacts. He had been taking on more and more work, and after a while he asked me to join him in a small company. I did. I took it on full time for one summer. It was intensely interesting work and further emphasized the uncreative-ness of the teaching for me. Because, though I loved teach-ing in essence, I didn't want it to degenerate into repetition and marking time. When I first branched out from teaching, it was really to enrich myself, to go out and test the theories against reality and bring back to class new and different emphases. But I did so well out in the business world that I was asked to stay on as a consultant. I decided to do so, temporarily.

"I asked the department for a leave from teaching without pay; it was granted and I repeated the request the following year, and that too was granted, but I returned to teaching in 1954. The pull back was both intellectual and economic. I had tenure, I was moving up in the profession: and I loved teaching. I was excited about returning with new skills and ideas. I could cite new applications of theories. My enlarged point of view took the boredom out of teaching. But I tried to set myself up so that I didn't have to sacrifice either field, or my security either. I arranged for a three-day-week teaching schedule, gave up the extra teaching and administrative work, and continued my private consulting work. Even then, at the very beginning, I earned more as a consultant than I did as a teacher.

"Almost at once I faced the animosity of my colleagues. I hadn't hidden any of my activities. They would know I was traveling to Washington or to other cities in the course of my consulting work. A certain amount of back-biting began. I was an assistant professor, slated to become an associate professor, but that was arbitrarily held up. My work was just as fine as it had been. My classes were better—much closer to the reality the students would be measuring up against when they went out into the world; I had even been publishing. Those were the days when you published or perished—but I *had* published. Still they held up my associate professorship. I could feel a pattern of animosity developing in my department. The academic atmosphere began to sour on me—all the pettiness was becoming distasteful—the infighting about salaries, rank, and special scheduling. The outside world seemed freer, more generous, and more attractice. I had always displayed good administrative ability; now my business experience had heightened this capacity. I served as sub-chairman of the department for six years, eager to take on administrative work in the university, but the attitudes I encountered were discouraging. Perhaps my position was giving me too close a view of the inner workings.

"During the late forties teaching had been a very exciting occupation because of the more mature students entering under the G.I. Bill of Rights. They were a different breed— serious, intelligent, eager. In contrast the students of the fifties were a dull, lethargic, unresponsive group. Nothing happened in the classroom—no sparks. That took the fun out of teaching. But my teaching post offered great security—an even ride on a highly predictable escalator. To give up teaching meant giving up tenure, pension, the standing of an associate professor (because in time I made associate professor)—everything that went with the fruits of academia. For a number of years I see-sawed between the two worlds, business and academia.

"I had been teaching for nineteen years when I was offered the opportunity to enter into a partnership with a new consultant firm. They asked me to leave teaching. I was a young man, not yet forty. I thought it over and made my decision to take the plunge, to leave teaching entirely and to cut off all ties to my profession. I sent in a letter of resignation to the department I had served for nineteen years. I received two telephone calls expressing regret, one from the dean of the School of Business, entirely outside our department, and one from my only good friend in the department. I never set foot in the place again. That says something about the nature of relationships in the academic community. I was happy to leave all the petty bitterness behind me. My reasons for leaving were complicated, but it finally came down to a value judgment about my own role, or perhaps it would be better put as a value question. Was I teaching garbage? Did the textbooks from which I taught reflect what the world was all about?

"Also, I like open competition. It's clean. In business the spirit is 'You have what I want and I'm going to do everything I can to get it from you.' In academia it's, 'You have what I want and I don't care if I can get it or not, I don't want *you* to have it.' That's mean spirited."

Jack Jasper and I are talking in the dining room of a private club in the Wall Street area. It's a spacious place overlooking the harbor, brilliantly lit on this sunny autumn day. There is an occasional woman seated at a table with other men but it's mostly filled with businessmen. The food is excellent, expensive, and excellently served. Jack tells me that the dining room has only recently been opened to women because of the changes taking place in the business world. (He entirely approves of the new policy.)

We have walked here from his offices, the New York headquarters of the firm he now heads. The suite of offices in the skyscraper building are so extensive that one takes a special elevator up, apart from the regular bank of elevators. Jack Jasper owns and runs this enterprise, encompassing hundreds of employees, with a wonderfully calm hand. He is as far from the frenetic, dynamic businessman in appearance as it is possible to be. His good looks are on the quiet, solid side; his manner is assured, deliberate, quietly amused, courtly. He imparts a sense of never being rushed or rattled—the epitome of the unflappable—one would instinctively trust him in any emergency. He smokes a pipe, wears conservative clothes, watches his weight, hardly drinks at all, goes in for almost none of the trappings of the newly wealthy. He has no summer place, no yacht or similar toy, and his home in a Long Island suburb is modest, though extremely comfortable.

His only luxury is traveling with his still youthful, pretty, trim wife. She sometimes accompanies him on business trips (a recent one to Thailand); sometimes the trip is unadulterated vacation. The Jaspers are extremely generous with their daughter and two sons, all of whom have moved steadily into maturity with the ease and success such a father makes an unspoken demand. The oldest son has entered the same field as his father. The daughter took a different vocational path, is doing well, and has just married a young man displaying great promise in his vocation. The youngest son is applying himself with energy to his college studies. Jack Jasper is proud of them, of course—a pride tinged with the reservation that anything less would be unthinkable—a standard that seemingly creates no visible tensions between parents and children. Family celebrations are frequent, warm, lavish occasions either at their home where Jack's wife prepares and often serves the meals herself with astonishing efficiency, or at exclusive and expensive New York restaurants. Birthdays, anniversaries, graduations, occupational or academic honors earned may spur the occasion. An ideal family, an ideal life? So it would seem for Jack Jasper.

We explore the question of whether his motivation in entering business had been expressly economic. Had he felt a strong drive to make money? No, excitement in the work was his major consideration. New concepts, new explorations intrigue him. Econometrics, for example. He has great reservations about its soundness, but it's interesting to him to observe how the newer members of the research teams explore its possibilities. He likes to think that the firm's findings serve the community as well as the big corporations who pay for its services. A study conducted by his firm was responsible for a reform in rates by a leading utility, he points out. He considers himself sensitive to the ramifications of the social issues involved in his work, and takes on litigation with zest, enjoying his appearances as a witness before a judge or jury or before a congressional committee or a regulatory agency of the government. He feels that his old teaching skills are very useful then, and that his larger view well serves the client and the community.

"Aren't statistics manipulable in any direction?" I ask.

He agrees, but also points to the danger of such manipulation. "The fellows arguing from an opposing view are just as intelligent, just as bright, and may be closer to the findings of the situation. It would be bad business, bad for the client to manipulate numbers. If our studies come up with findings that don't gibe with what the client's looking for, we'd be fools to try to make the numbers fit, it wouldn't work. In such a case we use our findings to try to alter the client's approach—that's the sound way to work."

We return to our original discussion about starting again. Was he conscious of taking a risk; did he entertain the possibility of failure; and what would he have done if he had failed, would he have returned to teaching?

"I had prepared so carefully for the move that I think failure never seriously entered the picture. Anyway, I didn't think about it."

What about his wife? Had she been totally supportive; had she pushed him; had she removed herself from decisions, had she any problems about pursuing an independent life? He said yes she had been supportive, no she hadn't pushed, and then he tackled the last part of the question, answering with no show of self-consciousness, no.

"My wife wanted to take a job when my youngest son left for college. I said, no, I need you at home and there aren't any money pressures. Why should you take a job?"

He informs me that she took his response well, and has been perfectly happy in following his demand. I know her to be an extremely active woman, busy with the innumerable charitable, social, and cultural events of the middle- and upper-class community in which they live. "Doesn't her volunteer work keep her just as busy as any full-time job would?" I ask.

"Yes, but she's not committed to that work. She can refuse to take on a particular task when I need her at home, or want her to join me on a trip. She couldn't do that with a full-time job. She's a volunteer, and that gives her freedom to think of her family first."

Without transition he follows this with strong words of praise for the women in his organization, and informs me that they function at all levels of the organization including the top. He uses terms like "native brilliance, dash, verbal skills, intuitive business sense" and he particularly praises women for their non-competitive, supportive attentions to one another. He clearly admires "the new woman" in his own organization. He doesn't foresee great changes in his career, or any basic changes in his style of living. He's content in his middle fifties to have reached this plateau of productive, good living. "But anything is possible," he adds and his quietly contemplative eyes light up, "and I like to think I'd be equal to a vital change if it presented itself."

Mark Rudnick
STARTING
FROM AN INNER DREAM

Mark Rudnick is also a self-made man, but he fits the typical notions of the mold more closely than Jack Jasper. Dynamic is the operative word for Mark Rudnick. He's the youngest man of sixty imaginable, with a full head of dark, carefully barbered hair; large, round, black eyes brimming with energy, laughter, and enthusiasm; a slim body in a suit as well cut as money can buy; and a personality charged with vigor and ego. He's fit, trim, and always tanned; he swims, sails, skis, travels widely. When he isn't living at his East Side duplex in New York, he's at his Fire Island beach house, or his chalet in the Alps. He is the head of a very successful business whose main base is in New York, but with divisions in Washington and Europe. My friendship with him goes very far back. Now we meet at his invitation at consistently elegant and expensive places—his box at the Met, an East Side French restaurant, his lush offices in one of the newer glass towers of the East Side.

When we come together to talk formally, it's in his large,

bright corner office fitted up like a living room—with the large desk off at one end. We sit in armchairs at a coffee table, sipping coffee. But first I check in with the receptionist; I admire a fresh flower centerpiece arrangement on her desk and "make myself comfortable" in a bank of deep, soft armchairs while I wait for Mr. Rudnick to be free to see me. Like most top executives he needs every bit of energy he's blessed with—he's a very busy man. In addition to owning and guiding a leading advertising and marketing agency, he is engaged in national and international programs for the public good as an adviser to government agencies, and he devotes time to writing monographs on such subjects as language and illiteracy; the media and social change: and mass media programs to change patterns of nutrition, education, population control, and education in the Third World.

He has come a long way from his beginnings. His background is similar to mine, the child of immigrant Russian-Jewish parents who arrived in this country about 1905. He was the last of four children—a daughter and three sons. His father was a traditionalist, tyrannical and rigid (except with Mark's mother with whom he was unexpectedly tender)—a father capable of breaking a chair over a son's head in a rage that parental discipline wasn't being heeded. The father's concern was for the son, that he be "a good boy," that the child would "amount to something." He was equally tough on himself. He drove himself hard, beginning as a teamster who delivered supplies to the innumerable small delicatessens dotted over the city. He then conceived of a franchise to regularly supply stores, and from that branched out into his own small delicatessen factory. He did well, continuing to work very hard himself.

Mark remembers that when he was a little boy he never felt poor. "At the Passover seders there were always extra chairs for guests. And we had our aspirations. There was a ten-volume set of Shakespeare in the house which my father had gotten with subscription premiums to the *Jewish*

Morning Journal. My father was an educated Jew. He had
attended a *gymnasium* in Russia and he could read and
write English. When I first started going out with Judy"
(Mark refers to his wife of approximately thirty-five years of
marriage) "I wanted to impress her. My father had been
dead for fourteen years by then, but I led her into the first
delicatessen we passed and I asked the proprietor, 'Did you
know Pincus Rudnick?' She was a little woman and she
dropped everything and came out from behind the counter
in her dirty apron and kissed me. Then she ran into the
back, shouting, 'Morris, Morris, get up from your nap, we
have a guest, Pincus Rudnick's youngest child'; and the two
of them treated us like long-lost relatives. That's the kind
of man my father was. Fourteen years dead, and his customers remembered him instantly.

"He died when he was fifty-seven. I was eleven years old.
My two older brothers were already dead, the first one at
age seventeen from spinal meningitis and the other two
years later, of TB. Two years after that my father had a
stroke. He was incapacitated for three years before he died.
I was eight years old when he first became ill. I remember
walking him through the neighborhood to the barber shop,
holding his hand. He had been the strongest man in the
world to me; now he was this pitiful creature. It was
frightening: I remember the neighbors out on the street,
the way they looked at us. I was afraid I might hurt him or
that something might happen to him while he was with me.
I remember another time being awakened out of sleep in
the middle of the night and seeing my father standing over
my bed and crying. I was his only remaining son.

"I was bar-mitzvahed at the age of twelve, because if
you're an orphan you become a man earlier. We weren't
comfortably off any more, though we weren't starving. I
worked after school as a delivery boy. Work was sacred. I
understood that. There was no way that I would ever spend
a day unemployed as an adult. I was never without a job,
not even for a day. Anything else would be socially shame-

ful, like getting an F at school; that was a crime I never committed. Either one, failing at school, or being unemployed as an adult, would be a violation of the self, the utmost humiliation. I was 'a good boy.' There was one very minor incident when I was a kid where I was caught doing something wrong, throwing rocks, or something. I was crushed when we were caught. It was disgraceful. I had the attitude that getting into trouble was a luxury I couldn't afford. It meant being drawn off the track, it meant I wouldn't 'amount to something.'

"I was a naive Brooklyn kid who didn't know what was what in the world. Our lives were very narrow. I felt that we had lost our connection with the world of affairs with the death of the males in my family. Me and two females— and the females didn't know anything of the world of affairs. Why, I never even ate in a restaurant until I was fifteen or sixteen years of age. My sister, who was six or seven years older than I, did her best for us, but she was naive too. My Uncle Harry had become the theater manager of Loew's, a movie house. One Saturday she dressed me up, took me by the hand, and led me in to ask for a job. Neither one of us knew that wasn't the way a boy got a job—led in by hand, by his big sister.

"I got to go to a summer camp on a scholarship and it was a revelation to meet such a different breed of people— people who lived in Manhattan and the Bronx. After the summer, the father of one of my bunk-mates gave me a job as a stock clerk at thirteen dollars a week. I really worked at that job. I didn't know enough then to know that the way to get ahead is not to be good at what you're doing, but to be good at the next step up. I concentrated on being good at what I was doing. That's a mistake.

"I attended public high schools and city colleges. I couldn't have gone on to school unless it was tuition-free. My plan was to become a teacher. I tried out for the football team and made it. I graduated class of '37. I was an English major; when I took the licensing exam to teach

English I passed the written, but I flunked the oral test. That was a blow. My esses were sibilant, or something. I was very defensive, easily hurt, something of a loner. I still am. I would much rather not be dependent on other people. There's been a lot of tension generated and a lot of struggle within me and with others on the question of inter-dependency.

"I finally made that ushering job at Loew's. I earned extra money while I was going to school, working weekends and evenings. Then I was promoted to outside work, as the barker, complete with resplendent uniform. I walked up and down and did the deep-voiced pitch under the marquee. I was teaching at the time and the kids I taught would gather out front to look at me. I was some kind of hero to them. It built up my confidence to the point that I actually took a girl out—to the movies.

"My aim in life was to be a writer and a teacher. But there was the matter of paying work, and I took what I could get. I worked at so many different things I get a bit mixed up about which came first. When I was a stock clerk, I also sold subscriptions for the *Jewish Examiner*, an English language newspaper with classy articles like "The True Nature of Anti-Semitism" or "Capitalism in Extremis." The whole paper was put out by one man. One day he taught me to put the paper together, and practically the day after that he left the paper to work for the United Jewish Appeal. I took over editing the paper. For twelve dollars a week. In my spare time. When I saw that I could do it, I asked the publisher for a raise. Seventeen fifty. He said, 'no,' so I went on strike, and he said 'okay.' I did that paper for two years. I was a substitute English high-school teacher by that time, and I was doing some rewrite for the *Brooklyn Eagle*. I remember telling myself, 'It can be done. It's easy. All I have to do is not sleep.' I also did some rewrite for the *New York Post*. I was a charter member of the Newspaper Guild," he adds with pride.

"One of my friends was doing radio script writing. I was

good at plotting, and I collaborated with him on scripts for *Inner Sanctum*, a mystery radio drama series. I did that for a year or so, evenings, spare time. We became part of the *Ellery Queen* stable of writers, and we did some *Bulldog Drummond* scripts too. I began to feel strongly about what we were writing. I began to express strong views about how the script should go. One night we were arguing some point and he said, 'Who the hell do you think you are? I'm the professional, not you.' So we broke up.

"I'm aware now of the fact that people find my enthusiasm overbearing, aggressive—that some people think me an objectionable fellow. Especially in the past. Now I'm more conscious of my effect on others. I've *become* very self-aware. I went through years of psychiatric analysis working through that kind of problem. Now I can hold myself in check. I've become my own spectator; I see myself more clearly. Then I was too concerned with 'amounting to something.'

"I had married Judy by that time. She had come out of the same sort of background I did, but had acquired such taste, such style, I wanted to live up to that."

"She set standards for me that I responded to, as if I had been starving for them all my life. I don't mean that she pushed me. Money didn't mean anything to her; it never has; she has no money sense at all. She imparted to me a yearning for style in living, good taste, class. I drove myself in every way to meet those standards.

"Through some publicity I was doing for the Sons of Israel, I met the chairman of a chain of retail stores, and I took the job of managing the chain. It was grubby work; the whole scene was grubby; but it was more money and I stayed with it.

"I went on writing. For me, then and now, an individual sitting down alone in front of his work is *it*. When I take on a task of writing, I'm imbued with a sense of myself, of my strength. When I want to feel really good about myself, I sit down to write. Writing is the only task I don't *have* to do, the only task I freely *choose* to do, the most liberating work of all.

"But there was always the practical push too. Because now Judy and I had two children; we were a family, that was a tremendous joy and a tremendous pressure. She created a solid home for us. That was very attractive to me, the solidity of her family feeling. I met her at a vacation place in the Poconos. I remember my first view of her as she entered the dining room—she was so clean, so elegant. The first time I called her on the telephone when we got back to the city, she answered the phone from her bedroom, and she told me that her two sisters were lounging on the bed with her. I could hear them giggling and teasing in the background, I could sense the warmth between them. I loved that about her, the way she was with her mother and father too. Her father's dead. But she and her three sisters and her mother are still like that." He clasps his hands together, interlocking his fingers. "Her mother's nearly ninety. Still spry. Wonderful woman.

"Judy had an iron-bound family rule: No matter what else was going on, I had to be home for dinner with her and the children. That was *it*, and no matter what was going on, I made it home for dinner. It became equally important to me to get home to her and our two sons. But it created a pressure too. All my life I've had a recurring anxiety dream. I'm trying to get out a paper, it's like the old days rushing to get out the *Jewish Examiner* single-handed. I'm all alone, I can't get it done, I'm failing—and I wake up—it's an awful dream.

"Judy wasn't a homebody in spite of the dinner stricture. She wanted to go back to work and of course I permitted her to do that soon after our second child was born, but her family always came first with her. I felt I owed her and my sons a certain style of life. I had the opportunity to buy into the retail chain. It was a good deal. I had been managing stores for four years, but I wanted out. That wasn't the life I wanted, and that wasn't the life Judy wanted. I began looking around. There's a lot of humiliation in putting yourself on the market. I remember how I was kept waiting in an executive's outer office for twenty minutes; once I was kept sitting right in the office of an executive while he went on with his work; it was an endurance test—let's see how much subordination I can submit this man to. I remember how coldly I was eyed by another boss type because I was coming on too strong. That cold evaluative look is killing. Having been the head of my own business for twenty years has satisfied a lot of hungers I carried around for a long time; my achievement has laid to rest a lot of past humiliation. Now I try never to humiliate others, as I was.

"I resisted the retail store possibility; I landed a job in a big corporation—in the advertising department—and later I joined an agency with that one account as my big asset. After a while the agency announced it was relocating outside New York. Judy and I talked over what it would mean to move out of town. We didn't want to leave New York. My account wanted me to go on doing their campaigns and they suggested that I open my own agency. It was 1956, nobody was starting agencies then. I didn't have any money saved; raising a family took every penny I was earning. I thought, 'I'll never make it.' Judy said, 'Do it.' The corporation whose advertising I handled offered a loan of $45,000 toward my new business; I borrowed $5,000 from a friend, and I was in business. Within two years, I paid every cent back at six percent interest. Judy's attitude, and the fact that my account valued me so much, meant the most to me—that they saw me as an asset, worth a $45,000 investment. I've done well.

"My sons kid me about being corrupt. They're socially aware, as I would want them to be. I've always been concerned about the state of the world. I believe in a humanist socialism, a democratic socialism—a worldwide just society. I try to contribute whatever talent I have to alleviate suffering, hunger, inequalities. After eleven years of being in business when I landed one of the biggest accounts in the business, a cigarette account, I thought, 'My sons are going to be disgusted with me! Selling cancer.' But they didn't react that way. They saw the development in the light of my life, my career. The oldest one actually said, 'I'm proud of you, Dad, that's a real acknowledgment of your talent,' and the other joked, 'Listen, Dad, you're corrupt anyway. Congratulations on your total downfall.'

"I don't think the businessman is exalted in our society. The business community and businessmen are courted for their money, their power is in their money, but if the establishment could get their hands on the money without taking the businessman's opinion into account, they'd do so. And within the business community advertising is on the lowest rung, not exalted in any way. That's always bothered me. Deep down. Perhaps I somewhat agree with that evaluation.

"What pleases me is when I'm sought after, not as a businessman but as myself. When a government agency comes to me and asks me what I think, that pleases me. I've branched out beyond the narrow sights of the advertising business. The things I love to do serve a much wider community than the business community—serve more than profits. When the White House asks me to become an active member of an international board dealing with starvation and nutrition in Third World countries, that pleases me—nothing is more stimulating to me than to work on problems of media approaches to population growth, planned parenthood, birth control, nutrition, health. I fly all over the world setting up media programs to educate, to inform, to change centuries-old harmful patterns. I've worked in India, South America, Africa studying the problems first-hand, then I come home to work out the media solutions, sometimes I return to the Third World country to put the plans into practice. I spend approximately half my time on these projects, while continuing to run my business.

"One of my unfinished dreams is to get that paper out.

I'd like to start my own publication. I tried to buy a national weekly that was up for sale; my oldest son would have edited it. That deal fell through, but I haven't given up on that dream. I'll get to it yet. I could start an entirely new project tomorrow with the same energy I brought to starting a new business twenty years ago."

Judy Rudnick
COMPROMISING,
BUT STARTING ANYWAY

To some extent men like Jack Jasper and Mark Rudnick are successful because of exceptional ability; to some extent luck plays a part in their good fortune (for example, both were exempted from conscription into the armed forces during World War II; and they were operating at a time when the economy was spawning millionaire entrepreneurs like cabbages in a garden); but their success derives as well from another factor. These men draw on all the world for a support system. Their aims took them down a path which went in the right direction; they were doing the right thing, succeeding within the mainstream goals set by the society; and even for the strength they drain from one of their most vital support systems, the long, happy marriages they sustained from their youth, they were allowed to function comfortably within a patriarchal framework that society applauded. From our present vantage point, we are shocked to read that one "did not permit" his wife to work, that the other graciously did "permit" her to do so. To throw a small

side-light on the inner workings of such outwardly serene
relationships, I sought out Judy Rudnick for an interview.
What was it like to be the wife of Mark Rudnick for thirty-
seven years?

Judy Rudnick is older than Mark by some years, but she
too is remarkably youthful for a woman in her middle sixties. She's a stunner, naturally stylish, showing off her expensive clothes to great advantage on a splendid figure. She
moves with ease on tall heels; her hair is fashionably cut
and tinted to just the right muted, blond color to make it
appear natural, and her makeup is appropriately quiet and
effective. She has wonderful multi-tinted eyes fringed with
lush, black, curly lashes. She strides into the art nouveau
lobby of her apartment house as the doorman is letting me
in. She's wearing pants, a tweed jacket, a silk shirt, all in
shades of beige; multiple, long strands of pearls; and a silk
scarf of brighter, warmer colors. She carries a brown
leather underarm portfolio and beige gloves. She has just
arrived by taxi from her office. Her smile is vivid, charming. We settle down in oversized white leather armchairs in
the living room of the penthouse duplex apartment where
she and Mark now live alone. A maid serves us coffee. The
views beyond the window are New York at its sensational
loveliest—bridges and buildings lit by a late afternoon,
hazed glow. The terraces beyond the windows are filled
with greenery. The room is both severe and lush in its tones
of stark white leather and creamy rugs; from the foyer beyond, lined with multi-mirrored blue glass, the light is dif-
fused by the reflected blue of the mirrors. A handsome
staircase mounts to the bedroom above. In the other direction, I can see into the dining room where a carefully arranged silk scarf appears as if carelessly thrown on the table
and pinned by a Chinese vase.

"I've always been living three lives," Judy begins. "First,
I am the wife of Mark Rudnick. Then I am the mother of
my children. Then I'm a worker. When the children were
little, that was the order. Now that they're grown and on

their own, work has moved into second place. Being the wife of Mark Rudnick has always come first with me. Perhaps if we were marrying today, I might have done things differently—then, there didn't seem to be any other way.

"I would have been very unhappy without my work. After my second baby was born (they were very close in age, eleven months apart), I ran into a friend in the neighborhood park. I had the infant in the carriage and the older infant on a chair attached to the front. I was pushing that load and my friend greeted me with 'Gosh, Judy, you look terrible. Are you sick?' I wasn't sick but I knew then I couldn't go on being a full-time mother. It wasn't for me; it would have *made* me sick. I had my children late, in my thirties, I had been working since I got out of college ten years earlier. I was miserable when I stopped working. The children were terribly important to me, and the pressure of society in the late forties and fifties was to be a homebody, but I couldn't do it. Yes, Mark was very supportive. He didn't try to block me in my needs at all. But there was an unspoken understanding that he and the children would come first—and they did. It was I who had the strong family feeling as well; and he was very supportive there too. He did come home for dinner, if not absolutely every night, practically every night.

"My life has hardly been one of suffering. It would be a lie to say I suffered from oppressive, male domination. What is true is that I have always allowed family interests to disrupt the pattern of my own interests. Even today I disrupt my work to go to Fire Island, to go to the Alps, because that's where Mark wants to be in the summer and for the three months in winter. His work goes on from these points—but mine is interrupted."

She holds an important post in an American-based organization aiding in the development of a Third World Asian country. She has been with the organization for many years and the organization accommodates its needs to her priorities in order to keep her valuable services. Her work is creative and varied, and has included such tasks as recruiting advanced personnel to man the growing industries and educational facilities of the Asian country, to setting up international academic conferences to explore questions of special needs and problems. She earns a good salary, but money has never been an objective with her. She does her work for the sake of the work, and for the sake of herself.

"The first time my work necessitated my going abroad for a long stay, that is two or three weeks, there was something of a struggle between us. Mark didn't like my going, but I went anyway. He pointed out that he never went for long periods, and he doesn't—a week or two at a time to India or South America is the most he'll be away. I pointed out that he didn't *need* me. But it seemed to be purely a question of my absence. He simply didn't want me gone. But I went."

Some of Judy's work deals directly with women, fundraising for women candidates, for example, pressing for upgrading of women in all areas. Had she experienced discrimination as a woman in her own work?

"I was always used as the charmer. When our organization had to deal with difficult representatives from other countries, or if there was a tight situation, I was always told, 'You go in and charm them.' I resented that, the emphasis on my good looks and on my manner and on my great legs. Imagine saying that about a man, 'Let's hire him. He has such great legs.' Once in a while, the fact that I was a woman would get shoved right in my face. There was an official occasion abroad once. We were waiting to enter the dining hall to open a state banquet. I was the only woman present. The minister of defense popped a button on his shirt, and he turned to me and asked me to sew it back on. The look on my face must have been so outraged that he quickly corrected himself, but that was his first response to the popped button.

"If I were twenty-five now I'd plan my career differently.

And my life. There has to be more give and take than we women demanded then—the woman's way has to become more of a two-way street. It's true that we both worked at the relationship, Mark and I, it's an immensely important relationship to both of us, neither of us ever wanted out of it. We love one another. We had our difficulties—there were differences between us on the question of authority in raising the children—but nothing we couldn't work out. But if I had it to do over again, I would value my own talents more. I would aim for real built-in professionalism, put my work on the same level as my concern for my family. I don't think it could have been done thirty years ago, but I think it's possible today. I approached the problem from a point of view that was prevalent then. A woman was always available to her husband and her children's needs. The woman worked to make it work—the marriage, the family, and if she insisted on it, her career too. I still would strive to make it all work together, but the basic premise would be different. It would be interesting to have a go at it, under the new rules of the game. What if women categorically refused to learn how to cook, to sew, to type—insisted on becoming solidly educated, or solidly entrenched in their careers?

"I think the most distasteful thing of all for me during the short time I stayed home as a housewife was asking my husband for money. But you know, I still have to ask for money—though I keep my own salary. Mark is the most generous of men, yet I've never felt good about our money situation. The attitude always seemed to me to be: 'Here it is, but you don't deserve it.' Everybody now claims a new heightened consciousness—men and women; but of course, the heightened awareness comes more easily and naturally to the women. It's our *lives*, after all. The men lag behind. One can't level yet all the way with men in terms of our new awareness. But I'd like to try. What would we have to lose, Mark and I, at our age? It would be interesting to start again as a couple on a new basis."

BOOK FIVE

Starting Late

Grandma Moses
FARMWIFE
INTO LEGEND

Of all forms of starting, starting late is probably the most fulfilling and liberating. It comes for most of those who do accomplish their aims as the icing on the cake—the dessert they have been longing for all their lives. Starting late is a risk, like all starting, but the older one becomes, the more one recognizes that all life is a risk. Why not throw it all on a chance to win? What *is* there left to lose after all? Most of us go through life with a minimum of individual courage, following the curve of what is expected, accepting a pre-packaged form to our lives; copying, like an example in a book, the personas of those who have met society's standards, while we by-pass the person we should like to become. Those who break out of this mold, in the late years of their lives, are a special breed.

Grandma Moses is probably the most famous late starter in our history. For those who moan about what they've put off doing, her story has been the great American consoling myth to persuade them that it's never too late to start. It can't fail to appeal—a startling flight, from nonentity to world-famous painter, accomplished by a quaint little farm woman well over the age of seventy, as real as the soil from which she sprang.

In the years of her fame, Grandma Moses put together a painstaking and touchingly inadequate autobiography at the request of the agents handling her paintings.

In it, she tells of being born Anna Mary Robertson in 1860 of Scots-Irish descent. She was poor, one of ten children. At age twelve, she left the farm "to earn my own living as then was called a hired girl."

Life was hard, but she was not the girl to whine about it. She remembers when she was quite small that her father would buy white paper by the sheet, "it was used in those days for newspapers. He liked to see us draw pictures, it was a pennie a sheet and it lasted longer than candy. I would draw the picture, then color it with grape juice or berries any thing that was red and pretty to my way of thinking. Once I was given some carpenters red and blue chalk. Then I was rich. Then came the days when I dabbled in oil paint and made my lamb scapes my Brothers said I called them, they had some brilliant sun sets, and Father would say 'Oh not so bad.' But mother was more practical, thought that I could spend my time other ways." She put painting aside for many years.

She was married at age twenty-seven to a farm worker, Thomas S. Moses, and the couple settled on a farm in Virginia, with the hope of prospering there. They had ten children, but "left five little graves in that beautiful Shenandoah Valley." A hard-working farmer's wife busy with the expected tasks of birthing, mothering, cooking, chores, baking, berrying, preserving, she had no leisure in which to nag herself about "fulfillment," and in any case she took pleasure in carpet weaving, quilting, and embroidering during the winters when the farm chores were lighter, and with her Robertson inventiveness, she earned some dollars making butter "in pound prints," shipping the product all the way "to the white Sulphur Springs, W. Va.," as well as producing potato chips, "which was a novelty in those days . . ." She was an enterprising woman.

In 1905 the couple picked up, and with their five remaining children, moved back home to New York State to continue dairy farming because they believed New York a better place to educate their children and put them "on their own footing." Tom Moses died in 1927. Grandma Moses remained on the farm. Her youngest son took over the running of it. She was then sixty-seven.

Time to pack it all in? Contemporary society would say so. *The New York Times* of January 1977 ran an interesting little story that illuminates our attitude to aging.

Testifying at the trial of a damage suit she brought in Jacksonville, Florida, Ann Sothern, who used to play wisecracking blondes in the movies, broke into tears when a defense lawyer suggested she was too old to work regularly. Miss Sothern, walking with a cane and complaining she was forty pounds overweight, is suing a dinner theater where, she maintained, she was injured by a falling pole during a performance in 1973. She became tearful when she was asked, "Don't you feel that when a person reaches the age of 67, you should not expect to work as often as you did when you were younger?" After she regained her composure, Miss Sothern replied: "Acting is my life. I love it. I've been acting since I was 15."

Working, keeping busy was Mary Robertson Moses's life. Bringing in a little extra cash was always a useful thing to do. Giving pleasure was a joy. She did so with whatever came to hand—making cookies, jams, rugs, yarn pictures, quilts, dolls, and finally, when arthritis made it too painful to pursue fine handwork, with the oil paintings she had begun to do, just for the fun. The "dabbling in oil" she refers to in her autobiography evokes an artist's palette, tubes of paint, studio light. Nothing of the sort. House paint, a single lightbulb, her work table "an old-fashioned contraption with panels on four sides" decorated all over with landscapes painted when Grandma Moses was approximately fifty-five, to pretty up the table.

For her first painting she found some exterior paint and an old piece of canvas which had been used for mending a threshing machine cover, and along with her yarn pictures, her jam, and her "cand fruits," it was shown at "the Woman's Exchange in Thomas' Drug Store in Hoosick Falls." It was there that Louis Caldor, an art collector and engineer, summering in the area in 1939, first saw Grandma Moses' paintings. He bought what was in the store, inquired where the artist lived, went out to the farm-house and bought fifteen others. Three were included in an exhibit, "Unknown American Painters," held at the Museum of Modern Art. The career of Grandma Moses was launched, and would extend from the tiny village drug store to the walls of the Metropolitan Museum of Art, in time.

In October 1940, Grandma Moses was given a one-man show at the Galerie St. Etienne in New York. It was a moment highly receptive to her unique appeal. The long wearying ordeal of the Great Depression was ending in a general binding up of wounds and an atmosphere of celebration of solid American virtues. The great waves of immigration had also been halted long enough before, so that masses of newly assimilated foreign born and first-generation Americans, well over the trauma of displacement, were ready for a love affair with traditional America. What could be more authentically American than a dainty, white-haired, eighty-year-old Hoosick Falls farm woman turned artist? She personified for a newly art-conscious rising middle-class an apotheosis of the ideal of the common man—all the better because in this case she was the little woman. Nothing about herself or her work was beyond the reach of ordinary men and women; all were eminently accessible—content, style, voice, and even price. Her canvases aroused a patriotism eager to proclaim itself in a popular-front spirit of democratic defense against a menacing fascism, particularly since it came clothed in such attractive freshness—a simple, joyous appeal to a recently hard-pressed people, eager for a family party.

What shone through her canvases, luminous as the white undercoat with which she underlay her vibrant landscapes, was a victory snatched from the hardships of rural American experience—one others could identify with in their quite different struggle. The modest country scene, seemingly aiming for nothing beyond a true and pleasing picture of itself, became for others a peaceable kingdom with which to connect. Louis Bromfield called this quality of Grandma Moses "a sense of space, and 'of the whole' . . . a satisfactory relationship with the universe." Her "primitivism" appealed as well to the ultra sophisticated: the composer Cole Porter was one of her earliest fans.

The show was overwhelmingly successful. By 1943, there was a large demand for the paintings of Grandma Moses. Though she was highly praised, the little woman was also patronized. Otto Kallir did a book on her in 1945. "Five years before nobody in the art world had ever heard her name," he wrote, "and eight years ago she herself was not aware of possessing an artistic gift." One must assume he means by that either a commercial artistic gift or a self-conscious one. There is a profound misunderstanding at work here. Grandma Moses did not draw an exclusive line between work in life and work in art in the manner of formalist artists or critics. For Grandma Moses, make-believe, legends, postcards, illustrations, jams, canned fruit, yarn pictures, paintings, work, babies, death, joy in being, in family, in horses, turkeys, in the glitter of snow were all part of the wonderful mix of a continuous fable of life in which the surface was more light than dark—serene, busy, joyous, enchanting as a child's vision.

She was entirely self-taught, never having even "seen a real painter at work. I mean one that has taken lessons." She was reported as being at a loss to describe the techniques by which she achieved her luminous canvases. She began to paint by copying what she had at hand—pictures on Christmas and greeting cards, nineteenth-century color reproductions in the few books she had access to, illustrations and advertisements in magazines, and the Currier and Ives prints which most influenced her; but in a short time she moved on to original subjects—scenes from her childhood, the paintings which describe farm life in idyllic tableau: apple picking, maple sugaring, arriving at grand-mother's for Thanksgiving, bringing in the Christmas tree from the woods, town landscapes before modern industrial-ization muddied the scene, and special moments hauled up from the shallow well of legends carefully hoarded as her unique inheritance. In these memorializations it was her natural gift to seize upon a homely detail with poetic in-stinct. The sensibility expressed is clearly that of an imagi-native artist.

Her daughter-in-law reported that Grandma painted in an upstairs bedroom of the farmhouse: "A large room with two windows . . . sitting in a straight chair, maybe on a couple of books, one a catalogue of Sears or Montgomery Ward, where she orders her brushes and tubes of paint, the other a very ancient Latin Bible, which was formerly used as door-stop around the house. . . . Grandma has her pic-ture she is painting, on an old mixing board covered with newspaper, and this is on an old pine table. That way she doesn't get any paint on her table. . . . Over the table is a wall light with a 150-watt bulb which enables Grandma to paint at all times of the day and on the darkest of days in the winter. . . . She often plans a picture while resting or when she can't sleep . . . or ill in bed and very discon-tented to stay there . . ."

She was eighty-five at that time. A photograph shows her—seated at her work table—to be a pretty, well-groomed, sharp-featured bird of a woman dressed in a white lace blouse. The hand holding an open catalogue is gnarled and twisted with the enlarged, knobby knuckles of an arthritic.

She could not have imagined being anything but useful and pleasing. When people who had seen reproductions of her work wrote to request another picture just like the one they had admired, it didn't occur to her to refuse, and she accepted a commission of this kind, just as she would have accepted an order for more jam or canned fruit or another yarn picture. She called these requests "those dreadful orders" and would make the burdensome work palatable by varying the position of the house, or the season of the year, or some detail of the scene. "The Old Oaken Bucket" was so popular, particularly after it won a $250 first prize at the Syracuse Museum of Fine Arts, that she became quite overwhelmed by requests for copies. It was widely reported that she painted belt-line fashion to fulfill these orders, though she denied working on many paintings at once.

The New York City department store Gimbels sponsored her second one-man show and brought Grandma Moses down to New York for it. It was held in a huge hall which overwhelmed the modestly small paintings and where a tremendous crowd, mainly women, overwhelmed the tiny woman, as well. Grandma, led to a microphone to make a speech about art, seemed to become disoriented, looking about wonderingly at her alien audience. There was a long, uncomfortable pause and then she told the well-dressed audience of women how she made her preserves, and how good they were, and she produced a few small jars out of her handbag and offered them as samples.

She said afterward that she never wanted to go to New York again. She didn't want to talk about her paintings to all those strangers. ". . . it was shake hands, shake, shake, shake, and I wouldn't even know the people now . . ."

If she could not articulate an expressive esthetic of painting, nevertheless she knew what she was about. She kept meticulously true to the scenes of the beautiful valleys where she had lived out her hard-working life, the Shenandoah, and the charmingly varied landscape of towns, valley, mountains, and falling streams of the New York-Vermont border country. The new paintings she produced in her last years re-stated the old simplicities in the luminous colors she loved. She used glitter on her winter landscapes. To some artistic adviser who tried to dissuade her from this practice she stubbornly insisted that they could not have properly looked at the country landscape on a sunny winter's day. "To me there is no winter landscape without the sparkle on the snow!" She went on painting into her nineties, incredibly with more assurance and artistic discretion. The Oriental delicacy of composition once noted by the late writer and art collector, Louis Bromfield, is most striking in these last works. When asked, she offered her recipe for doing art with the same straightforwardness she would have responded to a request for a recipe for preserving raspberries.

"Some one has asked how I paint and what on. Well I like masonite tempered presd wood, the harder the better. I prefer it to canvas, as it will last longer. I go over this with linseed oil, then with three coats of flat white paint, now I saw it to fit the Frames . . ."

She died in 1960 at the age of one hundred, having produced more than a thousand paintings of fair size and perhaps half as many postcard size. She was world-famous. The little old farm woman from Hoosick Falls, who ended her autobiography with the words "Now this is to give you an idea of who and what I am . . ." had certainly fulfilled her intent.

Mother Jones
STARTING TO FIGHT
AT FIFTY

In the past, notable women were often dubbed Grandma or Mother. When my first novel was published, I was over fifty. An otherwise professional and intelligent review in a Boston newspaper was given the cutesy headline "Mama Yglesias Has Her Say." The headline certainly had no relevance to either the review of the book or the book itself, other than a reference to the fact, stated by the reviewer, that Jose, our son Rafael, and I, had each published novels within some weeks of one another. Motherhood is proclaimed traditionally sacred in our society; in practice it's more often treated as a joke. There is surely no other way to read that headline than as a put-down. The Grandma, Mother, Mama appellations tacked onto the names of a number of notable women are a curious mannerism—perhaps a way of expressing discomfort with the idea of women becoming notable at all. Calling a woman Mama, Mother, or Grandma is an insistence on rooting women firmly to their biological destiny, as if to tie down the flighty creatures, keep them moored to the basic functions of birthing and mothering. I must have learned my own distaste for such nicknames from my mother. She was an immigrant woman who never dreamed of a career beyond mother-hood, but nothing infuriated her so much as being famil-iarly addressed as "Mother" by strangers. Men are seldom called Papa or Grandpa—certainly not notable men. At a time when most people died young, Franz Joseph Haydn lived into his late seventies and wrote two great oratorios at what was then considered a very old age—*The Creation* when he was sixty-six and *The Seasons* when he was sev-enty. Every child who ever took a music appreciation course knows that he was called Papa Haydn, but he seems to be a rare instance of cutting a male genius down to homey size.

Mary Harris Jones, an extraordinary late starter, lost her husband and four children in a yellow fever epidemic when she was thirty-seven. Though she never married again nor bore any other children, when she became one of the most colorful and persuasive labor organizers of her time, she was inevitably dubbed "Mother." A woman who went in for her sort of life in her day and at her age (she was then in her fifties), was considered a brash, exotic creature; if she was an old woman (any woman past twenty-five or thirty is old by decorative standards) her aggression was that much more difficult for a hostile environment to absorb and praise. But such women can't be ignored, if only because their style is so provocative. Since they won't go away or shut up, a gloss is put on their bizarre actions with the folksy glow of "Grandma" or "Mother"—a kind of coun-try-music touch to make the unacceptable more palatable.

It cannot be said that her nickname disturbed Mother Jones. She was a thoroughly liberated woman who exposed herself to great danger, even if she did outrage the suffrag-ists by her attitude toward winning votes for women—one that previewed differences that surface today in the women's liberation and equal rights movements. She was something of a working-class snob, eager to deflate and upstage middle-class women, but she was also a radical who genuinely believed that society needed more shaking up than granting women the vote would provide, and finally, her radicalism was heavily weighted with conservative concepts of the family and child-rearing. She scorned the illusion "that Kingdom Come would follow the enfranchisement of women," and she was bitter on the subject of careers for women, "especially a 'Career' in factory and mill where most working women have their 'careers.' A great responsibility rests upon woman—the training of the children. This is her most beautiful task." So it would appear that she took no insult in being called Mother Jones; indeed she may have invented the title herself, but if so, it was for a showman's reasons. At one point in her career, to discredit her, she was accused of running a whorehouse in her youth. Perhaps "Mother" seemed a good PR counter image.

Like Grandma Moses, she too wrote an autobiography.

Mary Harris claimed to be born on the first of May, in 1830, in Cork, Ireland. If true, she would have been over a hundred when she died. A considerable controversy has arisen over what is true and what invented in her autobiography, beginning with the very date of her birth and the number of children she bore. There are so many conflicting versions of the hard facts of her early life, and so many demonstrable inaccuracies in the autobiography, that one must inevitably come to the admission that Mother Jones suffered from a bad memory or that she lied a bit. Far be it from a fellow liar to point a finger at her. If she was busily creating her own myth, it's a useful one, and there is more than enough documented proof of a woman of amazing guts, talent, and spirit to let the case rest for our purposes. Let the historians, for whom the exact facts are crucial, settle the matter.

For the purposes of a story about starting late, there is enough for a saga. Like Grandma Moses, Mother Jones also took pride in her heritage—in her case one of hard-work, poverty, and militancy, with a string of family members fighting and dying in the struggle for Irish independence. Her father emigrated to Canada when she was five, obtaining work on the building of the railroads. He considered himself a citizen of the United States first and last—obtained his citizenship, and raised his children as Americans. Mary Harris attended common school and normal school in Canada and she also became proficient in dressmaking. Her first job was teaching in a convent in Monroe, Michigan. "Later, I came to Chicago and opened a dressmaking establishment. I preferred sewing to bossing little children." She doesn't explain why she returned to teaching, but she did in Memphis, Tennessee, where she met a staunch member of the Iron Welder's Union, George Jones, whom she married in 1861.

In 1867 a yellow fever epidemic swept Memphis, killing her husband and four children. Yellow fever was an untreatable, devastating plague. Its symptoms were terrifying and more so because it was highly contagious: fever, chills, congestion of the eyes, gums and tongue, nausea, headaches, pain, followed by jaundice, hemorrhaging from various parts of the body and the vomiting up of black blood, the famous "black vomit" of the disease. During an epidemic of that period, eighty-five percent of the victims died.

In Memphis, Mother Jones tells us the victims were mainly ". . . among the poor and the workers. The rich . . . fled the city. Schools and churches were closed. People were not permitted to enter the house of a yellow fever victim without a permit. The poor could not afford nurses. Across the street from me, ten persons lay dead from the plague. The dead surrounded us. They were buried at night quickly and without ceremony. All about my house I could hear weeping and the cries of delirium. One by one, my four little children sickened and died. I washed their little bodies and got them ready for burial. My husband caught

the fever and died. I sat alone through nights of grief. No
one came to me. No one could. Other homes were as
stricken as mine. All day long, all night long, I heard the
grating of the wheels of the death cart. After the union had
buried my husband, I got a permit to nurse the sufferers.
This I did until the plague was stamped out."

When I was a youngster attending my weekly Saturday
matinee film-gorgings, there were many movies in which
one could predict, beginning with the first frame, that the
heroine or hero who appeared so young, so happy, so fit
and adorable in the early stages, would inevitably be ground
through a mill of suffering beyond the demands of even a
childish taste for pain, which is, as we know, excessive.
Alerted to the agonies certain to come, I savored the early
scenes of innocent and doomed happiness. Sometimes I
had to stay through the end and come round to the beginning again to reduce the pain of the grim finish. Such ex-
cesses descended on the heads of real people as tastelessly
as in any melodrama, it would seem. Mother Jones, at that
time the childless widow Jones, returned to Chicago and to
custom dressmaking; but in 1871, the great Chicago fire
burned up the establishment she was building with the help
of a partner, and everything was lost again.

"The fire made thousands homeless. We stayed all night
and the next day without food on the lake front . . . Old
St. Mary's church at Wabash Avenue was thrown open to
the refugees and there I camped until I could find a place
to go. Near by in an old, tumbled down, fire scorched building the Knights of Labor held meetings. I used to spend my
evenings . . . listening to splendid speakers. Sundays we
went out to the woods and held meetings. I became acquainted with the labor movement. Those were the days of
sacrifice for the cause of labor," she continues. "Those
were the days when we had no halls, when there were no
high salaried officers, no feasting with the enemies of labor.
Those were the days of the martyrs and the saints."

Hyperbole aside, she entered the labor movement at a

239

time of savage warfare between capital and labor, when the rise of the national unions triggered a massive response on the part of the owners of the factories, railroads, mines, and mills. It was a period too when thousands of American children, some beginning at age five and six, worked hours intolerably long for even adults to endure in dismal sweatshops and killing mines and factories.

Child labor seems a long-ago cause for social anguish, but one of the advantages of keeping in touch with the mature and the aged is that what seems like dead history comes alive in their vivid rememberings. By the time I was conscious of my family as members of an economic community, they had lifted themselves out of the harsh confines of the sweatshop and home labor, but I was born less than a decade since my father carried his sewing machine strapped to his back, from shop to shop, allowing it to drive him relentlessly in pursuit of food for his family—or that my mother with little children underfoot and another one on the way, rode her machine at home, working to save her children from such a fate. Their joint triumph was this minimal advancement—that they had managed to survive without sacrificing their children to the misery they had barely endured and put behind them.

The harshness of the times extended beyond brutal working conditions to the entire ambience of a worker's existence, whether it was endured in the new tenements of the great cities or the deadly company towns of the mill and mine owners. To have been born into such circumstances was to be marked forever, no matter how far the victim subsequently rose. I know that, for myself, to have been born under the terrorizing thunder of the Myrtle Avenue Elevated was to shape my sense of life as nightmare. I responded with a coward's tactical strategy—withdrawal, cunning, silence. I don't mean to complain of no warmth or love in my childhood—given the punishing physical circumstances of our living conditions, it was a miracle how much family love survived—but slum living creates an ambience that cannot support life at an acceptable human level.

My family made its way out to the comparative working-class luxury of Franklin Avenue by the time I was seven. Yet I remained burdened with childhood sensations which I did not understand as social fact, validated and corroborated, but experienced as fantasies of derangement and illness. I myself couldn't believe that what I remembered had actually happened, in part because Myrtle Avenue was recalled by my older brothers and sisters as infinitely better than the family's earlier environments. "Myrtle Avenue was high-class, compared to the Lower East Side. What are you talking about?"

I was talking about a state of saturation in the filth of the streets, of nauseating smells, and dark, cold, menacing stairways; the terrors of the toilet in the hall, and of rats, cockroaches, and the bedbugs my mother fought a weekly losing battle against; I was talking about being too cold in winter and too hot in summer; of fear of the "others" roaming the streets in gangs, those Christians who for mysterious reasons beyond my comprehension thought it advisable to hound me for killing Christ; fear of drunks, and of the crazy lady rag-picker endlessly searching the gutters' accumulation of garbage, and of the raucous surface life of the streets and the greater fear of its subterranean, masked life; fear, finally, of the very air, as heavy with antagonisms and despair as with the coal dust and gases that strangled my breathing as I ran across Myrtle Avenue toward the equally grave dangers of the schoolyard. Overhead the rushing train chopped up the light with the rhythmic blows of an axe and its noise echoed and magnified my straining heart beat, as if I were having a fit.

My older brothers and sisters were quite right, however. The conditions of my childhood were a substantial improvement over the sufferings of earlier immigrant families. (More shocking is the fact that in the very places we fled, the Lower East Side, Brooklyn, and the South Bronx, children still sink or swim as I did. During the disastrously cold winter of 1977 the TV displayed tenements in the city of New York occupied by paying tenants where heavy icicle formations cascaded from broken pipes and the water froze solid in the toilets because of no heat.)

Mother Jones was not one to talk of pieties or of pie in the sky by and by. She took as her motto, "Pray for the dead, and fight like hell for the living," began her battles among the railroad workers, and from there moved on to the anthracite miners of Pennsylvania, many of whom were also of Irish background, men and boys like her brothers and father, whose wives and daughters worked in the mills. She set into motion one of the most remarkable careers in labor history.

Like Grandma Moses, she too composes into a perfect portrait of a sedate American elderly woman dressed in her widow's weeds, the black bombazine outfit of the period, discreetly ruffed with white at the neck, topped by a satiny black jacket gathered at the waist and tied to her pocketbook, thus freeing her small, capable hands. On her curly white hair she wore a flat-top black bonnet, secured with a hat pin, and on her sharp, fine, aggressive nose the inevitable granny glasses. A small, spare person, charming, pretty, modest, and pleasing in her appearance. There is very little exterior hint of the amazing guts of the woman.

It was a time of open warfare between owners and workers. Employers maintained intricate spy systems among the workers. There were armed guards at the plants, and goons to beat up labor leaders; imprisonment by way of frame-up was not uncommon; blacklists were circulated through the industry, and workers often had to sign contracts that pledged them never to join a union. Where legal means failed industry, illegal ones were used, and labor used similar tactics. That an organizer could end up dead on this field of battle was not an exaggerated possibility.

Mother Jones came on the scene of these violent strikes bearing peculiarly feminine arms—an intuitive, passionate, and unshakable conviction that she belonged on the side of the workers; tenderness; a flamboyantly dramatic flair; and the crafty wit of the powerless. She was considered to be weak in ideology, but that she knew how to talk to workers even her enemies conceded, and the like of her dramatized demonstrations would not be seen again on the American scene until the anti-Vietnam war demonstrations of the 1960s and early 1970s.

Her audiences of workers were instantly receptive to her straight, vivid speech. She would open with a salutation that became her trademark. "Fellow workers, comrades, and stool pigeons." And she knew how to stage a knock-out demonstration. She tells of being sent into a company-owned town to inject spirit into a strike threatened with failure. She traveled alone, stayed alone at the company-owned hotel. After her first meeting with the strikers, she was ordered out of her room when she returned to her hotel. One of the miners took her into his house to spend the night, but the sheriff arrived in the morning not only to put *her* out but to evict the entire family from the company-owned shack. She knew that the strikers were at a low point, ready to admit defeat and to go back to work. She made one more effort. She instructed the family to gather up "all their earthly belongings, which weren't much," and to put them in a wagon, along with their holy pictures.

"The sight of that wagon with the sticks of furniture and the holy pictures and the children, with the father and mother and myself walking along through the streets, turned the tide. It made the men so angry that they decided not to go back that morning to the mines."

To combat scab labor, she organized dishpan brigades. "I told the men to stay home with the children for a change and let the women attend to the scabs." She didn't join in herself "for I knew they would arrest me and that might rout the army. I selected as leader an Irish woman who had a most picturesque appearance. She had slept late . . . she grabbed a red petticoat and slipped it over a thick cotton nightgown. She wore a black stocking and a white one. She had tied a little red fringed shawl over her wild red hair . . . I felt she could raise a rumpus."

She instructed her leader and the army to carry their tin dishpans and hammers, and to bang and howl and to scare the mules for further confusion. "From that day on the women kept continual watch to see that the company did not bring in scabs. Every day women and children with brooms or mops in one hand and babies in the other arm, wrapped in little blankets . . . watched that no one went in. And all night long they kept watch." That strike was won.

In 1903 she staged a spectacular non-violent protest in the cause of ten thousand striking child laborers from the textile mills of Pennsylvania. "Every day little children came into Union Headquarters, some with their hands off, some with the thumb missing, some with their fingers off at the knuckle. They were stooped little things, round shouldered and skinny. Many . . . were not over ten years of age."

She gathered a group of these maimed children, parading them through the streets of Philadelphia to the public square before the city hall, where she spoke: "Philadelphia's mansions were built on the broken bones, the quivering hearts and the drooping heads of these children." Displaying their mutilated hands, she called upon "the millionaire manufacturers to cease their moral murders . . ."

The scene was widely reported in the press. "Universities discussed it. Preachers began talking. That was what I wanted. Public attention on the subject of child labor."

When the issue seemed to be "quieting down," Mother Jones stirred it up again. She gathered another band of mill children and a few adults ("they were on strike and I thought they might as well have a little recreation") and marched them from the city of Philadelphia to Oyster Bay, New York, the summer home of Theodore Roosevelt. "I thought that President Roosevelt might see these mill children and compare them with his own little ones who were spending the summer on the seashore."

On the road, the children were happy, according to Mother Jones, "having plenty to eat, taking baths in the brooks and rivers every day. I thought when the strike is over and they go back to the mills, they will never have another holiday like this." They had good advance preparation. Along the line of march, farmers met the demonstrators with wagon loads of fruit and vegetables. There were donations of clothes and money. Inter-urban trainmen would "stop their trains and give us free rides." Some towns yielded sleeping quarters and meeting halls for the real business of the march. Not everything went smoothly, however. They were impeded by a bad heat wave, and lack of rain made the roads heavy with dust. "From time to time we had to send some of the children back to their homes. They were too weak to stand the march." On the outskirts of Trenton, New Jersey, they were met by the police, hoping to head them away from the city. "There were mills in the town and the mill owners didn't like our coming." Mother Jones invited the police to lunch. "They looked at the gathering of children with their tin plates and cups around the wash boiler, and said nothing at all about not going into the city." In another town the mayor forbade a meeting on the grounds that he didn't have sufficient police protection. "These little children have never known any sort of protection, your honor," Mother Jones said, "they are used to going without it." In Princeton, New Jersey, they slept in the "big cool barn on Grover Cleveland's great estate," and a meeting was held opposite the Princeton University campus.

"Here's a text book on economics," Mother Jones said in her speech, pointing to "little James Ashworth, who was ten years old . . . stooped over like an old man from carrying bundles of yarn that weighed seventy-five pounds. He gets three dollars a week and his sister who is fourteen gets six dollars. They work in a carpet factory ten hours a day while the children of the rich are getting their higher education."

In New York City, they marched up Fourth Avenue to Madison Square where they were forbidden to meet, and shunted off to Twentieth Street, Mother Jones spoke before an immense crowd. An animal show at Coney Island invited the children's army to attend, and at the close of the exhibition of trained animal performers, Mother Jones was permitted to address the audience. "There was a back drop to the tiny stage of the Roman Coliseum with the audience painted in and two Roman emperors down in front with their thumbs down . . . in front were the empty iron cages of the animals. I put my little children in the cages and they clung to the iron bars while I talked. I told the crowd that the scene was typical of the aristocracy of the employers with their thumbs down to the little ones of the mills and factories, and people sitting dumbly by."

President Theodore Roosevelt refused to receive the marchers. The strike was lost; the children returned to work under the same miserable conditions; but the march "had done its work. We had drawn the attention of the nation to the crime of child labor . . . not long afterward the Pennsylvania legislature passed a child labor law that sent thousands of children home from the mills, and kept thousands of others from entering the factory until they were fourteen years of age."

There is a forced happy ending in Mother Jones's account. De facto child labor laws fought a continuing battle for passage. As late as 1918 and 1922, congressional child labor laws were declared unconstitutional by the Supreme Court, and it wasn't until the early forties that child labor regulation in industry was made constitutional, by which time Mother Jones was dead. And children still work, as we all know, working the streets of the slums, for one thing, in an apprenticeship where acquisition of a fast buck, legal or illegal, commands special skills and techniques; and they work as migrant agricultural laborers under conditions as dismaying as in Mother Jones's day.

It has been said, critically, of Mother Jones that she "lacked a consistent philosophy," by which is meant perhaps that she turned up among anarchists, socialists, communists. She refused to stay neatly put in one political camp. Her loyalty was always to what she considered the right cause. She disapproved when the leadership of the United Mine Workers settled for limited gains among the anthracite workers, leaving the bituminous coal workers out of the agreement. She took the lead in organizing the poorest of the poor in what she called "medieval West Virginia. With its tent colonies on the bleak hills! With its grim men and women! When I get to the other side, I shall tell God Almighty about West Virginia!"

She went out to Colorado disguised as a peddler to develop information that led to a walkout, and when United Mine Worker President John Mitchell disavowed the strike, she broke with him, publicly condemned him, and quit her job with the union. She went on to work with the striking machinists of the Southern Pacific Railroad. She supported the Western Federation of Miners when they closed down the copper pits in Arizona. She involved herself in the case of Mexican revolutionaries imprisoned in this country, bringing it all the way to the White House to demand and to secure a congressional inquiry. She worked in the mills herself to gain first hand information about child labor.

When she was eighty-three years old and active among the miners of West Virginia, she was tried by a state militia military court on the charge of conspiring to commit murder. She was convicted and sentenced to prison for twenty years. "She was never awed by jails," Clarence Darrow said of her. "Over and over she was sentenced by courts; she never ran away. She stayed in prison until her enemies opened the doors. Her personal non-resistance was far more powerful than any appeal to force." Protests by organized labor and a newly elected governor of West Virginia helped free her.

At age eighty-five she was busy among the carmen's wives during the New York street car strike of 1915–16. She had those women "fighting like wildcats. They threatened me with jail and I told the police I could raise as much hell in jail as out. The police said if anyone was killed I should be held responsible and hanged. 'If they want to hang me, let them,' I said. 'And when I meet God Almighty I will tell Him to damn my accusers and the accusers of the working-class, the people who tend and develop and beautify His world.' "

In a miner's strike in Pennsylvania she instructed a group of women pickets who had been arrested to take their babies with them when their case came up in court. ". . . while the judge was sentencing them . . . the babies set up a terrible wail." She told the women to sing all the way to the jail house and the sympathetic crowd that gathered and followed were encouraged to join in the singing. She kept the women singing once in jail also, day and night, at the top of their voices, spelling one another, endless medleys of patriotic songs and lullabies; and after five days of their thirty-day sentences they were released, having worn out the sheriff, the sheriff's wife, the town, and the sentencing judge.

In her nineties she was still visiting the shacks of the company towns in West Virginia, doing whatever she could among the miners and their wives during the bitter days of continuing lost strikes.

She was in Colorado when warfare between miners and the Rockefeller interests erupted into one of the bloodiest incidents in our national life, the "Ludlow massacre," where a tent colony of striking miners and their families burst into flames caused, it was believed, by the machine-gun fire of the company militiamen; and she testified, in her customary, feisty manner, before a congressional committee investigating the violent deaths of men, women, and children that were the result. She poured out a barrage of indignant words for two days running, a remarkable feat for anyone her age.

And then she shocked the suffragists. A dinner had been

arranged at which she was to speak to some five hundred activist women. She told the outraged women, "You don't need a vote to raise hell! I have never had a vote and I have raised hell all over this country! . . . don't be ladylike," she taunted, viewing them as middle-class, proper females born into privilege. "God Almighty made women and the Rockefeller gang of thieves made the ladies . . . I have been up against armed mercenaries but this old woman, without a vote, and with nothing but a hatpin has scared them all."

Folk singer, John Farrance reported her armed with more than a hatpin. He tells of Mother Jones in Monongahela, organizing in the mines, riding down "Pike Street in a buggy and horse. Two company thugs grabbed the horse by the bridle and told her to turn around and get back down the road. She wore a gingham apron and she reached under it and pulled out a special .38 pistol and told them to turn her horse loose, and they sure did. She continued on to the park and spoke to a large crowd of miners. She wasn't afraid of the devil."

She celebrated her one hundredth birthday in 1930. (Even if she had lied about her birthdate, she was certainly pushing ninety.) It was said of her that she liked to drink, but she appeared before a "talking picture machine" at the celebration with all her wits about her, and scored a public relations coup against her old enemy John D. Rockefeller, who had cabled his congratulations. Mother Jones thanked him. Then with an admirable display of militant diplomacy called him "a damn good sport" while adding, "I've licked him many times." It was her last public appearance before she died that year.

PART II

Born-Again People

Artur Rubinstein
STARTING AS CONTINUING

Inevitably, at some point in my talks with people who had changed their lives, the speaker would use the phrase, "I felt born again." To start anew and especially late in life is indeed to experience something like a religious conversion—resurrection and new life—the emergence of a new self, born in hope. No matter how small the step (or how great, and dangerously risky) it loosened a euphoria, a happiness unconnected to material rewards or any outer show of success. Some life changes do result in phenomenal success, not only in the ideal of self-fulfillment (I am doing what I have always wanted to do, even if it's beachcombing) but in the hard cash of the material rewards of our times—millions of dollars and world fame. The newspapers and magazines are filled with such juicy success stories. They're delightful to share in. We all live in hope and store up proofs against pessimism. Even modest attempts and successes win our applause. We gobble up stories of mid-life career switches. These feed our daydreams of swinging free of our old selves and our worn-out circumstances. But the "new me" confronts old personality problems and the actualities of harsh new conditions. Starting over may become a tough climb against bruising obstacles—a scaling of a sheer wall with one's fingernails, as one of the women interviewed put it.

There is a commercial jingle that advertises a brand of breakfast cereal, and surprises with a piece of valuable advice: "Today is the first day of the rest of your life. Start it right . . ."

To begin again and to continue day after day demands a kind of electric courage—the spark of reaffirmation to get things going. Sometimes it means dragging upward out of unspeakable depths. Perhaps one needs to go way down for the impetus to go way up. Or to rise at all. (I'm reminded of the author who was asked how he began writing every day. "I get up in the morning and get dressed," he said.)

Artur Rubinstein, the concert pianist now in his nineties, is a quintessential example of a man of affirmation, yet he tells of coming very close to killing himself in his youth. Like most performing geniuses, Rubinstein had started his musical career as a child prodigy, so that he had been a performer for many years when, in his twenties, he was overcome with despair that his career wasn't moving forward rapidly enough—a despair compounded by some trouble he was having in his love life. At ninety, Rubinstein spoke of the intensity of his desperation then, of how he longed for death, sitting alone in his room, almost unable to move. He forced himself out of his isolation. He described the stunning joy of coming out of darkness into light, air, and the movement of others—and to the decision to live. That he remembers at ninety the physical properties of the day long ago is proof of the vitality of the decision, one which, in a sense, he, like all of us, must make daily. Still performing brilliantly eighty-three years after he began, unbelievably youthful in his responses, Rubinstein continues actively affirming himself, gliding past the infirmities of old age with disarming bounce.

"My love of life is very, very unconditional. . . . You know . . . that I am not able any more to read nor to write. I lost the center of my eyesight. I don't see what I look at. I can still live; I'm not blind because I see around everything. So I am still independent in a little way, not very much. So, I discovered suddenly a new beauty of life. When I was seeing, I was reading too much. Some books which I shouldn't have read because they were not intelligent enough, I lost my time on it. They prevented me from studying more music and playing more. I had never got time to hear beautiful, beautiful compositions because I couldn't go to concerts. I was traveling myself, playing myself. Now I have endless records. I spend all my money on records. I listen to . . . beautiful performances by my colleagues, by . . . violins, by pianos, by quintets. . . . I get angry, I discuss it with them, when they play badly. I mean, I discuss inside, of course. They are not here."

His love of life included a greed to obtain everything he could get—perfection in his chosen art, fame, money, beautiful women, love—but he was prepared to pay in kind, with the full bounty of his unusual gifts. He was born in 1886 in Poland to Jewish parents, and his career moved steadily onward from child prodigy to world-renowned performer. He performed in the United States for the first time in 1906, but it wasn't until the thirties when the impresario Sol Hurok launched Rubinstein anew that his astonishing technique, his love for his audiences, and his presence as a performer came together for American concertgoers to make him one of the most popular performers of the concert stage, bringing him the overwhelming success, and all the rewards he ever dreamed of.

He became a United States citizen in 1946. He maintains an apartment in Paris, and it was there that he was interviewed when he became ninety years old and told the story of how he had wanted to kill himself. He described "the springs of his happiness" as having erupted from that moment when he chose life. "I was born again, in a way. . . . Of course, I believe in God, but my God is not a man with a beard—it is a power, an extraordinary power." A power that he is naturally keyed to, and is thus able to communicate to others.

"There is a thing which goes out, emanates from me, from my emotion—not from me—from my emotion, from the feeling . . . call it 'soul,' if you like to. . . . I always had a sensual, not sensuous, but sensual feeling of my fingers when I had to strike something which goes out of my inner self. When I have to sing out the nocturne of Chopin, I sing it inside. But I sing it like a love song, you see. And then, under my fingers I feel it. . . . I feel a rather sensual pleasure, you know, in touching it. I become excited when I touch an E-flat that will give that sound I need to hear."

The very old astonish us as wonders of nature do, even when there is nothing else astonishing about them, but when they appear in the form of an Artur Rubinstein, we are filled with inexplicable joy. He pokes fun at his own appearance, entering upon the stage like a "fat little man . . . in an evening dress . . . looking like an undertaker". He is not a traditionally handsome man, though he composes marvelously into a diminutive figure, powerfully and cleanly delineated, austere, and softly brushed by the "soul" emanating from his music. He is the quintessential example of starting as continuing. He was always a fantastic showman, and his great age now adds an additional, indefinable fascination. It is quite simply thrilling to see the controlled play of emotion on the aged, lined face, marvelous to watch the machinery of his hands, still expert and powerful, moving across the keyboard. It is a response similar to the one we give to the sight of mountains, great trees, open sky, fields coasting down to the sea. The very skin that has been covering a human being for ninety years, in its lines and transparency, is a wonder to us.

If everyone aged like Artur Rubinstein, there'd be no old

age homes, but there are many old age homes and few Rubinsteins. The other side of our response to aging is first fear, then a bit of ridicule to exorcize the fear, and finally horror in facing an image we shall soon become.

However, just to applaud mere survival may be another crippling form of sentimentalizing the aged right out of their true existence.

My husband's mother, who became eighty this year, mocks such attitudes. She resolutely refused the false position of being prematurely celebrated as one of the marvelous, surviving old. She maintains standards of austere truthfulness and accuracy, learned from a life of hardship, work, and the triumphs of the just. She's a beautiful looking woman, and in spite of her entirely white hair, looks much younger than her years. The nurse in the doctor's office she frequents likes to show her off to others as a gerontological heroine. "Look at her," she urges the other patients. "Would you believe that she's eighty?" Mother assumes a patrician manner in correcting errors. "I'm still seventy-nine until next month. So there isn't anything marvelous about me."

Alberta Hunter
DISCOVERING THE SECRET
OF HAPPINESS
STARTING TO SING AGAIN
AT EIGHTY

There is certainly something marvelous about Alberta Hunter, above and beyond her eighty-two years of age. I went down to Greenwich Village to Barney Josephson's Cookery in order to hear her sing and to talk to her. The Cookery is a fine little restaurant on Eighth Street that Barney Josephson opened after he was forced to close his famous nightclubs, Café Society Uptown and Downtown. "You know about me being a blacklisted saloon keeper?" he asks me, referring to the days when Senator McCarthy and Red Channels made the rules about which performers were permitted to appear where. After some years of running the Cookery solely as a restaurant, Josephson gradually introduced some jazz performers; and slowly all the greats of the old days could be heard there once more. Now Alberta Hunter is booked in, returned to singing after spending twenty years working as a practical nurse at Goldwater Memorial Hospital on Roosevelt Island.

We are talking between breaks in her performance. When she sings, she commands the space around her; sitting across a small table from me, she's smaller. She has pulled her frizzy, black and gray hair into a tight top-knot. Full-face, she is a little, aging black woman; in profile she's a strong piece of Mayan sculpture; performing she's a knockout of energy, charm, wit, and jazz musicality. She's wearing a simple skirt and loose, dark blouse. When she sings she uses a mike, but she doesn't need to. The strength and evenness of her voice is astonishing, given her age— not a quaver in it.

The long history of her singing career, starting at age twelve, rattles forth from her prodigious memory, studded with the names of performers who accompanied her (Louis Armstrong, Freddie Keppard, Sidney Bechet, Fletcher Henderson, Eubie Blake). She had begun making up her own songs: "Downhearted Blues," a classic made famous by Bessie Smith, was one of the first. She came to New York in 1923, a seasoned performer. "I left Chicago on a Saturday and by Wednesday I was the replacement for Bessie Smith in the musical *How Come?* It was my first time on a stage, but I just walked out and had no fear. I got a standing ovation, with Sophie Tucker in the audience, leading the applause.

"Then I was in another Broadway show at the George M. Cohan. After that I went back to Chicago and worked at the Royal Garden and the Phoenix and the Sunset Café with Earl Hines. Then I went to Cincinnati. That's where I met a handsome waiter and married him. He had beautiful eyes, a handful of gimme, and a mouthful of much obliged. I took him home to my mamma. I had brought her up to Chicago to stay in my little apartment. I was embarrassed with the two of them in that little place, so I took a vacation and went off to Monte Carlo and found a job singing. I never got back together with my husband, and it made a man of him. He went to school, and became the head of the redcaps' union, and got on the executive board of the CIO. Only Negro on it—Willard Saxbe Town-send. I never entertained the idea of getting married again.

"I've sung all over the world. I sing in six languages, Danish, German, Italian, Yiddish, French, and English. When I was in England I lived in the same apartment house as Marian Anderson while she was over there straightening out her middle register. I was appearing in the English company of *Show Boat* at the Drury Lane. Paul Robeson was Joe and my old friend Mabel Mercer was in the chorus. All that stuff they spread around about Paul Robeson wasn't true. He was sweet and unassuming. They said he was a dangerous communist, when all Paul ever wanted was for them to treat the colored people right. But that's the way it goes. You don't take tea for the fever, it'll never cure it. But after my mother died I didn't want to sing anymore. I studied nursing and I became a practical nurse and I did that for twenty years. I didn't mind that work one bit. I like to be of service. I went over to Roosevelt to feed a patient I'm particularly fond of, just today before I came to work. How I got to be singing again is that Bobby Short had a party for Mabel Mercer. I've known Mabel nearly fifty years. Mr. Charles Bourgeois saw me at the party and asked me to sing something. So I did, but real soft, just for him. He told me he was going to call Mr. Barney Josephson because I should be out performing, but I didn't pay much attention. I hadn't performed in twenty years. Right away I got a call the next morning. I was so excited I almost dropped the phone. I never sang at the Café Society, but I knew who Mr. Barney Josephson was. He asked me was I interested in singing for him. I got right to work on my songs, and a few days later I came down here and auditioned and he said, 'I want you.'"

She looks at me with her calm, jolly eyes. The brown skin of her face is remarkably smooth; it's more wrinkled on her expressive hands with their curiously shaped long, slim fingers and deeply curved tips. She clasps my hands, excusing herself for having to get back to work. "I'm working for the finest man in the world, Mr. Barney Josephson, a wonderful man. I've never been happier in my life than I am now."

She does two shows a night, three on Saturday night. She's written a couple of new songs for her return to show-biz. She opens with one, a rousing number that puts the audience solidly in her hand. "Come on up some night, my castle's rockin'."

Her diction is precise, her singing is rich in depth, color, and her musical phrasing is always perfect. Her body movements are stylized yet free; and she keeps up an intercourse of witty intimacy with the audience. Every song tells a complete, unique story. One of her own compositions, "I Want a Two-Fisted, Double-Jointed, Rough-and-Ready Man," is a marvel of risqué song at which she excells in expressing innocence and wit. "I want a man who won't let his children play with neither dog nor cat, but will bring in a skunk or a lion and say, 'Here, kids, play with that.' " She bounces up and down to the beat, twinkles at the audience. Everybody is thoroughly enjoying themselves.

She knows how to pace her act. She does a heart-tearing love song in Yiddish, "I Love You Much Too Much," then a fast number, "The Whole World Smiles With You," with its funny lines, and then "That man of mine has a scheme/ That man of mine has a scheme/ It's amazing the way he handles my machine." She ends with a gospel song she's written, "You're Gonna Reap Just What You Sow," gesturing upward to a stern God of judgment with her long tapering fingers and fixing the audience with clear-eyed weighing of our collective sins. For her second show, she does a completely different group of songs.

She is a firm believer in God. "If it hadn't been for God, I couldn't have gotten where I did," she tells me when we talk again. Isn't the routine exhausting for her at her age? She is not only performing at a top pace, but she has been taken up by the media and has appeared on all the major morning talk shows and been interviewed by leading newspapers and magazines. "I was at the last Newport Jazz Festival and I heard somebody saying to somebody, 'Alberta Hunter? Is she still alive?' Well here I am born again, alive and singing, and so excited I can hardly sleep nights. I'm happier than I've ever been. I tell you, I'm *happy*, I'm *happy*," she repeats—with perfect phrasing.

PART III

The Icing on the Cake,
Finding the Life You Really
Want to Live

Helen and Scott Nearing

There are feminists who might argue that Mother Jones was lucky in the ghastly tragedy that wiped out her family—that Alberta Hunter was smart to have taken off for Monte Carlo, forgetting her marriage to her handsome young waiter. They would argue that women who devote themselves to love are wasting themselves.

Before she married Scott Fitzgerald, Zelda thought she wanted nothing more in life than the man she loved.

"There's nothing in all the world I want but you," she wrote him before they married. "I'd do anything—anything—to keep your heart for my own—I don't want to live—I want to love first, and live incidentally . . . if you should die—O Darling—darling Scott—It'd be like going blind. . . . I'd have no purpose in life—just a pretty decoration. Don't you think I was made for you? I feel like you had me ordered—and I was delivered to you—to be worn—I want you to wear me, like a watch-charm or a buttonhole bouquet—to the world. And then, when we're alone, I

want to help—to know that you can't do *anything* without
me . . ."

Scott and Zelda's love played itself out at a high cost in
individual despair and mutual destruction. The prize at
stake in these tumultuous wars between lovers is the self—
autonomy of the individual—harder in every way for a
woman to establish than for a man, though hard enough
for both. How to win autonomy when to win seems to lose
the whole show?

We have seen in women's life stories how love, marriage,
and children contend with the fierce struggle to define the
self. Do all human ills begin here then at the same fount—
man-woman romantic love, marriage, and the family? And
then is the only way out destruction of the whole machinery? Psychiatry contends that the person who commits
suicide has given up hope for love. This bathes love in a
different light, as a guide to hope, continuity, and fulfillment rather than the rampaging monster of the "battle of
the bedroom." A narrow community of love within the
widest community of love is perhaps everybody's ideal of
personal and social happiness. That such communities
don't exist much is no big secret. Despair is easily documented. One of the major causes of death in the United
States is suicide—about 26,000 a year is the official figure.
A truer estimate is considered to be 35,000, covering those
suicides not reported as such for reasons having to do with
insurance coverage or with social shame or religious scru-
ples. The World Health Organization estimates that
throughout the world about 1,000 persons a day kill themselves. That makes for a half a million individuals a year
who cannot bear to go on living. There are many more
who feel the same way. These figures stand only for those
who succeed in wiping themselves out. Perhaps ten times
as many try and fail.

When Virginia Woolf committed suicide she left the
message that she couldn't bear to suffer any more of the
bouts of the madness with which she was periodically af-

flicted, and that she equally couldn't bear to subject her husband, Leonard Woolf, to the accompanying agony of seeing her through. There is love demonstrated on her part; and her husband loved her for sure, even if he couldn't help her ultimately. There are despairs which no amount of love seems to have the power to penetrate. At least the poetry of such suicide poets as Sylvia Plath and Anne Sexton tell us so. Like Keats, they are half in love with easeful death. Simone Weil starved herself to death, even though she was seemingly driven by a loving passion to do good in the world. Leon Trotsky, disappointed in the development of her views, unsympathetically grumbled that Simone Weil's mission was "to defend her personality against society." Trotsky, no doubt, had Marxist solutions in mind, but the point he makes is crucial, nevertheless, whether or not it applies to Simone Weil. To defend one's unique self against society, yes; and always to defend the *others'* unique self as well; and to defend or to help create the society which makes room for each. Because if it's only the first that's sought, if *only* the self is gratified, then anything goes and not even a Messiah will help.

Love, fidelity, marriage, family, commitment—these are old-fashioned concepts, as hard to define as to defend in our times. The cultural idiom has advanced beyond them, or at least it says it has. Perhaps such concepts need no definition and no defense, but simply exist side by side with all the newer forms, and sometimes in as exciting, fresh, and natural states as the latest fashion. Many of the men and women we have been listening to were special in their intense drive to express a single self. But there are some for whom community is the great prize sought—personal community, societal community. They want to be born again in a situation where they are joined to others in communal effort. In a sense this is true of artists; it is certainly true of Mother Jones; it's true of people involved in great social experiments; and it's true of the hundreds of thousands who have fled urban centers for new living on the land. Mostly they come in couples.

It's in this spirit that communes sprang up in what open country remains of our original wilderness. Maine has become a mecca for such seekers, and much has been written about the young people who comprise these groups, dedicated to subsistence living. But many older people have been similarly searching for community and meaning. Retirees come to live in Maine, not at retirement communities (there are virtually none in Maine) but in search of a more private, less artificial, and more challenging environment than condominium living offers. Like other younger pilgrims, they may be very wealthy or moderately poor. What draws them to the exquisitely harsh landscapes of Maine's brave fingers of land, holding their own against a brilliant, sustaining, and damaging sea, is a yearning new settlers find difficult to express. The word used most often is "meaningful."

Even if retirees are rich enough to concentrate solely on play, they want their play to be "meaningful." If they swim, they pit their bodies against water almost too cold to endure on a shore where no white hot sand beckons for lazy hours of lying about getting tanned, but where vigorous tides in their fierce, daily work alternately yield and claim a teeming territory of rocky shore torn from the rising slopes of evergreens and aspens. Beyond them, magnificent forest stands of pine, birch, beech, oak, cedar, and larch reclaim the ground wherever farmlands have been abandoned. Where cleared fields still exist, the winds sweep across subtly colored surfaces of hay, clover, and a succeeding variety of wildflowers sloping toward the always changing waters of the bays that surround.

If retirees play at being sailors, these waters command skill and the wisdom to understand that harm may overtake good with alarming speed and little warning. If they play gentleman farmer, they must respect the rigorous seasons, the lack of sun, the sudden frosts, the short growing time, the stony ground, and endure black flies, slugs, and bugs of every kind bent on destroying the garden. If they stay through the winters they must endure intense cold, days of short light, nights of long darkness, loneliness and dullness which may become hard to bear. For those who love it there is unutterable joy in Maine's coastal combination of high pure skies, brilliant sea, and stubborn land. There is no explaining this passion to those who don't share it. Among those who do, there is communion—and among people who might otherwise find nothing else in common.

For those espousing subsistence living the patron saints are, of course, Helen and Scott Nearing. The Nearings are friends and neighbors. Their famous farm is on the other side of the peninsula on which we live, and we are not only indebted to them for the modestly successful kitchen garden and compost heaps that Jose copy-catted from Scott's techniques, though in the most casual and surface fashion, but for our much loved little house. (It was Scott and Helen who informed me, through mutual friends, that a house jointly owned by two writers, Mabel Louise Robinson and Helen Hull, had been willed to the Author's Guild and was up for sale. The low price made it possible for us to buy and to start the life we have been living in Maine for the last eight years.)

The Nearings are also prime practitioners of the art of starting again. Even now with Scott in his ninety-fifth year and Helen in her seventy-fifth, they're off on a new venture, moving on to a new stone house they built with their own hands and with the help of volunteers and some paid labor. At their age, such a venture is heroic; but for the Nearings heroic ventures are commonplace activities. Scott Nearing is certainly something of an American saint, and Helen is a gracious and practical disciple. Literally excluded from the mainstream of American society because of his iconoclastic views, Scott Nearing, at the age of fifty, almost a half century ago, accompanied by a twenty-year-younger companion, Helen, abandoned urban living for a Vermont farm, and initiated and perfected the art of contemporary subsistence living. When Vermont became too chic for Scott's fierce conscience, they sold out at no profit and began again in Maine, once again establishing a farm and a life which would serve as a model for thousands of others.

Quite apart from anything else about Scott Nearing at ninety-five, one applauds him as a physical object. Visitors make the pilgrimage to the Nearing farm in Maine looking for political or organic gardening guidance, but they pause in awe, much as they do to the still wilderness at Katahdin or the dramatic action of the sea against the rocks at Schoodic Point, before a similar mysterious power of nature in the sight of a short, bent, dour-faced man working his enchanted garden, and the vigorous, youthful woman at his side.

What kind of people and places are these, so far removed from contemporary concepts of success? From the old Nearing small clapboard house to the new one is a short climb. The Nearings pretty much left that house as they found it twenty years ago. They kept it in good repair, but went in for no improvements or extensions. Bordering it is a traditional New England garden, cultivated, but with the charming effect of a wildflower plot, and then a small patch of lawn where visitors would gather to listen to Scott's political talks when they were given from time to time. To one side is the barn that held the tools and implements of Scott and Helen's non-mechanized gardening. Beyond is the vegetable garden, surrounded by Helen and Scott's handmade stone wall, built to keep out animals and as a sanctuary against the early chilling winds of Maine's autumns. One enters by way of heavy, barred wooden doors. The yield is beautiful to see in orderly lush green rows, staked where necessary to branches and saplings, and wonderful to sample (green peas off the vine, or young green beans) as one wanders down the paths. The visual effects vary with the time of year—as effectively as the most artful scene changes—now decorated by flowering fruit trees or the much-prized florist's asparagus fern, the spiraling towers of the pole beans, the fence of delicately colored sweet-pea blossoms, the flowering and fruited strawberry plants, the fragrant herbs which border the narrow paths leading to the sun-warmed greenhouse. The earth beneath the healthy growth of vegetables is rich and dark; not a weed to be seen.

Outside the garden are the carefully numbered compost heaps, fortresses of decaying matter, each held in a kind of open log-cabin container made of criss-crossed saplings. The pond that Scott dug out by hand is complete with spillway and dam, also handbuilt, and across a wide expanse of cranberry bog is the site of their cash crop— bushes of amazingly large, vividly colored hybrid blueberries, existing in their separate Eden, an enclosure made safe from birds by a high canopy of Japanese fishnet and carpeted underfoot by a deep, firm mulch of hay. This is fenced in by wire and admission is through a number of rustic barred doors. (Characteristically, there is a small area left free for the birds to gorge on.) A secret garden, a garden of earthly delights—phrases that start up in one's head when entering the workmanlike, productive usefulness of these tracts.

At the far ends of the open fields, tall logs of drying timber are stacked in the shapes of tepees. There may be piles of onions drying in the open. Perhaps the Rugosa roses are in bloom, or past bloom, when the fat little apples of the hips shine red and glossy. They too are fenced in, to stop the rough disorderly pushiness of their claim to the whole territory.

Now we are on the path to the new stone house. A dip into the sweetness of a patch of trees, down the pine-needled slope to a level still high above Penobscot Bay. Scott doesn't join the little tour to the new house. He stays busy at something more productive. Helen leads the way, traveling at a walking pace hard for much younger people to keep up with on this uneven ground she knows so well. She moves like a dancer—her head balanced on a straight back, her feet placed flat and firm with assured, muscular grace. None of her actions are taken with deliberate, self-conscious show. She is usually dressed in baggy wool pants, if it's cold, or droopy shorts if it's warm, with a sweater or shirt completing the costume. Helen can also be stylish. Run into Helen at a Kneisel Hall chamber music concert in Blue Hill, and she will be colorfully dressed and very likely topped by one of the subtly colored mohair ponchos she knits with great rapidity and a minimum of attention whenever she finds herself sitting down for more than five minutes. That may be when she's visiting or entertaining visitors, listening to Scott address an audience, or waiting her turn to speak at their joint lectures.

The Nearings don't entertain in the usual manner. Forest Farm held a regular three to five in the afternoon open house while Helen and Scott went about their work, and put their visitors to work as well.

During one of the hottest July Fourths on record, Jose and I arrived at the Nearing farm with some friends. One was Louis Schwartz, Benjamin Franklin Professor of Law at the University of Pennsylvania—a vigorous man in his sixties. Jose and Louis were promptly put to work gathering brush and wheelbarrowing it over rough ground to an indicated compost heap where they pitch-forked it to the height of the pile. Louis's wife and I were each presented with a can dangling from a leather thong to place around our necks and fill with blueberries. That's routine procedure at Forest Farm. Scott and Helen were both working, though Scott and the temperature had gone past ninety. We all quit long before the Nearings did. On a return visit, Louis Schwartz made sure to check out his compost heap whose number he remembered because of his proprietary and satisfied interest in it. There are hundreds of men and women, visitors from all over the country and from other countries as well who have worked a bit at Forest Farm.

Scott teaches as he directs, explaining and guiding. One leaves with valuable advice on an aspect of cultivation. (There were other gratifications in the meeting between the University of Pennsylvania's distinguished Professor Schwartz and Scott Nearing, because Scott Nearing was one of the first academic freedom cases on record. He was kicked out of the University of Pennsylvania without notice in 1915 because of his strong anti-war stance, and his activities on behalf of child-labor regulations.)

The rise and fall and rise again of Scott Nearing is a much told tale. Most tellings split the man and his history down the center of his two great passions—politics and the conservation of all living things. Scott holds his passions as one and indivisible; it is his public that insists on a separation. If he is hailed as almost a sainted leader by thousands of admirers and acolytes of the movement toward subsistence living, this group is likely to be totally uninterested in and even hostile to his radical politics. Conversely, to the comrades of his political actions, Scott Nearing's lifestyle is something of an embarrassment.

To have removed the fascinatingly disparate elements from Scott's political radicalism is indeed to have turned him into a bore. Scott is fascinating as a quintessentially American phenomenon—a mix of messianic, visionary apocalypticism, puritanism and the American spirit infused with the practical hard-headedness of a businessman or scientist. Scott is sometimes compared to Thoreau. But Thoreau is not a good fit any more than Vladimir Ilyich Lenin is. Aimee Semple McPherson, Isadora Duncan, Thomas Alva Edison, Charles Lindbergh are better matches—though there isn't an ounce of charlatanism or commercialism in Scott.

On the surface, nothing seemed more unlikely at the time than a long, lasting partnership between two such disparate personalities as Scott Nearing and Helen Knothe. Helen and Scott met in 1928 when Scott was forty-five and Helen twenty years younger. She was a beautiful young woman, as the photographs in *The Good Life Album* illustrate. They met as neighbors in the New Jersey community where Helen's parents lived. Like Scott, Helen was the child of comfortable people. Her parents were members of the Theosophical Society, and Helen became deeply involved in it in her teens. Summering in Holland among her mother's people, prime movers in the Theosophical Society, she studied music (Helen was on the path to becoming a concert violinist) and Theosophy. She was seventeen—in love with the city of Amsterdam, dazzled and petted by the elders who surrounded her, and quite drunk on a heady mix of Theosophy and music. She moved with the group to Switzerland to one of the posh settings made available to the Society by its wealthy followers. There she met Krishnamurti, the impoverished Indian boy who was being groomed into an elegant mystic for presentation to the world as the coming Messiah by Annie Besant and the Theosophical Society. Krishnamurti fell in love with Helen.

From Theosophy, the love of Krishnamurti, and the concert stage, it seems an impossible leap to the hard radicalism, the materialist economic views and the spartan life of Scott Nearing. But what emerges from Helen's two incarnations are the points of connection between them. She left Theosophy for Scott at the point that Scott became a social outcast and remade his life into the shining example it now is. Theosophy embraces a holistic concept of existence—the interconnectedness of human, animal, and natural life within the universe and the cosmos—all of these are present in Scott's philosophy.

Their love story is special, highly complicated, and would take very long to tell. It is only possible here to sketch the lightest lines.

I have never heard Scott put Helen down in any way. She calls him Scotto, and at dinner, if he forgets to eat in the excitement of developing his ideas, she plants herself in front of him and feeds him with a wooden spoon from the wooden bowls that are the only utensils they use. There is no put-down in her feeding him either, but the sign of close, deep affection. When I ask Scott to name the contemporary who most influenced him, apart from those he speaks of in his autobiography (Gandhi, Tolstoy, his grandfather, his mother, his early teachers), he ponders the question long and seriously, and then says, "Helen." With a young girl's cry of happiness, she rushes across the room to hug and kiss him for that ultimate tribute. He smiles into her face with wonderful sweetness.

Sue and Bob Ridge

Perhaps lasting couples performing equally, individually and together, need the peace and nurturing properties of a perfect environment to survive and prosper. Is it Maine, then? The peninsula on which we and the Nearings live is bounded by Blue Hill Bay. Across the waters lie the peaks of Acadia. Penobscot Bay and the hills of Camden border the opposite shore. The land mass is filled with other waters—fresh-water lakes and ponds, rushing streams, salt ponds, and the brilliant surprise of the reverse falls at Blue Hill and the Bagaduce.

For devotees everything on this peninsula delights the eye—from the whiteness of its simple church spires, its trim little capes, tall farmhouses and Victorian cottages to its falling down barns and heavy mists. We would swear that the color of any flower grown here is deeper, more heartbreakingly soft and suffused with the nature of itself. One connects the harshness of the climate to the delicacy of flowering color—the purple of a wild Japanese iris springing up between boulders is astonishing and touching, as is the sea lavendar, battling a daily tidal sea and proclaiming its victory with a stirring splash of violet blossoms. It is only one short step to connect such miracles with oneself, and to celebrate this struggle and survival as a personal victory.

It is poetic nonsense to leave a description of the Maine coast at that. Rural life displays its exquisite exterior view of unspoiled elegant simplicity, but this enchanting coating "straight out of central casting" is a cover for an underpattern of complex and frightening problems. Maine suffers one of the highest rates of unemployment in the country; there is insufficient industry, no public transportation, mediocre schools; and the spread between the poor and the rich is as wide as that in any underdeveloped country. The spread between their interests and intimate knowledge of one another is even wider. The farmhouses dotting the Maine landscape and inhabited by locals are seen as places in which "nothing ever happens." On the contrary, a subterranean, unreported life of intense social melodrama exists—alcoholism, incest, illicit love, illegitimacy, homosexuality, madness, a high incidence of feeble-mindedness; violent and lasting family ruptures; couple-switching; drugs, vandalism, and rebelliousness among adolescents—in a setting where the ratio of living space to human beings should insure a bucolic peace and soaring mental health statistics. (A recent study contrasted a section of New York City residents with the natives of a small village in Nova Scotia, measuring for contentment, stability, mental health. The New Yorkers came out way ahead.) Yet pilgrims fleeing what they have experienced as the ugliness and madness of urban life continue to pour into Maine searching to be "born again" (and into Vermont and Oregon and some other spots), seeking a new road to community, personal joy, fulfillment—and social good. Their individual histories are as variously colored as the hundreds of species of wildflowers that dot the open fields and woods of the area—that is to say that though one can categorize the new pioneers as belonging to a particular species, adequate description demands minute attention to the differences.

Still it may be said of the general species that a certain number instantly fail in their attempt at a new life and return to the lives that they quit; some stay on but not within the vision they brought with them; some succeed with glory; some even become public figures (Helen and Scott Nearing and their most celebrated disciple, Elliot Coleman; John Coles, the editor of *Maine Times*, the leading journal of the new lifestyle; many others); some, particularly among the older pilgrims, combine the old life with the new, taking what they consider the best from each. They grow their own vegetables and store them in huge, expensive freezers; they stay through the harsh winters and set up amateur theatricals or a choral group, or they skip out entirely for a six-week trip to Europe.

What the young find most dispiriting is what they most sought—hardship. Many young couples split under the strain. Young women, their heads befogged by an earth mother-pioneer-goddess fantasy crack up under the strain of back-breaking labor, childbirth, child bearing, and an intensity of loneliness they could never have imagined. Some create their own communities, bunching up in shared living quarters, or in separate houses on shared acreage, or join together in farming shared ground—sometimes under the compelling drive of an esoteric religion.

Some barge into local life as carpenters, clam-diggers, yardmen, chimney cleaners, caretakers, berry-pickers; or they drift back into what they were trained to do and take jobs as local teachers, reporters, performers; some go into business selling organic vegetables, health food, gourmet kitchen gadgets, antiques; or go off on a new tangent and learn how to cane chairs, to refinish furniture or to make objects from scratch; they may dye wool and weave it into cloth or fashionable ponchos selling at large prices; make rugs or patchwork quilts; leather goods; ironwork; pottery; basketry; Christmas wreaths, candles—the crafts offer a wealth of activities. Perhaps the most surprising news that pilgrims pick up is information about an eroticism among the natives more wild, asocial, and individualistic than anything they experienced back in Cambridge and Berkeley. Though newcomers may split up, pair anew and split up again, they are changing partners no more rapidly than in the houses of those who have stayed put in Maine for generations; and never before had they heard of so many sons and mothers, fathers and daughters, sisters and brothers in all combinations, running to one another's beds, as happens among the local population.

Is then the dream of a more humanly scaled life utterly false? Many among the newcomers would swear that their new life makes a better stab at obtaining inner and outer harmony than they've ever known. Sue and Bob Ridge and their life seems to prove it. The Ridges are in their sixties—of retirement age, though they retired young, about seven years ago. They are good looking, intelligent, cheerful, vigorous, sound people, the sort that are welcomed as a "credit to the community." They are rare birds, having married only once—to one another. They come from similar, WASP backgrounds and were given good educations. Bob, fresh out of Williams College, with a major in English, was taken into a brokerage firm owned by his uncle, but he loathed the work and the ambience, and in six months quit it for a job in publishing, where he remained happily involved with books for the rest of his professional life. He didn't stay at one publishing house, since musical chairs is the name of the game in publishing. He began in the publicity department of Appleton-Century.

When he married Sue, she was a teacher, then a librarian. They lived in a New York City apartment at first, enjoying the first years there before they had children. World War II speeded up the child-bearing, as it did for so many couples of the period. Though he was a father, and on the borderline of being overage, Bob was drafted into the armed services, and assured that he would never be sent overseas. His I.Q. and his education qualified him as an officer's training candidate, but what he was offered was a course in locomotive engineering, which he refused. He took his basic training at Ft. Bragg, where he edited the camp newspaper. Sue and a woman friend whose husband was also an "old-man draftee" traveled together to cheer up their old wrecks. Both women were big-bellied pregnant, and after hours on the train they arrived exhausted and disheveled to find their two men looking marvelously fit, young, and cheerful. Almost immediately Bob was sent overseas. His division was a part of the American forces that held out against the huge German counter-attack known as "the Battle of the Bulge." Before victory was secured, the Allied forces suffered more than 77,000 casualties in that action. Bob was lucky. He was unhurt; but what he saw and experienced left him with strong feelings about war and peace. Both he and Sue were actively opposed to the war in Vietnam.

By the late sixties, Sue and Bob's children (four daughters) were grown and out of the house, leading their own "messy young lives." Sue had spent many years birthing and mothering; then she returned to teaching and being a librarian. Bob had moved steadily upward from one publishing job to another, relocating when the job demanded it—from New York to Boston, then back again to New York. Bob worked in the city; their home was in a suburb. He commuted to Boston from Hingham, and to New York City from Middletown, a community near Red Bank, New Jersey. They had moved there after the coming of the children made living in New York too difficult and too expensive to contend with. They lived well but under a constant, grinding, and oppressive pressure. It was hard work keeping a family going at the level the Ridges required, particularly when it came to putting the four girls through college.

Their work was not without profound compensations,

other than sustaining them through satisfactory material needs. They both love books and loved working in the same field. Sue had become head coordinator of the children's book department of the county in which they lived. Bob's position was such that he made the important decisions about how a book was launched—a crucial aspect of book publishing in the sixties. Though their daughters were no longer at home, their days and nights seemed to be as crowded and busy as ever—commuting alone took many hours out of Bob's day—with less and less time left for what they particularly craved—space, silence, fragrant air, the sea and sailing, planting seeds—the sense that they were improving life on earth rather than adding to its exploitation. They returned from vacations dissatisfied with their lives.

(Sue and Bob's facade is smooth and pleasant, well-mannered, good humored; their responses are quiet, sensitive, fine, intelligent; but in spite of the exterior smoothness one senses a rich interior life embracing the knowledge of much pain in the world even if such disquieting information must be reined in by the duty to keep a cheerful countenance and to act, always, in the smallest and the largest contingencies, as far as possible to make the world a better place. One would say that they are splendid examples of the best of our white, middle-class America, if it's still possible to utilize such terms without pejorative intent—as I am.)

Theoretically for Bob to commute from Middletown to New York City should have taken about forty minutes to an hour, but, in fact, the daily back and forth stint had become a horror. There were frequent breakdowns of all kinds. The trip would often take hours. Bob would fortify himself with a lot of reading matter. There was the matter of the trestle bridge over the Raritan River which was frequently out. That meant getting off the train, taking a bus across to the other side, and then picking up another train to continue the journey into New York City. Bob bore these strains with his customary sense of humor, though he found himself wondering more and more often what his fifty-year-old self was doing, still trudging the same old treadmill, carting his heavy briefcase, loaded with books and manuscripts.

During a particularly uneven ride home one evening, the train jolted wildly. Bob's briefcase, heavy with books, but safely stowed away in the luggage rack, rose like a poltergeist from its nook and hurled itself at Bob's head, where it opened a deep gash from which an astonishing amount of red, red blood poured forth to cover him with gore. "Am I being given a clear message?" Bob asked himself as the conductor attempted to tend him.

The emergency first-aid kit on the train dated from the turn of the century. It was a glass enclosed, virginal territory which had to be broken open with its attached little hatchet to yield up its treasures—motion sickness pills, spirits of something or other to revive the faint, a small package of bandages—nothing adequate to staunch a heavily bleeding head wound. Bob was rushed to the emergency room of a nearby hospital. Sue was called to pick him up. He left with her, in his bloody garments, and still carrying the offending briefcase, whose innocent, unmarked air probably derived from its virtue in having acted as a beneficial agent.

They decided to move to the country. They had a limited amount of money: savings; a small, independent income; retirement funds. They sought a place on the water, where they could farm and also keep a boat and continue to sail. After much looking, they found a small town in Maine, on the Bagaduce, a tidal river which will lead a boat out to the great bays of the area. A farmhouse with a "For Sale" sign seemed to ideally answer their need. They called the owner, but in a typically Maine response, he told them that the house wasn't for sale. "I just put that sign out to irritate my neighbors." But the Ridges persevered, and the man sold them the farm and about twenty acres of land.

Their acquired wisdom about farming and animal husbandry was slim. They had started a victory garden way back during World War II, and they liked growing things well enough to keep up a modest kitchen garden wherever they lived. They had done their reading in the classic literature of subsistence living: John Seymour's *The Fat of the Land: Family Farming on Five Acres* is their favorite; but they had read everybody—Borsodi, Bromfield, Rodale, Scott and Helen Nearing, of course; and Eliott Coleman's parents were old acquaintances, so they knew of Coleman's development into Nearing's pupil, and they had visited the Nearings' farm nearby. They bought in 1971. They rented a house in the area while they brought the farm into shape to live in. Using skilled, paid help and a good deal of their own labor, they renovated the farmhouse and repaired the outbuildings, and started to work the soil for the gardens.

Today, they are so far successful that they raise enough of their own food to buy very little. The Ridges cultivate about three quarters of an acre of assorted gardens, growing a sizeable variety of vegetables for the table. What they produce is stored, canned, frozen, preserved, dried and, when in need, traded. They may exchange eggs for milk, pork for beef, shallots for horse manure, or any other plentiful item for a scarce one. The fields of hay yield animal bedding and garden mulch. They cultivate raspberries, strawberries, fruit trees, and grape vines. Their woods supply enough fuel to keep the wood stoves and open fireplaces fed during the winter, though back-up central heating is also in use. (In some ways, the Ridges are less than pure to the ideals of radical subsistence living; but they make no claim to being purists. They are meat eaters; they drink alcoholic and caffeine beverages; they use electricity, modern plumbing, and gadgets; they ski, sail, keep pets, own two Toyotas, play bridge, lead an active social life and take a European trip almost every year.) They raise their own protein—pigs, sheep, turkeys, geese, chickens. They don't hunt. They "couldn't bear to shoot a deer." What about killing their own animals? They hire a man to shoot the pigs and the lambs. (Sue hides in the house and turns on music very loud so as not to hear the sound of the shot.) The hired man scrapes off the coarse hog hairs, skins the lambs and splits the animals down the middle. Sue and Bob spread out the halved sections on the kitchen table, and following a mounted map as a guide to the parts, they butcher together. They pay again to have the hams and bacon smoked. The rest is frozen for winter use. They kill their fowl in traditional fashion. Bob turns them upside down, swinging them by the feet until they're dizzy enough to be laid out on a table; then he chops off their heads with a hatchet. Bob plucks the feathers; Sue removes the intestines and completes the cleanup.

There is a temptation to renounce flesh altogether, perhaps a bit more on Sue's side than on Bob's. Bob says, "I love the animals. I like having a relationship with animals. It's true that we kill our animals in the end, but the killing isn't the horror that commercial slaughtering is. Unless you give up meat altogether, it's better to raise your own."

He doubts that it's cheaper to raise animals than to buy meat. "That's not why we raise our own animals. Our meat certainly tastes better." (It does; I've eaten it.) "And I do believe we give the animal a better life than the brutal commercial raising does."

Sue waited five months after the pigs were killed and butchered before she was able to face the decapitated, frozen head of the pig and make head cheese. She also prepares scrapple, and Italian and regular sausage. They trade cuts of their meat for beef and veal, and they raised enough turkeys to sell a few at one dollar a pound for Thanksgiving dinners. There again the quality was superb; and anybody who has eaten a farm fresh egg knows that it is a product as different from the supermarket variety as garden tomatoes are from the flannel and rubber articles sold by that name in the stores.

This season they hope to grow enough grain to feed their animals, because commercial feed is laced with chemicals and additives they'd rather not be using. They're organic gardeners, and in addition to the vegetable gardens, this year they also plan to grow enough corn to dry and grind into cornmeal. The big problem is that there aren't any small machines for home threshing or grinding, and the local mills which used to service the family farm no longer exist. The Ridges like to try to do everything the way it was done "in the old days," but that's not always possible. (We joke about the Cuisinart as a substitute, enjoying the irony of the use of such posh technology applied to subsistence farming.) She wants to grow wheat this year, in spite of the problem processing it. "I want to see how it grows," she says and moves her hands in an upward, seeking gesture ending with an opening outward of all her fingers. It's clear that growth is a miracle to her. She starts her garden seedlings early in a glass-enclosed porch, where she tends them carefully and they repay her lushly. "Don't you find it a miracle, the way the seeds come up, every time?" Bob says, putting Sue's feelings into words.

Is it possible to be self-sufficient without the extra income that the Ridges regularly count on? How do the kids do it without that crutch? Bob and Sue don't know, but they're glad they didn't have to try. Sue works at the local library. (Every tiny town in Maine contains its own little library, a sign of the power of the word in the highly literary New England mind.) But she does it more as a public service than a money-earning task. She is paid a little for her work. Bob writes literate, witty, skillful notices of cultural and other events for a small local paper. They are both actively involved in the life of the town, joiners and leaders of the organizations that keep things moving locally. They have many friends, more social contacts than they can manage. They're the sort of people friends and neighbors turn to first in an emergency. They always help—instantly, and with no fuss.

For themselves there has been only gratification and pleasure in their new life. Bob sounds like a Maoist on the subject of working with the body as well as the mind.

"That's the most stimulating aspect, that you're using your body." He enjoys the whole process of hauling in the wood for the stoves, caring for the animals, tending the gardens. "I've done things I never would have thought possible while I was sitting behind a desk," he says. "I had to learn how to use these huge syringes on the pigs, when they took sick." He takes the measure of an enormous needle, laughing and proud. Sue laughs at herself, too, describing how she stuffed pig's intestines with sausage meat, with the not very efficient aid of an old-fashioned sausage machine which she said was literally unworkable unless one had three hands. "So I used my chin to keep a certain part steady." It was an amusing vision—pretty, dainty Sue struggling with hog's intestines, sausage meat, and the recalcitrant machinery.

It's not easy to define happiness in other's lives, but I'd risk describing Sue and Bob as happy people—within themselves as individuals, together as a couple, and as part of a community.

CONCLUSION

If the stories in this book lead to any conclusion it is that there are as many different aspects to starting as there are manifestations of being. Only a few have been touched on here, and only a few of the kinds of circumstances that spark it. If there's a common denominator in the experience it is the mysterious driving power at the center of being that the longing to start expresses, no matter how different the starters. Those who felt born again, those deliberately changing careers, those growing into new persons, those daring life-and-death risks, those stubbornly becoming themselves, those working on their insides and the ones working on the outside world, the creators and the businessmen, the planners in advance and the ones that are pushed, who jump first and see where they've landed later—all are swimming toward a similar shore. "I must be myself," Emerson said, "I cannot break myself any longer for you, or you."

In the last volume of *Remembrance of Things Past*, the

celebrated passages occur that bring the narrator full circle to his earliest memories and to a moment of dedication toward his work as the recorder of his unique experience. Proust arrives at this almost religious vow during a fashionable party among dissolute gossips and social climbers.

The happiness which I was feeling was . . . an enlargement of my mind, within which the past was re-forming and actualizing itself, giving me . . . something whose value was eternal. This I should have liked to bequeath to those who might have been enriched by my treasure . . . I felt myself enhanced by this work which I bore within me as by something fragile and precious which had been entrusted to me and which I should have liked to deliver intact into the hands of those for whom it was intended, hands which were not my own.

A very different kind of reaching out is described by Golda Meir. She had just arrived in what was in the twenties a primitive Tel Aviv, and seeming more so since she had come from the comparative high comforts of living in Milwaukee:

I was in my very early twenties, doing exactly what I wanted to do, physically fit, full of energy and together with the people who meant most to me—my husband, my sister, my best friend. I had no children to worry about and I didn't really care whether we had an icebox or not, or if the butcher wrapped our meat in pieces of newspaper he picked up off the floor. There were all kinds of compensations for these small hardships, like walking down the street on our first Friday evening in Tel Aviv and feeling that life could hold no greater joy for me than to be where I was—in the only all-Jewish town in the world, where everyone from the bus driver to our landlady shared, in the deepest sense, not only a common past, but also common goals for the future. . . . I knew we would remain bound to each other for all our lives . . . here Jews could be masters, not victims, of their fate. . . . I was profoundly happy.

Her happiness expresses the euphoria attendant on starting together with many others on a great work of social organization. I saw the beginnings of the new Jewish state myself in the thirties and recognized the phenomenon when I saw it again many years later in a number of newly emerging Third World nations where virtually entire populations exhibited a joyous people's rush toward social autonomy, toward what they conceived as mastery of their own destiny, and exuding an exuberance so palpable it throbbed in the impoverished streets and in the country air like a great collective heartbeat. These are beginnings which take off with a blinding rush that obscures the problems of going on toward middles and endings.

But we have heard how starting means continuing.

Having made the decision to become an artist even if it killed him, Vincent Van Gogh still faced the meticulous mastery of working techniques. He writes his brother of a small water-color,

. . . a corner of my studio with a little girl who is grinding coffee. I am seeking for tone, a head or a little hand that has light and life in it, and that stands out against the drowsy dusk of the background, and then boldly against it that part of the chimney and stove, iron and stone, and a wooden floor. If I could get the drawing as I want it, I should make three-fourths of it in a green-soap style, and only the corner where the little girl sits would I treat tenderly, softly and with sentiment. . . . I cannot express everything as I feel it, but the question is to attack the difficulties, and the green-soap part is not yet green-soapy enough, and on the other hand the tenderness is not yet tender enough. But at any rate I have hammered the sketch on the paper, and the idea is expressed, and I think it a good one.

And another extraordinary artist, the composer Igor Stravinsky, describes a sideways approach to starting: "When I start a work, an idea from inside has taken me, and, when starting, I may see the end or the middle but *not* the beginning. That has always to be found, has to be developed in the spirit of the composition, that discovery of the correct entrance to a piece."

When I myself started on the work I had always wanted to do, I wasn't sure I had really started. In the back of my mind there was a nagging pull tugging at my energy, repeating the possibility of failure. To write a first novel at the age of fifty-four seemed a fool thing to do. Novelists

284

had passed their peak by that age, usually. I had no money to fall back on; no proof of skill as a story-teller; no rainbow promise that editors, publishers, book-sellers, or readers were eagerly waiting to reward me as a bearer of gifts. I sat down before my typewriter the same person I had always been presumably. Why should this attempt be any different from the ones before that had ended in failure? Ended in my rising dissatisfied to put the work aside once more?

I was in our rundown cabin on the grounds of the Maine property we had just bought. There was no electric power in the cabin and I attach to that moment, always recalled with intense and exact vividness, certain physical details of the play of light in the small space I occupied—a sense of darkening air enriched by the sad, good, dying smells of earth, leaves and grass moving inexorably toward the end of autumn, dead winter, and spring with its new birth. I was conscious of a strange, internal hush as if some fixed inner agitation had been quieted finally. The late afternoon light existed in its slanting cast for only this one uniquely beautiful moment of time, and I found myself entertaining the notion that held fast in individual consciousness such moments deserved reproduction as specimens of human happiness. Because with my decision to start, that's what I was feeling—a happiness I could only liken to the happiness of love. The story that I had for so long a time wanted to write had quietly become whole in the room, insisting on its presence.

It was the same story of a young woman dying of tuberculosis that I had tried before, a young woman dying in the midst of the busy, busy living going on around her, surrounded by the grotesque, cruel, frightened, loving, comic, and startling reactions of those standing by. My intention had always been to write about death in the midst of the life we live. When I had first planned my book, I was a young girl and the symbolic illness of the time was still tuberculosis; but by the time I reached my typewriter in the dimming light of the cabin in the late autumn of 1969, the symbolic illness of our time had been confronted by me again and again as cancer, and with this change at its heart, my story leaped into a contemporary frame and into the words that would tell it.

The work existed in my mind, intact and shining, a pale, full moon. Yet like a vision of the moon that an onlooker may delight in without knowledge of the coarse physical matter of which it is composed, I knew that my shining object too must be composed of plain matter—words, sentences, paragraphs, on sheets of thin paper—any aspect of which might ensnare me in failure, and blot up all the light I hoped to shed. No matter. Starting is continuing. Just as moonlight reflects the power of the sun, inevitably a work, an act, a destiny taken on as an act of faith in the self reflects the glow of autonomy. Between me and the work a compact of hope and trust had been sealed. For its sake, I was prepared to face the risk of failure, and of rejection and criticism, exposure and ridicule, while of course hoping for acceptance and welcome.

This moment, inexplicably different from preceding ones seemingly just like it, was different in its dedication. Nothing would be allowed to come between my self and my work this time until the task was finished.